Covered Wagon Women

Diaries and Letters from the Western Trails 1852

Volume 5

The Oregon Trail

Edited and compiled by
KENNETH L. HOLMES and DAVID C. DUNIWAY

Introduction to the Bison Books Edition
by Ruth B. Moynihan

University of Nebraska Press
Lincoln and London

♾ The paper in this book meets the minimum requirements of American National Standard for Information Sciences—Permanence of Paper for Printed Library Materials, ANSI Z39.48-1984.

First Bison Books printing: 1997

Library of Congress Cataloging-in-Publication Data
The Library of Congress has cataloged Vol. 1 as:
Covered wagon women: diaries & letters from the western trails, 1840–1849 / edited and compiled by Kenneth L. Holmes; introduction to the Bison Books edition by Anne M. Butler.
p.   cm.
Originally published: Glendale, Calif.: A. H. Clark Co., 1983.
"Reprinted from volume one . . . of the original eleven-volume edition"—
T.p. verso.
"Volume 1."
Includes index.
ISBN 0-8032-7277-4 (pa: alk. paper)
1. Women pioneers—West (U.S.)—Biography.   2. West (U.S.)—History.
3. West (U.S.)—Biography.   4. Overland journeys to the Pacific.
5. Frontier and pioneer life—West (U.S.)   I. Holmes, Kenneth L.
F591.C79   1996
978—dc20   95-21200   CIP

Volume 2 introduction by Lillian Schlissel.
ISBN 0-8032-7274-X (pa: alk. paper)
Volume 3 introduction by Susan Armitage.
ISBN 0-8032-7287-1 (pa: alk. paper)
Volume 4 introduction by Glenda Riley.
ISBN 0-8032-7291-X (pa: alk. paper)
Volume 5 introduction by Ruth B. Moynihan.
ISBN 0-8032-7294-4 (pa: alk. paper)

Reprinted from volume five (1986) of the original eleven-volume edition titled *Covered Wagon Women: Diaries and Letters from the Western Trails, 1840–1890*, published by The Arthur H. Clark Company, Glendale, California. The pagination has not been changed and no material has been omitted in this Bison Books edition.

To Clyde A. Duniway (1866-1944),
historian, academic President,
fourth of the five sons of
Abigail Jane (Scott) Duniway.
He read her Journal of 1852
to his sons at bed time,
and selections to students
and public audiences.
Its publication here symbolically fulfills
his contract with the Arthur H. Clark Co.
of September 28, 1928.

Introduction to the Bison Books Edition

Ruth B. Moynihan

> Where other folks have gone *we* certainly
> can go; at any rate we think so.
>
> —Abigail Jane Scott

This volume in the *Covered Wagon Women* series includes the diary of one of the most important women in Pacific Northwest history. Abigail Jane Scott, who married Benjamin Duniway only ten months after she arrived in Oregon in September 1852, became a writer, editor, mother of six children, and Oregon's "Mother of Woman Suffrage." During the sixty years after she wrote this journal, Abigail Scott Duniway was one of Oregon's most notable women—writing, lecturing, traveling, publishing a weekly newspaper, and fighting for equality of opportunity and the right to vote.

Oregon finally approved woman suffrage in 1912, following several other western states. Abigail Duniway had prepared the way through her weekly newspaper, *The New Northwest* (1871–87), and her frequent lecture tours, by stagecoach and buck wagon and even horseback, throughout the rugged pioneer country of the Pacific Northwest. Having survived the overland trail, there were few other obstacles that could ever faze her.

Seeing so much death and suffering at such a young age was undoubtedly one important factor in transmuting the character of sensitive Abigail Jane Scott into that of the redoubtable Mrs. Abigail Duniway, a woman of suffragist zeal, indomitable energy, and fearless conviction. She recognized this herself when she used the diary as source material for her first published novel,[1] written when she was only twenty-five and published in 1859. The heroine was a woman's rights advocate, fiercely independent and often angry about the way women were "forced" by their husbands to make such a dangerous and life-destroying trip. Abigail Scott Duniway wrote the story again in 1905,[2] transforming her passion into nostalgic sentimentality and heroine-worship. But the anger and the women's rights zeal remained a prime component.

One of Abigail Duniway's farm neighbors in Clackamas County when she was first married was Cecilia Adams, another of the diarists in this book. Cecilia was the wife of William Adams, sharp-tongued newspaper editor and founder of the Republican Party in Oregon. It was in

Adams's weekly *Oregon City Argus* that Abigail Duniway published her first poems and articles. After moving to Hillsboro, the Adamses and Parthenia and Blank, Cecilia's sister and her husband, undoubtedly knew Tucker Scott, who settled in Forest Grove in 1859. All of them were involved with the Tualatin Academy and Pacific University, to which Tucker Scott contributed land. The world of these frontier pioneers was small and interconnected, despite the great distances of their journeys. The bond of a shared overland trail experience was powerful—and never forgotten.

The journey itself was usually a joint venture, involving brothers and sisters and in-laws and nephews—whole networks of families, seldom just independent individuals. One has only to look at the names and relationships of those who traveled with the Scotts, or with Polly Coon, or with the twins, Cecilia Adams and Parthenia Blank.[3] In each case, other relatives had already made the trip in the 1840s, settling in Oregon and providing crucial help to the newcomers in the last stages of their journey as well as when they arrived.

Historians know that such group relationships have been common in all the great migrations that make up American history. It was not just the Native American Indians who moved from place to place (especially under the pressure of other population movements). Immigrants—from seventeenth-century English Pilgrims to eighteenth-century Scotch-Irish, from nineteenth-century Italians, or eastern European Poles and Jews, or Scandinavians, to twentieth-century Central Americans or southeast Asians—have followed similar patterns of family and village migration. People go where they already have relatives or friends. People survive by means of networks of communication and mutual aid. America's frontier travelers and settlers were no exception.

In fact, looking at these diaries, one sees that in each family history there were several previous migrations. Over several generations the Scotts had moved from western Virginia to North Carolina to Kentucky to Illinois before going to Oregon. Polly Crandall Coon's father had moved from Connecticut to western New York to Wisconsin before they went to Oregon. Martha Read was born in Massachusetts, married and moved to western New York, then moved with her family to Illinois before they decided to go to Oregon. The twins Cecilia Adams and Parthenia Blank were born in New York and married in Illinois before they and their husbands and their father and other relatives all traveled to Oregon to join an older brother.

When seventeen-year-old Abigail Jane Scott began writing about her family's journey westward in 1852, she already shared in the sense of high purpose and great loss that marked almost all women's narratives about the trail. One can see the loss in her first entry, where she speaks of "bidding farewell forever" to "the home of my childhood." But one can also hear the youthful excitement in her reference to being "seated by a blazing fire with Heaven's canopy over my head trying to compose my mind."

It was painful to say goodbye to grandparents the Scott family would never see again, but one of Tucker Scott's sisters (married to Deacon Elijah Browne) was caring for them—and would inherit the farm. And Yankee settlers in the nearby community of Tremont had already begun to take over the political and commercial possibilities of the area. Many close relatives traveled with the Scotts, and others were already in Oregon. A new beginning "across the plains and over the mountains" meant new land, new hope, new prosperity.

One of the losses Abigail knew about was her mother's grief at having to leave behind household goods, symbols of the comfortable domesticity finally achieved after years of log-cabin pioneering. Tucker Scott insisted that everything be auctioned off before departure. But an admirer of the oldest sister, Fanny, bought some treasured "gawdy Dutch plates" and returned them to her as a farewell gift. Secretly, the girls and their mother carefully sewed the plates inside the "Mother's wagon" featherbed. Anne and Tucker Scott slept on it all the way to Oregon. The plates survived, and one was still proudly displayed by Abigail's grandson 125 years later.[4]

The illness of Abigail's mother, Anne Scott, an "invalid" since the birth of her twelfth child the previous September, was another incentive to migrate. It would get her away from the yearly malarial fevers that plagued midwesterners in the nineteenth century. And Anne's sister and brother-in-law, Neill Johnson, who emigrated in 1851, were among the many who reported back to Illinois that the climate of Oregon's Willamette Valley was far more mild than the harsh winter blizzards and summer droughts of the Midwest—supposedly a "new garden of Eden" for someone trying to recover her health. The Scott party included another "invalid" too, Abigail's twenty-two-year-old cousin Malinda Goudy with her baby daughter born the previous October. Aunt Martha Caffee, Anne Scott's sister, was also ill during the early part of the trip, as was her husband, Levi, who was trying to recover from alcoholism.

The idea of carrying sick women in wagons for six months could seem like a chance for them to rest to those starting across the plains with little perception of the actual difficulties of the trip. Most of the emigrants had never even seen a mountain. Tucker Scott had carefully studied all the guidebooks—Abigail mentions them several times in her diary—but these tended to gloss over the difficulties. Abigail expressed the family optimism on June 1: "Where other folks have gone *we* certainly can go; at any rate we think so."

However, the overland trail experience severely tested family networks. Plagued by death from a major cholera epidemic and from measles and mountain fever and pneumonia and accidents, the 1852 overland migration was the largest in American history and the most devastating. Disasters could be deeply destructive of family relationships and established behavior patterns. As these diaries catalog the deaths and graves and occasional murders, one is reminded of wartime narratives. Wagons pass by, people keep moving, the sick and dying get left behind, the wagons roll on right after a burial. Grief must be contained and put aside as people go on with the desperate business of staying alive and getting over the mountains before the food gives out and the snows begin to fall.

To read Abigail Duniway's overland trail diary is to see her as an enthusiastic young girl, curious, observant and opinionated, optimistic even in difficulty. Although the sadly eloquent description of her mother's grave, on June 21, is perhaps the pivotal entry of the diary, Abigail continued for three more months to record details of the landscape and events of the trail with precision and pleasure. We see Independence Rock in a hailstorm, Devil's Gate inscribed with names, details of a murderer's grave, a description of the Soda Springs and how to add sugar and vinegar to make "a drink equal to any prepared soda in the States." Finally, after a harrowing journey over the Barlow Trail around Mt. Hood to Oregon City, the Scotts "reached the residence of uncle [Neill] Johnson in French prairie. . . . They were of course glad to see us."

On June 20 the sudden death, from cholera, of Anne Roelefson Scott—who had been reluctant to travel and exhausted by the exigencies of frontier farm life and giving birth to twelve children—was a loss that none of her daughters ever forgot. Two months later four-year-old Willie Scott's death on August 27 was another tragedy; it took him days to die of a slowly debilitating "*Cholera Infantum*," as it was called, while Tucker Scott and others in the party were severely ill.

Abigail Jane Scott was also grief-stricken by the drowning of John MacDonald on July 30. Family lore always claimed that the two had been "smitten," though Abigail never admitted such a thing in print. On August 30 she described the necessity of leaving behind a dying young man from Maine. But she never even mentioned the imminent death of her young cousin Miranda Goudy, who on September 17 left the train at The Dalles on the Columbia River, along with the Stevensons. George Stevenson died there, too; his wife became Tucker Scott's second wife the next spring.

Oregon's Willamette Valley was so fertile and its potential markets for produce so lucrative that, despite initial reluctance and despite the difficulties of the journey, successful immigrants quickly encouraged their eastern relatives to follow. In the letter Martha S. Read sent her sister just before departing, she fearfully remarked that "it looks like a great undertaking to me but Clifton was bound to go. . . . I hope to live to see the day to come back and live among you but life is uncertain." By the time she wrote again from Oregon, she spoke of being near "the best kind of timber for building," "the best kind of flour," and "the best kind of wheat." Oregonians even raise "the best kind of vegitables here," and can sell them to miners at high prices. "I suppose I shall not mind it so much when we get into a house," she concluded, adding, "I want you to make up your minds whether you will come to Oregon or not."

One can hear the sense of loss in Cecelia Adams's poetic June 4 tribute to "Home / what so sweet! / So beautiful on earth!" immediately after the diary tells about "a day long to be remembered for hard work" as the party had to ferry themselves across the Missouri River in a flat boat. But one cannot ignore the enthusiasm of her final entry on October 24, describing her boat trip down the Columbia to Portland, "the largest town now in the Territory and a fine town it is and would compare favorably with many eastern cities. . . . it is bound to be the great commercial emporium of the North west."

One purpose of keeping a diary was to describe the trip in detail to potential travelers. With hundreds of wagons all around them, immigrants felt themselves part of a huge historic enterprise. For example, on June 3, Abigail Scott rode her horse to some bluffs near the Platte River and described "a romantic spectacle. . . . The emigrants wagons cattle and horses on the road in either direction as far as the eye could reach, the plain below in which all this living, mass was moving." Women as well as men developed a pride of achievement that lasted for a lifetime.

Despite the difficulties of the journey, the "garden of the wilderness" turned out to have great money-making possibilities. Carefully listing the prices of items purchased along the way, women also listed the prices and wages in Oregon when they got there. A farmer could make very good money selling to miners and other new settlers, they said. Labor too was much needed in the West; Martha Read reported that her fifteen-year-old daughter had gotten a job as soon as they arrived; she was to "work out" at "$2 per week." Men's wages, she reported, were up to $2 per day on a farm, while "mechanics get from 5 to $10 per day."

The Donation Land Act of 1850 entitled Oregon settlers to the first *free* land claims in the nation's history. Each immigrant could claim 180 acres, and his wife could claim another 180 acres in her own name; 360 acres of prime land in the Willamette Valley seemed better than gold to many a practical man and woman.

Land ownership gave many women a sense of financial independence they had never had before. It also enhanced women's chances of marriage, although that was a mixed blessing. The number of available women was so small that men of all ages were wooing fourteen-year-old girls just for the sake of land. If a woman became a widow, she could seldom manage so much land alone unless she had strong sons. But, like Polly Coon, she could sell lots to build a town. Some women as well as men quickly discovered the wealth-building possibilities of land speculation—buying in order to sell at a profit a few months later. Abigail Scott Duniway kept doing that all her life.

Abigail Jane Scott, with less than a year's formal education, became a schoolteacher soon after arriving, while the rest of her family managed a hotel in order to recoup their losses. Women assessed the quality of their husbands' land and the potential for trade and commercial development. Although each of these diaries mentions meeting people on the trail (usually traders or herders) who were heading back eastward, few families did so. If they survived the trip, they were ready for a new life in Oregon.

The original editor of Abigail Jane Scott's manuscript, as printed in this book, was her grandson, David C. Duniway. He had a distinguished career as historical archivist for the state of Oregon. He died in 1993. David's father, Abigail's son Clyde Duniway, had been a Stanford University historian and president of the Universities of Montana and Wyoming, and of Colorado College and Carleton College. Abigail Duniway's fierce devotion to her "bailiwick" (as she always called it) was a defining part of their lives.

David Duniway's story of her life introduces the diary, which was a prized family possession for nearly 150 years. But it was not until late 1977 that David Duniway found out about the second copy of the diary which had been sent back to Illinois in 1853. His unknown cousin, R. Edwin Browne of Independence, Missouri, brought it to Oregon and inquired at the Oregon Historical Society whether anyone had ever heard of Abigail Jane Scott. Indeed, as David says in his introduction to the Scott sisters' letters, which follow the diary in this book, it was the kind of fortunate "miracle" that delights any historian or genealogist. The second copy of the diary as well as the family letters had been saved and handed down by the Brownes, who remained in Illinois with Grandfather Scott. They provide more details of the trip, and also evidence of the warmth of family relationships. (There are other letters too, about a family scandal, which are not included in this volume. They are discussed in my biography of Abigail Scott Duniway, *Rebel for Rights*.)[5]

With this reprint edition, a new and larger audience can share the words and the courage of some great American women on one of America's greatest adventures—the overland trail to Oregon.

NOTES

1. *Captain Gray's Company, or Crossing the Plains and Living in Oregon*, (Portland OR: S. J. McCormick, 1859). Only a few copies of the book now remain in rare book libraries.

2. *From the West to the West: Across the Plains to Oregon* (Chicago: A. C. McClurg, 1905).

3. See the introductions to the diaries in this book and also references in the diaries themselves.

4. See Moynihan, *Rebel for Rights: Abigail Scott Duniway* (New Haven: Yale University Press, 1983), 29.

5. See Moynihan, *Rebel for Rights*, 46–50.

Contents

Editor's Introduction to Volume V . . . 13

Journal of a Trip to Oregon:
Abigail Jane Scott
Introduction, by David Duniway 21
The Journal 39
Accounts of John Tucker Scott 135
Letters of the Scott Sisters 139

Journal of a Journey Over the
Rocky Mountains: Polly Coon
Introduction 173
The Journal 177
Epilogue 201

A History of Our Journey:
Martha S. Read
Introduction 207
The First Letter 209
The Diary 212
The Second Letter 246

Twin Sisters on the Oregon Trail:
Cecelia Adams and Parthenia Blank
Introduction 253
The Diary 256

Illustrations

ABIGAIL (SCOTT) DUNIWAY 10

HARRIET, MARGARET AND CATHERINE SCOTT . 10

AMOS AND FRANCES (SCOTT) COOK 11

POLLY COON 11

MARTHA READ 11

ABIGAIL (SCOTT) DUNIWAY
As a teacher, at 27, in 1862-63.
From a carte de visite, in the
custody of David Duniway.
McEwan Photo print.

HARRIET, MARGARET,
AND CATHERINE SCOTT
From a daguerreotype, 1852-53,
in the custody of David Duniway.
McEwan Photo print.

AMOS AND FRANCES (SCOTT) COOK
From a daguerreotype, October 1853,
in the custody of David Duniway.
McEwan Photo print.

POLLY COON
Courtesy of Gladys Foss,
Portland, Oregon

MARTHA READ
Courtesy of H. Daraleen Wade,
Salem, Oregon

Journal
of
a journey over the
Rocky Mountains
by
Mrs P. L. Coon
of
Albion Dane Co
Wisconsin

2d At night came within
a half mile of the Platte
& camped for a day to do our
washing &c About half an
hour after we camped one
of the celebrated Platte river
storms came upon us & lasted
nearly all night — The wind
blowing from nearly every point
of the compass. I never witnessed
any thing of a storm before
Some of the tents were blown
down & those that were not
required two or 3 men to hold them
all night. Those that slept in
the wagons were nearly as bad
off. It seemed every moment
that they must blow over — Dr
S's wagon cover was entirely blown
off & his provision much wet
and damaged.

3d Found our mess very
much dejected with their
nights watching & drenching
but consoled themselves that
they had seen some of the
Elephant. Every thing being
wet we concluded to lay 2
days & dry & repair & wash
4th We are nearly ready
again for a move in the
morning. Some of our men have
been sick but are better
4 wagons more have joined us
we are now 14 wagons & over
30 men. A boy died today in
a camp near us of Diareah.
5th Started out & in about
3 miles crossed Wood Creek
Among the camps on this
creek there was much sick
ness & 5 had died since yesterday
Dr S. visited them & gave them
medicine

THE DIARY OF POLLY COON
Title page and June 2-5 entries of 1852
Courtesy of Mrs. Gladys Foss, Portland, Oregon
At 85% of original size. Photos by Randy McCauley, Monmouth, Oregon.

Introduction to Volume V

An added feature of volume five of our series, center-ing on those who traveled the Oregon Trail in 1852, is that we have the valued assistance of a co-editor, David C. Duniway of Salem, Oregon. He is now retired as the distinguished Oregon State Archivist, having served in that position from 1946 to 1972.

David Duniway has edited for us the diary of his grandmother, Abigail Scott [Duniway], a family treasure in his possession. Abigail was a 17-year-old teenager when she wrote the 1852 diary. She later became the vigorous advocate of suffrage for women in the American West and is often designated the out-standing woman in Oregon history. Not only that, but David Duniway has edited for us the letters written by the Scott girls to their grandfather in Illinois soon after their arrival in Oregon. Over the years he has taken a special interest in the overlanders of 1852 because of his relatives having traveled west that year.

As in the other volumes of this series, the records are arranged in relation to the time they crossed the Missouri River. Dates for the Missouri crossing are as follows: Abigail Scott, May 10; Polly Coon, May 18; Martha Read, May 21; Cecelia Adams and Par-thenia Blank, June 1.

The introduction to Volume IV, which records the overland journeys to California in 1852, will serve equally well for Volume V, which tells of the over-landers on the Oregon Trail for the same year.

It might be noted that there was precious little trouble with Indians all the way across. This was one result of the great Indian treaty council held at Fort Laramie in September of 1851. It was really engineered by that man of the fur trade and master of Indian relations, Thomas Fitzpatrick, who was known as "Broken Hand" by the tribes. The Plains Indians attended in large numbers: the Sioux, Cheyennes, Arapahoes, Pawnees, Crows, and even the Shoshones from farther west on the Oregon Trail in the Snake River basin of present Idaho. The treaty called for lasting peace among the signatory tribes and with the whites. It made depredations by both Indians and whites punishable and restitution obligatory. After the council, Fitzpatrick took a delegation of eight Indian leaders to visit President Millard Fillmore at the White House.[1]

One distinctive aspect of the 1852 overland experience was the death by disease of countless cattle on the Oregon route. This happened all along the way in what is now Idaho State. The women's diaries document this clearly. In fact Martha Read's diary is a major historical source in this matter. She jotted down day by day the number of "dead beasts," totaling 557. The number of deaths for the whole breadth of the trail must have been much greater.

Martha's letter from Oregon suggests that many of the cattle "died with the horn oil." In her diary it is designated as "hollow horn" on July 24. John N. Winbourne describes this as "An imaginary disease arising from the erroneous belief that loss of appetite and listlessness in a cow was due to *hollow horns.*" One cured

---

[1] LeRoy R. Hafen, and Francis Marion Young, *Fort Laramie and the Pageant of the West, 1834-1890* (Glendale, CA, 1938), pp. 178-96.

it by boring a hole in each horn just above the base, then filled the hole with salt, pepper and sugar and plugged it with a wooden peg.[2]

The real cause of death was probably anthrax, or "murrain." William Cornell, on his way to Oregon the same summer, wrote on September 1:

> This morning Mr Nichols had a cow to die in good flesh   I had the curiosity to examine her   I first sawed off the horn to see if she had hallow horn   I found it sound but upon opening her I found an unusually large gall   nearly a quart and the melt swolen bloodshot or purple and upon cutting it seemed nearly putred   The blood a bad color   Not hunger hollow horn nor murrain and if poison whether vegetable or mineral I cannot tell   still plenty of stock is found dead.[3]

In researching the diary quoted above in 1961, David Duniway, our co-editor, wrote to Dr. William D. Prichard, then of Prineville, Oregon, a veterinarian with the United States Department of Agriculture Animal Disease Eradication Division, asking for comment. Dr. Prichard wrote to Dr. L. M. Kogen, D.V.M., of Ontario, Oregon, right on the Oregon Trail, asking for his opinion. Dr. Prichard described Dr. Koger as "a very exceptional person." Other Oregon veterinarians confirm this judgment and regret his later death. Here is Dr. Koger's answer:

> In reply to your interesting inquiry of October 11, 1961, concerning Mr. Duniway's question of the probable cause of death loss in the Lower Snake River Valley in 1852, emigrant cattle, I fear that positive answers are improbable. That there were

---

[2] John N. Winbourne, *A Dictionary of Agriculture and Allied Terminology* (East Lansing, Mich., 1962), p. 382.

[3] Karen M. Offen and David C. Duniway, eds., "William Cornell's Journal, 1852, with His Overland Guide to Oregon," *Oregon Hist. Qtly,* LXXIX, No. 4 (Winter, 1978), p. 388.

such losses are attested by the place name Dead Ox Flat, and
the recollection of old timers of the amount of cattle bones that
were picked up and shipped out by railroad. . . There are several
poisonous plants in the area, but we do not in these times observe
death loss from them in September. . .

However anthrax causes occasional losses and probably has
done so since pioneer days. No doubt many causes were involved
in the death loss, but it seems reasonable to me that anthrax
might well have killed the cow described in the William Cornell
diary, despite his elimination of "murrain" which was the term
that was in common use probably for anthrax at the time.[4]

For those who have not read the introduction to the
first volume of this series, we reiterate some salient
points which have been used to guide the editorial
hand. It is a major purpose to let the writers tell their
own story in their own words with as little scholarly
trimming as possible. The intent in this publication of
primary sources is to transcribe each word or phrase
as accurately as possible, leaving mis-spellings and
grammatical errors as written in the original.

Two gestures have been made for the sake of clarity:

1. We have added space where phrases or sentences
ended and no punctuation appeared in the original.

2. We have put the daily journals into diary format
even though the original may have been written continuously line by line because of the writer's shortage
of paper.

There are numerous geographic references that are
mentioned over and over again in the various accounts.
The final volume in the series will include a geographi-

---

[4] A ready reference on anthrax is Chapter IV "Koch the Death Fighter"
in Paul de Kruif, *Microbe Hunters* (N. Y., 1926), pp. 105-44. This is the
story of Robert Koch who identified the anthrax organism.

cal gazeteer, in addition to an index and bibliography to aid the reader.

The scarce and unusual in overland documents have been sought out. Readily available accounts are not included, but they will be referred to in the final volume along with the bibliography. If the reader knows of such accounts written while on the journey, please let us know. Our goal is to add to the knowledge of all regarding this portion of our history – the story of ordinary people embarked on an extraordinary experience.

KENNETH L. HOLMES

Monmouth, Oregon, 1985

The Diaries, Letters, and Commentaries

Journal of a Trip to Oregon

ᛦ Abigail Jane Scott

INTRODUCTION

Abigail Jane Scott, better known by her married name — Mrs. Abigail Scott Duniway, was an Oregon and Pacific Northwest leader in the suffrage movement for forty-one years. Called Jenny by her family, she became a teacher, farmer's wife, poet, novelist, milliner, newspaper editor and lecturer. She first met her husband, Benjamin Charles Duniway, near the end of the Oregon Trail, when he came out from the Willamette Valley to succor his father and family who also migrated in 1852. His support, with that of her children, was essential in the long fight for women's property and voting rights. It began with the publication of her newspaper, the *New Northwest,* in Portland, 1871-1886.

She told her story in her autobiography, *Path Breaking* . . . (1914). Recently it was retold by Dorothy Nafus Morrison in *Ladies were not Expected* (1977); by Helen Krebs Smith through 1876 in *The Presumptuous Dreamers* (2 vols., 1974 and 1983); and by Ruth Barnes Moynihan in *Rebel for Rights* (1983). Further sources are listed in the bibliographies of these biographers.

THE FAMILY AND THEIR ORIGINS

This *Journal* is significant because of the Oregon family to which it relates. Abigail's brother, Harvey W. Scott, who disagreed with many of her ideas, was for forty years editor of the *Morning Oregonian* in Portland, a leader and molder of thought and the Republican party. Their sister Catherine Scott Coburn shared in editing both their papers.

Other sisters, the children of the next generations and many of their cousins who came to Oregon, also contributed to the history of the west.

Abigail was the second daughter, one of twelve children of John Tucker Scott, better known as Tucker, and Ann Roelofson. The parents were married in 1830 in Tremont, then county seat of Tazewell County, Illinois. Both the Scott and Roelofson families had migrated several times before they reached Illinois.

Knowledge of the first James Scott family in America begins with family papers and the will of his father-in-law, Benjamin Terry, probated Sept. 26, 1771, in Pittsylvania County, Virginia. It is amplified by public records which include James's estate, filed in Halifax County, to the east, during the French and Indian War in November 1757. Family tradition has it that James came to America as a prisoner from the battlefield of Culloden and the defeat of Bonnie Prince Charlie, the Stuart heir to the British throne. Pittsylvania County was carved out of Halifax in 1766/7 and the Terry lands were near Peytensburg, the old county seat on the eastern border.

Keziah Terry Scott, James's widow, married Col. Richard Murphy, who by 1770 was transferring his interests to Rowan County, North Carolina, and eventually to the Mitchell River, a northern branch of the Yadkin on the western border of Surry with Wilkes County. The Colonel was a Tory, remained loyal to the King, and lost his lands because of his service. The family relationship "fled" to Washington County, Kentucky in 1797 or 1798 as part of a Baptist migration. The grandson, James and Abigail's grandfather, moved in 1824 to Sangamon County, Illinois, to free slaves, and two years later north to Tazewell County where they were first settlers in Groveland township.

The story of the Roelofson family begins with the memoirs of a grandson of the first Lawrence Roelofson, Isaac Knight: *A Narrative of the Captivity and Sufferings of*

Isaac Knight from Indian Barbarity (Evansville, Ind., 1829). Isaac was born in Washington County, north of Pittsburgh, Pennsylvania. In 1785 or 1786, his family (including the first Lawrence) migrated down the Ohio River to Fort Vienna in what is now Muhlenberg County, Kentucky, and in 1792 on to Henderson County, where they were among the farthest west of the American settlers. About 1793, Isaac crossed the Ohio to cut cane on the site of Evansville, and was captured by Kickapoo Indians. He had been vaccinated for smallpox and spread the disease among the Indians. He eventually escaped from his Indian family at Michilimackinac over two years later.

Lawrence Roelofson, Jr., Isaac's uncle, migrated in 1821 down the Ohio to Carmi, White County, Illinois, and then north to Tazewell County about 1829. He was an early follower of the Cumberland Presbyterian Church organized in 1810, and this church was the center of the life of the Roelofson and Tucker Scott families. Members of the Roelofson sisters' families were migrating to Oregon in 1852. Much of the story of the Roelofsons is preserved in the Roelofson Clan Archives, gathered in Oregon by their descendants who met annually for over sixty years.

OREGON FEVER

Tucker Scott was first siezed by "Oregon fever" in 1838 or 1839. He and an uncle, Peter Scott, could have been present October 1, 1838, when Jason Lee gave an inspired talk at the Main Street Presbyterian Church in Peoria, a "New School" Church. Lee, a Methodist missionary to the Indians of Oregon, had just returned from his Willamette Valley Mission. His description of the country and its climate was printed in the *Peoria Register and Northwestern Gazette* of October 6th. The speech sparked the organization of the Peoria party of eighteen young men, which set out May 1, 1839, for Oregon. They were the first Americans with the announced intent of becoming permanent settlers. Tucker knew some of them, including leader Thomas J. Farnham, a lawyer from Tremont, Tazewell County seat.

In October 1838, Lee's enthusiasm resulted in the organization of the Oregon Provisional Emigration Society at Lynn, Massachusetts, and the publication of a magazine, *The Oregonian*. In February 1839, this periodical began to list its agents. Two in Illinois were Peter Scott in Warren County and J. T. [Tucker] Scott at Groveland, Tazewell County. Peter and his family would migrate in 1847.

Tucker was delayed in his migration by family and economic problems resulting from the brutal death of his brother at the hands of "road agents." He was responsible for half his brother's debts, and this ended in Tucker's bankruptcy in 1842. As agent for the politician, Edwin Dickenson Baker, Tucker recouped his finances through the sale of portable lumber mills.

Immediate impetus for the 1852 migration came from the migration the previous year of the Rev. Neill Johnson and his family. A Cumberland Presbyterian minister, he was married to a Roelofson sister. Tucker's migration attracted members of the families of three other Roelofson sisters. They would leave behind the Roelofson grandparents in the care of the youngest brother. Tucker would also leave his grandmother, Chloe Riggs Scott, who would die that winter, aged 100, and his father James Scott and second wife, in the care of a sister and her husband.

THE JOURNAL

Since he had nine living children, Tucker assigned each older child specific duties for the trip. Jenny was given the task of keeping the journal. In 1925, her sister Etty, who was eleven in 1852, remembered Abigail "as a slight young girl — evenings after the weary stretches of travel with the old book in her lap sitting either by the tent or perchance one of the waggon wheels — sitting on the ground — while our father was giving her 'commands' to keep the 'Diary' correct! — she was too weary — at the time to write — But always did her best —" Abigail had had part of a year in an Academy, plus country schooling and a background of family reading.

From contemporary letters it has been possible to compare handwriting and identify passages written by the next youngest sister, Margaret Ann Scott, or Mag, and by Tucker. Each hand betrays itself by personal characteristics. Abigail creates elaborate punctuation which occurs at points where the subject changes. It was as if she were stopping to think. She is also the best speller, and must have used her old "blue spelling book" to good purpose. Mag uses only occasional periods or commas, while Tucker rarely uses punctuation and is terse. This co-authorship and direction is acknowledged by two inscriptions added to the old book which describe the *Journal* as being written "with the help of the old man." Revisions in the original manuscript, Scott Journal and Letters, appear in this book as italic words in parenthesis.

Margaret would attend Tualatin Academy at Forest Grove, and marry a local merchant, George Fernside. They moved to Tillamook Bay where he had a store on a barge that visited settlements around the Bay. Margaret died of tuberculosis, and hers was the first burial in the Tillamook Pioneer Cemetery. Her four daughters were raised by her sisters. Abigail raised Anna.

Abigail wrote her *Journal* in a blank book, 8" x 12", bound with paper covered boards and a brown leather spine. It has become fragile with hard use. At the end of the volume is Tucker's record of his income and expenses for the trip, and this is reproduced after the *Journal*. There were at least nine unused pages filled by the family with poems and sometimes scribbles.

In the winter of 1852-1853, the *Journal* was copied and sometimes revised by Abigail thru June 9th, and by Mag and occasionally by Tucker for the rest of the manuscript. It was sent back to the grandfather James Scott of Groveland, Illinois, with opening "General Remarks" by Tucker. In footnotes, references and selections adding to our knowledge of the Scott party will be identified as the "1853 Revision." The original manuscript is in the possession of R. Edwin Browne of Independence, Missouri, along with the letters to James Scott, who was his great-grandfather. They are quoted or reproduced with his permission. Entries in the *Journal* were often shortened in the revision, and changes reflect consciousness that James would be interested in details initially unrecorded.

The *Journal* was used by Abigail for two of her novels, *Captain Grey's Company. . .* (1859) and *From West to West. . .* (1905). It was also used by Leslie M. Scott, son of Harvey, in compiling a composite account of the 1852 migration for the "Compiler's Appendix," volume 3 of Harvey W. Scott, *History of the Oregon Country* (1924). He added comparative data from other diaries and journals, from books used by his grandfather, and from data furnished by State Highway staffs of states along the route of migration. He also consulted two surviving sisters, Fanny and Etty, who furnished significant details and clarified some *Journal* entries. Anyone wishing to understand the route of the Oregon Trail as it was in 1852 will find it rewarding, although it has been replaced in some aspects by more recent studies.

The *Journal* was first transcribed in 1924 by the editor's father, Clyde A Duniway. His manuscript has been used to furnish bits of now-missing text. Missing fragments are indicated in the text by brackets. It was read at bed time to "us boys" and selections were read in his senior pre-seminar each year at Carleton College, Northfield, Minnesota. It has been quoted in speeches over the years by Clyde and his son, David, the editor of this version, as well as by Abigail's biographers.

Publication has been made possible by the surviving heirs,

all grandchildren of Abigail Scott Duniway. They assigned their literary rights in her writings to David Duniway. They are Dorothy Duniway Ryan, Willis S. Duniway II, Robert E. Duniway, Katherine Duniway Murray, and Ben C. Duniway.

PREPARATIONS AND DEPARTURE

Vivid are memories of three of the six Scott sisters of preparations and the departure from their family home in Illinois. Two miles south of Groveland, six miles east of Pekin and four miles northwest of Tremont, it was located in section three, township twenty-four north, range four west. Catherine Scott Coburn published her account in the *Morning Oregonian*, June 17, 1890, and Leslie Scott reprinted it in his "Compiler's Appendix." This quote is from pages 239-241. Kate was 13 in 1852:

. . . Through all the winter preceding the April morning when the final start was made, the fingers of the women and girls were busy providing additional stores of bedding and blankets, of stockings and sunbonnets, of hickory shirts and gingham aprons, that the family might be equipped for the trip, and not left destitute in case of failure to reach the goal in season, or of opportunity to replenish the stores from the meager and high-priced stocks of a new country. Ah! the tears that fell upon these garments, fashioned with trembling fingers by the flaring light of tallow candles; the heartaches that were stitched and knitted and woven into them, through the brief winter afternoons, as relatives that were to be left behind and friends of a lifetime dropped in to lend a hand in the awesome undertaking of getting ready for a journey that promised no return. . .

But this time was past. The sale of surplus belongings had been made, the wagons, five stout vehicles, had been bought, and, gorgeous in green and yellow paint, with stout canvas covers snugly adjusted over supple hickory bows, stood just beyond the yard gate, ready for human occupancy. The stores of bacon and flour, of rice and coffee, of brown sugar and hard-tack, had been carefully disposed, a hurried breakfast was taken, and the oxen,

drawn by from two to five yokes to each wagon, soon drew the
five wagons into line. Into three of these were stowed the belongings of the family, an old-fashioned group, consisting of a wife
and nine children. The word was given, the sluggish oxen started,
and the journey of more than two thousand miles was begun.
Memory returning to that morning in the long ago, paints a
picture of moving wagons, of whips flourished with many a re-
sounding snap, of men walking beside them with a forced show
of indifference, though now and then the back of a brawny hand
was drawn hurriedly over the eyes; of silently weeping women
and sobbing children, and of an aged grandfather standing at his
gate as the wagons filed past, one trembling hand shading his
eyes, the other grasping a red handkerchief, his thin gray hair
blown back by the fresh breezes, and the soft spring snowflakes
falling gently, around him. "Good-by, good-by!" say these memory children with flushed, tear-stained faces, grouped at the open-
ings in the wagon covers. The old grandsire's response was choked
with emotion and drowned in the creaking of the wagons, the
shouts of the drivers, and the creaking of their whip lashes, and
the little caravan moved on out of sight.

One of our five wagons was occupied by a little family of three,
a man and his pale-faced wife, who held closely to her bosom,
on that trying morning of last good-byes, a babe of six months.
Since the advent of this child, the mother had daily drooped and
faded, and this journey was resolved upon in the hope of restoring
her to health. A health journey! Think of it, ye who travel in
palace cars, supplied with every luxury that modern ingenuity
has brought to bear upon travel to make it a delightful pastime.
A heavy wagon without springs, surmounted by strong canvas
stretched smoothly over bows of new hickory, drawn together in
a circle at the rear by a strong cord and made fast to the front
bow; a canvas door, thrown backward over the wagon sheet
when opened, and fastened with large horn buttons when closed,
was provided to protect the weak women from night dews and
invading storms. A rifle, dread suggestion of possible encounters
with Indians, hung from leathern straps against the bows on one
side, and on the other dangled a canteen, a compass and a sun-
bonnet. The wagon bed was packed with boxes and bundles neatly
stored; a feather bed and pillows, rolled together and tied with

cord during the day, were at night made up for a couch, with quilts and blankets, in a space made vacant by the removal of the boxes; a low chair, sitting sideways, with barely room in front to place the feet, a space utilized by the babe, when tired, as a place to sit, the mother providing the handbreadth of floor at the expense of her own comfort, by lifting one foot to the side of the wagon.

Thus equipped, a weak woman with her babe started on a transcontinental journey of between 2000 and 3000 miles, across mountains, streams and arid plains, in search of health, and in this wagon home she lived and journeyed patiently, even cheerfully, during the months of weakness and homesickness, jolting over the uneven roads, hungering, with an invalid's feverish longing, for proper nourishment, yearning for rest and caring daily, with such assistance as her kind husband could render after the discharge of other wearing duties that were his portion during those months of trial, for the tired, restless babe. Finally The Dalles was reached, and here the heroic health seeker found a grave. Her faithful husband prepared the worn, emaciated body for burial, and was one of three men comprising the entire funeral cortege, to bear his wife to the peaceful rest of the earth's sheltering bosom. A health journey, begun in expectancy, pursued in hope, ending in disappointment. There are many health journeys of which all these things can be said, but few, indeed, the details of which are so full of silent pathos and heroic struggle as was this.

The day of departure was described by Mary Frances Cook in a letter to Leslie Scott, December 20, 1920, quoted from his "Compiler's Appendix," page 249. Fanny was nineteen in 1852:

The weather that morning was quite spring-like, the sun shone through fleecy clouds, birds were singing and vegetation was rapidly springing into life. Groveland (a small country town), through which we passed, was 'lined' with people on each side of the street, waving us *bon voyage*.

That first day, Fanny remembered another parting which she described in 1925 in an answer to a questionaire from Clyde Duniway:

. . . Our dog followed us till we came to the the – Illinois
River – where we had to cross on a Ferry boat – to reach the
City of Peoria – The wagons were all settled, on the ferry boat,
when Father discovered our dog – Watch & he told him as he
placed *back* on land – "Go back home Watch & stay with Grandfather." After we reached Oregon (six months later) we had a
letter to the effect that the poor Canine went back (Our Grand
Father Scott lived near our old Home) to the Family Home &
refused food & in a short time he died!

Harriet Scott Palmer also remembered the dog. Etty was
eleven in 1852, and in her memoirs *Crossing over the Great
Plains by Ox-Wagons,* page 2, she speaks of the ferry:
". . . We looked back and saw our old watch dog (his name
was Watch) howling on the distant shore. . ."

THE CARAVAN

The five Scott family wagons included one for the William Gowdy nephew and his family, and one for the Levi
Caffee family. There were sixteen Scott yokes, or thirty-two
oxen, used on the wagons, ten extra oxen belonging to
cousin Levi, as well as three cows, two horses and a pony.
Six oxen were procured en route to replace those which had
died, or three yoke, and a fresh yoke was received from the
Rev. Neill Johnson on the John Day River, Central Oregon. The wagons are identified by Mary Frances Cook, or
Fanny, in an interview with Fred Lockley published in the
Oregon Journal, March 21, 1925:

The provision wagon was drawn by five yoke of oxen. John
and Robert Dickson [Dixon] were the drivers. The camp equipage wagon was drawn by three yoke of oxen. Levi Caffee and
Robert King were the drivers. What was called the family wagon
also had three yoke of Oxen, with Mitchell and Burns as drivers.
What was known as "Mother's wagon" was drawn by two yoke
of oxen. John Tucker Scott, Harvey Scott and John Henry Scott
took turns driving it. What was known as the miscellaneous
wagon had three yoke of oxen. John Goudy and Fisk serving as
drivers. . .

Etty in her "Memoirs" (page 3) reported that her "mother kept the two youngest with her always in "Mother's wagon."

Tucker Scott wrote his father April 4th, two days after leaving home that "we have as fine a company of men as could be desired and from our limited acquaintance I think a good deal of them —"

April 15th, after crossing the Mississippi to LaGrange, Missouri, Tucker reported to his father that "there is in my company 26 souls all told that is 8 teamsters and one man is a passenger besides our own families." By prior arrangements, the train was enlarged when it was joined by a party led by Stull Swearengen of Vermillion County, eastern Illinois. This party caught up with the Scotts April 24th or 25th, just after crossing the Chariton River west of Kirksville. At St. Jo, Missouri, where the caravan crosses the Missouri River, May 10th, they join a party of men from Groveland who are awaiting them. This included Mr. Lyford and Mr. Wafer, who had accompanied the shipment of provisions by the Illinois, Mississippi and Missouri rivers to St. Jo. There were three packets per week to St. Louis from Pekin, Illinois, the Scott market town. As Tucker reported in a letter to his father May 6th, "I found my provisions & stores all stored & in good order & I now have them loaded up and ready for a start tomorrow that is I can get across the river but the crowd of emigrants are so great that it is difficult to get to the boat at all. . ."

From Fort Kearney, May 28th, on the banks of the Platte, Tucker reported to his father that "we now have in our train 12 waggons 113 head of oxen & 12 head of horses." June 9th, from above Ash Hollow, he reported that of the 12 wagons, 5 "are from vermillion County Ill (Mr Swearengins) 1 from Brown Co. the Groveland boys & our own & *52 souls.*" The Groveland wagon belonged to Frank Gay who also had his own stock. All but two members of the party can be tentatively identified.

MEMBERS OF THE PARTY
Scott Family

John Tucker Scott, 43, or Tucker (February 18, 1809-
September 1, 1880), father, shared driving the "mother's wagon," which was abandoned on Snake River. It
was used by men of the party as a boat down the river
to Fort Boise, where it became a ferry. Arriving in the
Willamette Valley as a widower, Tucker would marry
Mrs. Ruth Eckler Stevenson, also widowed and from
the party. He would run a hotel at Lafayette, Oregon,
farm, move to Scott's Prairie, Puget Sound, fight in the
Yakima Indian War, and return to Clackamas County,
Oregon and then to Forest Grove to farm and run a mill.

Ann Roelofson Scott, 40 (July 26, 1811-June 20, 1852),
the mother, and wife of Tucker. An invalid, she died of
cholera on the Oregon Trail, thirty miles west of Fort
Laramie.

Mary Frances, 19, or Fanny (May 19, 1833-September 9,
1930), was the oldest daughter, assigned to cook. She
married Amos Cook at Lafayette, Oregon. He was a
member of the "Peoria Party" of 1839-1840, the first
overland emigration. At the July 5, 1843, meeting of the
citizens at Champoeg to form the Provisional Government, he was elected constable (or "first sheriff") of
Yamhill County, Oregon. He was a farmer. Fanny was
a prohibitionist, and spent the last years of her long life
in Portland, outliving all the family.

Abigail Jane, 17, or Jenny (October 22, 1834-October 11,
1915) was the principal author of the "Journal," and
her life has been described above.

Margaret Ann, 15, or Mag (October 27, 1836-September
24, 1865), assigned to help with the cooking and became
co-author of the "Journal." Her life is described above.

Harvey Whitefield, 14, or Harve (February 1, 1838-
August 7, 1910), shared in driving the "mother's wagon"

until it was abandoned. Fought in the Yakima Indian War of 1855, first graduate of Pacific University, first librarian, Library Association of Portland, Collector of the Customs, Portland, he served forty years as distinguished editor of the Portland *Oregonian*. He would die at Baltimore, Maryland.

Catherine Amanda, 13, or Kit (November 30, 1839-May 27, 1913), was responsible for the care of the two youngest children. She married John R. Coburn, and was widowed early. She helped edit Abigail and Harvey's papers, as well as her own.

Harriet Louise, 11, or Duck or Etty (March 9, 1841-January 3, 1930), drove the loose stock riding "Shuttleback," an old mare. She became a spiritualist and a medium. She married William R. McCord, carpenter and inventor, and then Isaac A. Palmer. She died in Seattle.

John Henry, 9, or Henry, Jerry, or Sonny (October 1, 1843-May 1, 1862) helped drive "mother's wagon." He died of tubercluosis at Forest Grove, Oregon.

Sarah Maria, 5, or Maria or Chat (April 22, 1847-November 24, 1901), became a musician. She married James Munroe Kelty, a Lafayette merchant, who would be sheriff of Yamhill County, Oregon.

William Neill, 3, or Willie (December 30, 1848-August 27, 1852). He died in the Burnt River Valley on the Oregon Trail.

Roelofson and Scott Relatives:

Levi Caffee, 37, (November 16, 1814-January 16, 1867), shared in driving the "camp equipage wagon." He was first cousin of Tucker, an orphan brought up by Tucker's father, James, who was his guardian. He came west to cure his alcoholism. He ran hotels at Champoeg and Lafayette, Oregon, was a teamster, had a stage from Champoeg to Salem, and later a dairy outside Lafayette.

Martha Roelofson Caffee, 37, or Aunt Mattsie (September 4, 1814-December 15, 1892), was a sister of Ann Roelofson Scott, and wife of Levi. She was cook and second mother to the Scott children.

Charles Clifford Caffee, 9 (February 2, 1843-September 18, 1925), was son of Levi and Martha.

Edward Taylor Caffee, 4 (1848-January 8, 1917) was also a son of Levi and Martha. He served as a bridgetender on the Steel Bridge in Portland for fourteen years.

William H. Goudy, 29, or Bill (July 2, 1822-July 12, 1897), was the oldest child of Stinson Anderson and Naomi Roelofson Goudy, a sister of Ann Roelofson Scott. He taught school in Marion County, Oregon, where he married September 14, 1854, Mrs. Rosaline Purvine. With the Purvine children, she received Oregon City Donation Land Claim 2462. They farmed near Hubbard, Marion County, the rest of his life.

Malinda Jane Brown Goudy, 22 (August 11, 1829-October 2, 1852) was the wife of William Goudy. She died at the end of the Oregon Trail at The Dalles on the Columbia.

Mary Goudy, 5 months (October 22, 1851-June, 1932), was the daughter of William H. and Malinda Goudy.

John Tucker Gowdy, 16, or Teet (November 21, 1835-March 26, 1917), was a son of Cyrus Finley and Tabitha Roelofson Gowdy. Cyrus was a brother of Stinson Goudy, but used a different spelling, and Tabitha was sister of Ann Roelofson Scott. John shared in driving the Scott "miscellaneous wagon." Tucker, in a letter to his father, James Scott, July 3, 1853, reported that "Teet is at work on a farm for $300. pr year and found he is a good boy!" On February 4, 1861, John married Anne Eliza Kemp, also an 1852 pioneer, who would publish her own memoirs. John farmed in Marion and Yamhill counties, and served in the 1895 Oregon Legislature, House of Representatives, from Yamhill County.

Travelers who paid fare to Oregon City to Tucker Scott:

G Burns paid $50 and helped drive the "family wagon."
Leslie Scott says he joined at St. Joseph and left August
15th down the Snake River.

John H. Clason paid $100 as a traveler. He died August
30th on Burnt River. A son of Maine, he joined the
party at St. Joseph.

John Dixon, 20, paid $50 and helped drive the "provisions
wagon." He was born in Illinois, the son of William and
brother to Robert. He first worked in Oregon City as a
carpenter. He died at Lafayette on March 4, 1896.

Robert Dixon paid $50 and also helped drive the "provisions wagon." He was John's brother. He surveyed during the summer of 1853. On November 22, 1860, he
married Louise J. Scott, daughter of cousin Lemuel and
granddaughter of Tucker's Uncle Peter.

Robert H. King, 21, or Bob, owed $50 for his fare. He
had been farm hand to Tucker Scott in Illinois. He was
born in Pennsylvania according to the U.S. Census of
1850. He helped drive the "camp equipage wagon" and
left by the Snake River, August 15th, rejoining the
Scotts after Fort Boise. He worked at a sawmill at
Milwaukie, Oregon, the first winter.

Sommers, paid $50. As "Summers" he sent word to a Mr.
Childs in Groveland, Illinois, according to Mag's letter
of April 25th. Tucker Scott reported on July 3, 1853,
"Sommers is at Marysville [Corvallis, Oregon]; he is
doing well."

J. L. Wafer paid $55. He was a photographer. He accompanied goods sent by boat to St. Joseph, Missouri from
Pekin, Illinois. A John F. Wafer married Lydia Barrell,
March 13, 1854, in Polk County, Oregon.

Others from the Groveland, Illinois, area on their own
or working their way:

J. B. Chamberlain died May 10th at St. Joseph. He joined

at Peoria. The U.S. Census of 1850 for Peoria records a J. B. Chamberlain, 30, an Episcopal minister, born in New York, wife Mary 28, born Ohio, and son Sherrill, two, born in Illinois.

Mountain Fisk shared driving the "miscellaneous wagon" occupied by the William Goudy family.

Franklin B. Gay, 25, born in Vermont, traveled with his own wagon according to Tucker's letter of June 9, 1852. He would abandon the wagon and leave by the Snake River, August 15th. On July 3, 1853 Tucker reported that "Frank Gay has just returned from the Dalles with the fragments of the stock that he sold to Swearengin before the storm out of 170 head only 9 lived through Frank is the only person that went through in our train but got entirely *Strapped* he saved himself in fact he made money . . . Frank acted the man all over with me and I want to tell his mother of the esteem I have for him". Frank served as the surveyor for the road over the Cascades for the Free Emigrant Road Company of Eugene that October. The "bill of Exchange" for $250 to pay for his services he assigned to Mr. Swearingin who had to sue for payment in the Lane County District Court. Frank is listed in the U.S. Census for 1850 in Tazewell County, Illinois, where he appears to have been the oldest child of Franklin and Debora Gay, both born in Vermont.

John Hancock, 24, was listed as a cooper in the U.S. Census of 1850 for Tazewell County. He was the son of John and Nancy Hancock, and all of them were born in New Hampshire. According to the "Journal" revision of 1853, he left the party August 2nd. On March 24, 1853, Tucker reported that "John Hancock is at Milwaukie doing about as one would expect *him* to do his snake river story that you speke of is truly a snake story he did swim the river ore & back again & did bring over Franks old ox but more than this he did *not do* than *brag &* *yarn* he was the laziest man I saw on the plains!"

Mr. Lyford with J. L. Wafer accompanied the goods sent by boat from Pekin, Illinois, to St. Joseph. The U.S. Census for Tazewell County lists a Joseph Lyford, 22, brickmaker, living in the same house as John Goudy, 14, with others.

Mitchell shared driving the "family wagon" which he turned over July 24th. Reprimanded, he took French leave. On July 3, 1853, Tucker reported "Mitchell is at Portland tho it but little difference where [he] is."

Crawford Morrison sent word to his father Esq. Morrison, June 9th by Tucker's letter. According to a letter from Mag, June 7, 1853, Morrison wrote the *Tazewell Mirror,* published in Pekin, Illinois, about going down the Snake River in wagon beds.

Jefferson Vandervort was reported by Mag on June 7, 1853 to be in Portland. According to Leslie Scott, he died soon after arrival in Oregon.

From Mt. Sterling, Brown County, Illinois:

John Jordan joined the party at St. Joseph with a wagon, oxen, and John McDonald. He tried to rescue cattle that swam the Snake River on July 30th. He left the train August 2nd.

John McDonald, approximately 20, traveled with John Jordan. He drowned in the Snake River on July 30th.

Charles Estes, Peter Smith and William Reed are listed as Brown County boys by Leslie Scott.

The Richards brothers from Brown County were remembered by Etty when she answered Clyde Duniway's questionaire in 1925.

From Vermillion County, Illinois:

John Buoy, about 21, arrived in Oregon October 29th and obtained Roseburg Donation Land Claim 461 in Lane County, TWP 19S, R2W, Sec. 19. He appears to be a brother of Mrs. Stull Swearingen. Other Buoys who

arrived in 1853 all had claims in the same township:
Laban, b. 1801, James, b. 1829 and Thomas, b. 1833.

George Stevenson traveled with one of two wagons and
horses from Danville. He died at the Cascades of the
Columbia River.

Ruth Eckler Stevenson, 25 (1829-March 30, 1906) was
George's wife. She would marry John Tucker Scott on
March 15, 1853.

Stevenson — Five-year-old son of George and Ruth Stevenson, not found in U.S. Census records.

Jacob George Stevenson, 3 (born November 21, 1849) was
a son of George and Ruth. He married Helen McCornack of Eugene in 1878, and built for her a fine house
in that city. A teacher and farmer, he was executor of
Tucker Scott's will. Jacob lived in Klamath Falls, Oregon, when his mother died in 1906.

Isaac Stull Swearingen, 39, or Stull (1812-January 8, 1883),
arrived at The Dalles, September 25th. He had three
or four wagons with horses and oxen. He is listed as a
lawyer in the 1850 Census, Vermillion County, Illinois.
Stull obtained Roseburg Donation Land Claim 2000 in
Lane County. On July 3, 1853, Tucker wrote that "Swearingen is settled about 75 miles above here and has a
good claim, now a word with regard to him he deceived
me and abused my confidence and tried to swindle me in
various ways he only succeeded however in swindling
me out of 40$"

Evaline Buoy Swearingen, 27 (December 24, 1824-Febru-
ary 20, 1909), married Stull November 22, 1849 in
Vermillion County, Illinois.

Lydia J. Swearingen, 1, daughter of Evaline and Stull. She
married Casseus Macy on April 30, 1870, and married
a second time, G. H. Shipley, November 1, 1874.

Working his way west:

A "Butler" was listed as a driver by Leslie Scott, p. 232.

DAVID DUNIWAY

JOURNAL OF A TRIP TO OREGON

April 2d; Leaving home, home friends and home associates in Old Tazewell, we are this evening snugly quartered in the open prairie 15 miles from Peoria and 9 miles from Farmigton: Have had but little difficulty in our journey so far; – crossed the Illinois river (for perhap[s] the last time) with but little difficulty and in a word have had no trouble at all except what has been occasioned by bidding farewell forever to those with whom most of us have associated all our lives; and to me it was a great trial to leave the home of my childhood, the place where, when care to me, was a stranger, I was wont to roam oer hill and dale, and where; when I came to know more thoughtful days I have loved to silently muse over the varying vicissitudes of life and loved to wander alone to the seqeste[r]ed grove, to hold commuion unseen by mortal eye with the works of nature and of God–[1]

But here we are, and here I am seated by a blazing fire with Heaven's canopy over my head trying to compose my mind and trying (almost in vain to see how

---

[1] *April 2*: "We, having made up our minds to emigrate to Oregon, have left home, home friends and home associates, and are this evening snugly encamped in the prairie between Peoria and Farmington, We crossed the Illinois river without difficulty, and have had no trouble at all except that occasioned by bidding farewell forever to relatives and friend[s] with whom many of us have associated all our lives; – and to me it was a great trial to leave the home of my childhood the place where, when care, to me, was a stranger, I was wo[nt] to roam over hill and dale, listening to the song of birds and gathering "sweet wildwood flowers", the place where I came to know more thoughtful days, I have loved to silent[ly] muse over the ever varying vicissitudes of life, and loved to wander alone to the sequestered grove, to hold communion w[ith] the works of nature and of God." 1853 Revision. [For a key to source abbreviations used in these notes, see end of document.]

form my thoughts into writing by the flickering and
uncertain blaze of the large wood fire; all with us is
animation (and not a little confusion) and all are
quite anxious to go to ahead

April 3d   Eat breakfast this morning in a snow storm,
and altho. the prospect *did* look rather gloomy, still
we kept in good cheer, and our victuals, crusted, (not
with sugar) but snow, certainly disappeared in a manner that plain[ly] showed that we had not lost our
appetites even in we were experiencing all the 'delights' of (*a*) snow storm in the open prairie; Camped
this evening near Ellis Ville timber, two miles west
of Fairview [*&*] 6 miles from Ellis Ville

The South wind blows very hard, and rather cold
and the sky and atmosphere portends an approaching
storm

April 4th   Sabbath day and consequently we will not
go on; Rained very hard last night but ceased in time
to prepare a breakfast to which we all paid ample jus-
tice; The wind blows very disagreeably and the cold
blasts make us willing to keep in the tents; Intended
to have attended church in Fairview to-day but it was
too muddy; so we will try to spend the Sabbath as best
we can. :.

April 5th   Snow this morning four inches deep and
we were not allowed to stir until nine o'clock, when
a humane and kind-hearted gentleman whose (*house*)
is situated at a short distance from (*our*) camp came
and offered us one of his rooms to use until the storm
should abate (*&*) we could get ready to (*continue*)
our journey and I am now writing by the blazing fire
and enjoying all the comforts which this truly hospita-

ble family can afford; It is certainly pleasant to be
allowed to sit by a blazing fire once more after having
been out for three nights in the cold winds and storms

April 6th – Morning – The snow still lies on the ground
four inches deep, but we think it quite as pleasant traveling and lying by, under the circumstances;, We are
now making arrangements to pack up and start on our
journey;; The morning is warm, and the snow appears
to be preparing to take, a final leave of us; Evening –
Traveled 15 miles to-day, – passed through towns, Vir-
gil and Elks Ville

Camped in the prairie in a place that looks as if it
were two miles west of nowhere   Cloudy and all ap-
pearences of rain

April 7th   Two of our company taken sick; one with
ague, one with the lung fever;– Traveled till about
dark when we stopped at a house to try to get permission to remain all night, but there was no feed for our
cattle on the premises, nor [c]ould we get any under
th(r)ee miles   Leaving our sick folks at that house in
charge of one of the company the rest of us almost
tired out set out for three miles ahead; We got here
with but little difficulty considering the state of the
roads; I, in company with my sisters concluded to
take a view of the (country) around us and in running
over the hills and adniring the scenery; around us, we
got so belated we had to walk the distance alluded to
and [i]t was actually the muddiest road I ever saw
Though we got very tired we lear[n]ed one lesson not
to loiter behind the wagons unless we wanted to take
a long walk: We succeeded in getting hay at the
rates of twenty dollars a ton and were glad to get it,
even at that price

April 8th   Mother so sick she cannot travel and we will have to stay here until she gets better;. The morning is fine; and if we were all well we would certainly be a jolly crew

April 9th   Rained very hard almost all night, Mother still unable to travel; Mud shoe mouth deep around our camp;

April 11th   (*Morning*)[2] Cannot get (*hay*) here any longer, have had no corn since we came here; and not withstanding it is the Sabbath we must move on – evening.. got corn to-day by sending one of our company two miles and a half off the road in search of it: camped this evening in front of a (*house*) where we have bought plenty of chickens and eggs and we intend to have quite a feast Sick folks are better, and we are all straight again and all in good spirits

April 12th   Passed through some of the worst roads that can be found in this Sucker state and traveled 18 miles; Are now camped in the superbs of the beautiful village called Chili   The evening is fine and the scenery around us is beatiful and picturesque enough to cause any intelligent lover of nature's works to feel contented & happy

Expect to attend a prayer meeting this evening;

April 13th   Traveled 18 miles to-day; Passed through Mendon, a beatifully situated town about two- o'cl[ock] The roads are excellent,- sick folks (*almost*) well again the weater is fine and we have really spent a pleasant day). (Camped near a village called (*Ursa*) a rugged looking place containing a grocery, tavern and store;) Had considerable difficulty crossing a little stream

---

2 Inserted in pencil.

called Bear Creek but fortun[   ] got over safely-)

April 14th   Arrived at Quincy at twelve o'clock–
Waited till five, for an opportunity to (*cross*) the majestic Mississippi; Are now safely quartered in a large
steam ferry boat and while I am now writing we are
launched on the unruffled bosom of the great Father
of Waters bound for a landing place seven miles N.W.
of us;[3] and while I look with a feeling of calm con-
tentment upon the placid current of this great river, I
at the same time think with feelings which defy description of (*the*) loved hom[e] of my childhood, my
own native state; Safely landed and encamped for the
night upon the river bank upon the Missouri side

April [   ]th   Old Illinois I say farewell
              Tho long in thee I'd love to dwell
              Yet I must go perhaps no more
              To reach this lovely land and shore

April 15th; Traveled 17 miles; Noticed quite a contrast in the conditions of persons on different sides of
the river. Farmers in Illinois near Quincy were seen
as we passed along, contentedly following the plough
while on this side the negroes do the work and to me
the contrast was so great that I could think of little
else all day;[4] Saw a ma[n] who said he owned seven
slaves of a good stock- he had raised them himse[lf]

---

[3] "near the town of La Grange." 1853 Revision.

[4] *April 15*: "We traveled seventeen miles; the country through which we
passed looks extremely dull; – but little improvement has been made upon
the naturaly 'hard looking' farms. We often saw slaves at work in the fields,
but they did not appear to care *how* any part of their labor was performed;
to me, the contrast between the enterprising farming, of Illinois, and the
dull, careless work of the negroes, (*here*) was so great that I could think of
nothing else all day"   Note: rest of the original entry omitted from 1853
Revision.

and two of them were worth one thousand dollars apeice but he had not got enough of work out of them yet, and in a few years they would be worth more; May none of *us* ever be guilty of buying and selling the souls and bodies of our fellow creatures; slavery is a withering blight upon the prospects happiness and freedom of our Nation

April 16th Made 15 miles; Mr Caffee tawken dangerously ill with the pluerisy: The weather is fine although the roads in some places are almost impassable Camped where we are obliged to use slough water which is well thickened with the blackest kind of mud and is hardly fit for (*even*) the cattle to drink

April 17th Mr C. so sick that we cannot travel— have sent him to a house where he will receive the kindest attentions the family can afford We cannot get a physician anywhere to attend him and we will be obliged to use our own skill [u]ntil we get where medical aid can be procured The boys, to-day, killed four pheasants and fifteen squirrels and we intend to have a great feast when we get them rightly served up

April 18th Sabbath day— Get plenty of hay at $5 per ton and therefore no necessity of traveling Mr C. is considerably better and we hope out of danger .:. We think he will be able to go on by tomorrow

April 19th Made 20 miles— The cold North West wind blowed very disagreeably into our wagons all day and made us feel willing to walk most of the time to keep warm: : Camped where we can get corn a 50 cts. per bushel but no hay can be obtained at any price

April 20th Made 18 miles: The wind blows very hard and we have had rather a hard time of it all day .. Looks more like November than April Mr C. has gone to a house to spend the night He is considerably worse and we begin to doubt his recovery: : Engaged two physicians from Kirksville (a vallage about half a mile from us to attend him during the night; ;

April 21t Mr C. still no better– have taken him to a tavern and have left one of our company to attend him, (*and*) the rest of us have moved forward five miles and intend to remain here until he gets better

April 22d We still entertain little hope of Mr C's recovery:: We have repaired to the banks of the Charitan a small but dangerous (*looking*) stream near our camp to do our washing:: The (*weather*) is fine but prospects for going ahead at present look rather gloomy

April 23d 'Tis indeed a dark picture that has no bright side. Our sick man is getting much better and is convalescing so rapidly that we apprehend no dangerous results from traveling with him and we are preparing to cross the stream before mentioned in a crazy looking ferry boat which will carry one loaded wagon and one yoke of oxen at a time provided they keep some one busy bailing the boat; We intend to move on three miles after crossing where we will encamp for the night

April 24th Came 15 miles:: Stopped two miles from the road we get corn a 76 cts. per. bushel We came to-day through roads where the mud was in some places at least two feet deep [5]

---

[5] *April 24*: "We traveled, this day, about fifteen miles. The cattle were scattered (*in the morning*) and it was late before we could get started: Mr. Swearingen from Vermillion county Illinois, with his family, joined us

April 25th   Sabbath day: The boys killed a turkey
yesterday and we had a great feast to-day As there
(*have*) four other teams joined us there a good many
of us when all collected together and we concluded
to have preaching in our camp to-day— a considerable number of the neighbors collected and we had
a fair specimen of back woods life and meetings both
in the sermon and congregation [6]

April 26th   Got an early start and traveled 20 miles
A sharper tried to make us pay $10 for the privilege
of grazing cattle on a piece of prairie land near his
dwelling but we knew what we were about and saved
our money

April 27th   Came 6 miles to a stream called Madison
creek, which owing to recent freshets is too deep to
ford and we will be compelled to wait here until the
water has time to run down; Our sick folks are all
about well again and we get along very well though
we do not much like the idea of remaining here very
long;

April 28th   The stream is still too high to cross and
we begin to feel a little impatient; Notwithstanding
we have a great deal of sport and no small amount
of work to do; yet the time passes very slowly when
we are unexpectedly detained;

April 29th   We raised our wagon beds some six inches

to-day, making our company quite large The boys killed a fine turkey,
which we have reserved, for a tomorrow's feast. We found the roads extremely muddy;: We got corn at 45 cts." 1853 Revision.

6 *April 25*: "The neighbors collected together around our camp in the
afternoon to hear a sermon, which at Father's request was delivered in
camp. We had a fair specimen of back woods life in both the sermon and
congregation." 1853 Revision.

and managed to cross the stream safely to-day, although the mud on either bank looks sufficiently deep to completely mire every horse and and ox in Missouri

April 30th   Came 18 miles : ; The country through which we have passed for the last two weeks has almost without a single exception looked entirely unfit for the abode of men and we have seen no signs of civilization worth mentioning – in fact nothing (*at all*) but here and there a shabby log hut which exactly corresponded to the destitu[te] and desolate scenery around us: But the portion of country we see to-day begins to look more and more like civilization as we pass along over hill and dale   We are now rolling over a splended looking prairie while the blue tinged timber in the distance, the wild flowers and shrubs (*beneath*) our feet and the (*numerous*) herds conteantedly grazing near us presents an appearance at once picturesque and sublime

The roads are excellent and the weather charming

May 1t   Came 20 miles over a splendid portion of country: I rode on horseback all the afternoon and got so far ahead that the teams stopped for the night two miles from the house where I had halted to waited for them and I had the pleasure of going that distance back in a hurry;, Camped in the open prairie where the grass is rather poor ;.

May 2d   We were obliged to go ahead until we could obtain better grazing for our cattle which we could not procure until we had traveled 16 miles when we encamped in the out skirts of a little grove and we intend to remain here until tomorrow

May 3d   Came about 19 miles over good roads gen-

erally though we passed through some miserable mud
holes; The weather is much colder than we have had
for a week past and the heavy clouds loud thunder
and off repeated lightning, portends approaching rain

Camped in a little point of scrubby timber with the
prairie almost all around us   We are within eleven
miles of St. Josephs

May 4th   Came within 6 miles of St Joe when we
halted until some of our company who had gone ahead
to see if it were practicable for us to get into the town
on account of the (*great*) rush of emigration,–   returned and advised us to move on; We then went within
4 miles of the town and halted for the night;.

May 5th   Rained very hard last night, and our camp
and everything around it, looked, this morning as if
it were just ready to swim off;; In consequence of
this we concluded to move on to town and we are
camped within half a mile of the main body of the
town, and all are busy cooking and packing provisions, which reached us safely at St. Joe. having been
sent that far by water.;.

May 6th   Mr Chamberlin, a young gentleman belonging to our company has been complaing considerably
for several days and yesterday we moved him to a
house just opposite to us, a he was much worse:. Had
a physician sent for who pronounced his disease to be
pneumonia and lung-fever   We intend to remain here
for some days until we see how his disease will termi-
nate;;

May 7th & 8th   Mr Chamberlin is very ill and we
will be obliged to cross the river next Monday and
leave him, if he gets no better which we have at pres-

ent little reason to hope   He is staying at a private
house where he receives the kindest attentions and
some our company watches with him constantly   It
will be a hard trial for us and him to leave him behind but is the only way for us to do, as we should
have been on the plains by the first of May at the
farthest

May 9th   Sabbath day has come once more, and with
it have come sad and melancholy feelings for us all,
at the thought of leaving one of our company behind
us sick, perhaps never to see his face again ;; We intend to cross the Missouri in the moring, and have
made preparations accordingly

May 10th   Crossed the river without any difficulty
Left our sick man some better this morning and two
of our company remained with him, with the intention
of staying until he gets either better or worse, when
they will overtake us on horseback   Moved on six
miles to a place where a company of five men who
are old acquaintances have been waiting two weeks
for us to join them.: The surrounding scenery is delightful   The soil is fertile and lacks nothing but
improvement to make it one of the firt places in the
world in agriculture;; My sister [7] and I ascended to
the summit of a hill and with the aid of a spy-glass
took a farewell view of St. Joe. and the United States.:

May 11th   Came about 12 miles over a very hilly and
disagreeable road. ; Though we found it better towards
evening than it was in the forenoon   Canped in a
beautiful and altogether romantic spot where we get

---

[7] Mary Frances or Fanny according to Leslie Scott, p. 257. Leslie miscalled
J. B. Chamberlin, "George," and said he died this day, p. 256.

some dwarf trees to burn by carrying them a short distance and tolerably good water can be obtained from a kind of spring in a ravin near us

May 12:; Found the roads very good to-day.; Grass is plenty everywhere that we have been since we crossed the river The portion of country we to-day, is not so hilly as that of yesterday.;. Camped near a little grove where we obtained wood, and water.;. We have passed 7 new graves (*belongs to May 14th*) to-day. passed a place, where some folks were busied consigning to its last resting place the remains of a young man who had (*died*) with the measles The family had emigrated from Pennsylvania— had lost three of their company in St. Joe, and with a wish to overcome evry obstacle, they determined to push ahead little knowing that the extent of their ambition would be to come this far on their journey, only to lay the remains of a son in the ocean like and seemingly boundless plains.;. They have become entirely discouraged and when we left them, they were making preparations to go back to the home of their natvity-: (We came about 18 miles)

May 13th Came about the same distance as yesterday and found wood and water by turning out our road about a mile:: There are near forty teams camped within sight of us ::.

May 14th Came (I should think 18 miles;.. The country as we pass along, looks more and more level; and the *plains* certainly wear a charm which I little expected to see; The weather is fine which aids them in wearing a brilliancy which certainly cannot be surpassed in any country or in any prairie.;. We roll along over, level roads for the most of the time, and those who are walking, or on horseback by going off the main road a little can see a sight which looks fit for angels to admire; The little hollows which at a short distance from the road we can see at almost any time are generally filled with flowers and var (*i*) egated with ten thousand tints which are almost sufficient to perfectly enchant the mind of every lover of nature

May 15th   Came about the same distance as yesterday (&) over much the same looking country. Crossed the big Nemaha a dangerous stream and encamped for the night upon its shores.:. Broke two ox yokes in ascending the bank of the stream

May 16th   Sabbath day: 'Tis well that we crossed the Nemaha last evening for it is rapidly rising ;: The cold wind blows very hard and very disagreeably, and the atmosphere, is cold enough for a drear November morning

May 17th   One Thousand Eight Hundred and Fifty One

We came about 18 miles;. The country is gently rolling, and ever and anon we could see at perhaps a mile or more from the road a small but beatiful little grove, adding, alike, beauty and variety to the scenery; We passed the *little Nemaha,* to-day;. before we came to it the road which had been going almost due West turned North about ¾ of a mile, passing around the bluffs to afford an opportunity of crossing the stream:; These bluffs are beautifully rolling, and as high as many we see on the Illinois river.;. The stream is only about 15 or 20 feet wide and meandering among small clusters of trees bounded on either side by (*these*)

high, rolling bluffs;: We passed five other new made
graves, We found an excellent and beautiful camping
place a half mile from the road by the side of a little
stream;; We have seen no Indians for several days

May 18th   *We* have come according to Platts Guide [8]
about twenty three and a half miles; The road and
country as far as we could see was much more level
than any we had seen before.;. The wind (*has*) blowed
very hard from the S. S. W. ever since 10 o'clock :;
We passed three new made graves again to-day:: We
are encamped in a bend of a clear running brook at
no great distance from the "Big Blue"

May 19th   Traveled about 19 miles to-day:, Crossed
the Big Blue without any difficulty:; The road to-day
has been more hilly than that of yesterday;: We passed
four new made graves:: The deaths are principally
occasioned by colds and diarrehea brought on in (*some*)

---

[8] "Platt, Philip L. The travellers' guide across the plains, upon the overland route to California showing distances from point to point, accurately
measured by roadometer, and describing the springs, streams of water, hills,
mountains, camping-places and other notable objects along the route; with an
appendix containing the routes from Council Bluffs to Fort Laramie; . . .
and a general summary of distances, by P.L. Platt and N. Slater, A.M. Chicago. Printed at the Daily Journal Office, 1852." This was republished in
1963 by John Howell, San Francisco.
   Leslie Scott discusses the numerous books published prior to 1852 which
were read and studied by John Tucker Scott, p. 237. "He used *Pratt's Guide,*
published in 1848, and Palmer's *Journal,* published in 1847. Hastings' *Emigrants' Guide,* published in 1845, was in his travel library; also Colton's
maps, which contained the best geographical knowledge of the time. He also
had the Oregon Trail map of Charles Preuss, 1846, and the *Report* of Frémont's exploring expedition to the Rocky Mountains, 1843, which covered
much of the route followed by the Scott party; also Frémont's map of Oregon
and Upper California (1848)." How Leslie dated Pratt's Guide as 1848
he does not say. John Tucker Scott could use this guide from St. Joseph to
Fort Kearney, and the upper ferry of the Platte to Fort Hall, in the main
Guide, and Appendix 2, Route from Council Bluffs to Fort Laramie, from
beyond the ford at Fort Kearney.

instances by exposure and fatigue, but we think most generally from imprudence in eating and drinking We have however known several cases of the measles and two deaths have been caused within our knowledge of this diease.:, Several of our company have been attacked with diarrehea attended with violent hemorrhoids but by taking a strong preventative at first and abstaining almost entirely from eating a day or two they get along without any dangerous consequences

We have encamped a half mile from the road where we get good wood but not very good water

May 20th   We came according to the best conclusions we can form about 19 miles.;. Passed two newmade graves– one person died of measles another from causes not mentioned on the inscription at the head of the grave;; I have not seen an Indian for several days though, we are now within the midst of a tribe of Pawnees who are reported as being rather hostile and and very theivish.;. We crossed the Little Sandy about four o'clock and encamped I should judge about one mile and a half from it near a natural hollow, which contains some standing water in places and in one place within reach of our camp a kind of spring where we get tolerably good water   We can also obtain wood in this ravine tho, it looks as if camping were not done here very often or it would not supply the wants of emigrants a great while

May 21t   Traveled according to Platt's guide about 14 miles over a very hilly road.;. There has been rain slowly falling all day, and we concluded that on account of this it was best to go no farther to-day and we therefore halted about two o'clock with the intention of remaining here until morning.;. The rain has

now about ceased to fall and we begin to think it is all
over   We get very good grazing for our stock at this
place; it is off the main road a half mile and about
two miles west of little Sandy a stream (*which would*)
hardly be worth a name at all if it were not for the
bad hills on either side and the difficulty of crossing
on that account which, certainly ought to render it
worthy of note;: We found in some natural hollows
and along some hill sides several pieces of something
exactly resembling iron ore, which occasioned the beleif that iron mines of great value are to be found in
this vicinity;:[9] Since writing the above we have found
that (*big*) Sandy is 3 miles ahead of us, and the stream
we crossed yesterday was probably a branch of big
Sandy

May 22d   We traveled about 12 miles;; 2 miles
brought us to Big Sandy .:. We went very slow on
account of the bad state of the roads which owing the
rains of last night and yesterday had become very
muddy.:. The weather has been clear and beautiful
this afternoon, tho' it was very dark and foggy this
morning;: Last night Mr Stevensons horses five [10] in
number took a stampede and we were compelled to
leave him and his family as he could not come on
until he found them.;: This evening however two of
our men who remained with him to help him in searching for them overtook us and brought the joyful news
that they had all been found and they will overtake
us tomorrow.;: We are camped 9 miles from big Sandy

---

[9] "I strolled in the evening down the precipitous banks of a deep ravine,
where I found some peices of iron ore which occasioned the beleif that iron
mines of great value can be found in this vicinity." 1853 Revision.

[10] "six in number." 1853 Revision.

on the margin of a little stream where we get plenty of wood and water and good grass

May 23d   Sabbath day;; Owing to the Indians being reported as numerous us we do not consider it best to remain more than one night in a place and we therefore traveled some 7 or 8 miles to-day, till we found another camping place where wood water and grass could be obtained– this we found on the banks of a (*small*) stream called Ale Ness, but which we thought it best to denominate Tadpole Sandy as the warter is littrally filled with these little animals and in many places the sand is so much higher than the water that we can walk on its surface, but anywhere that we have made the experiment we can obtain good water by spading down two feet, The day is clear and warm;, Mrs Caffee is very ill

May 24th   Came about 18 miles to-day:;. We are following the little Blue a stream about one hundred feet wide.;. The water is rather muddy but has no unpleasant taste.; Its banks are ornamented with Cottondwood ash and elem trees

We encamped for the night upon the banks of the Blue, in a very loely spot.

May 25th   Came about 12 miles, rained yesterday afternoon and last night almost incessantly, though slowly, making the roads bad and traveling disagreeable,;. We met a large train coming from fort Laramie, loaded entirely with buffalo robes,;; The men who drove the teams were a set of French and Indian half-breeds– and spoke a kind of French, Indian and Elglish jargon when talking, with eachother which mingled with a host of curses, (in English) sounded strangely to our ears

May 26th   Came 18 miles–   The weather is fine, but
the dust flies so thick that in some places it was difficult for us to see our way   &   We passed four new
made graves–   One was that of a man who was murdered–   and found on the road by some passing emigrants, lying off a short distance from the road; Upon
examination it was found that he had been killed with
buck shot– and (*stabs*) with a buoy knife:; Those who
found him, buried him by laying him upon the ground
and covering him with earth,: left him, with a notice
to the effect of the above, posted by the road side,:,
He had probably got into some effray with his company who had served him in this manner   We are
camped again on the banks of the Blue

May 27th   Came 22 miles ;: The roads are good and
the country beautiful.;; We were informed this morning that it would be twenty five miles to wood and
water; We accordingly laid in a supply of these necessary articles before starting, which we were afterwards very much pleased as we camped on the prairie where neither could be obtained:: Our men saw
several antelopes off at a distance from the road, and
gave close chase to one, but it proved too smart for
them   A man shot a hare to-day and brought it to our
train for us to see;; It looked very much like a common rabbit but was much larger and was a kind of
dirty white color.;. The antelope resemble sheep in
form though they are larger and rather more graceful
in their movements   They are almost white, with a
few red spots on the side and back

We find the health improving as get farther on,–
we passed no fresh graves to-day   Mrs Caffee who
has been very sick is much better and only requires
care to keep her from exposure

May 28th   Came about 18 miles; We found no water except one or two mud holes, and (*but*) one place where any wood could be procured until night when we struck the Platte, river ;;. We halted (*for the night*) on its banks opposite to Grand island, which is covered with wood and very good grass; We drove our cattle on to this island to graze and the men waded across to it and got wood for cooking purposes.;. The stream where they crossed over to the island was about three feet deep and one hundred yards in width with a quick-sand bottom; The water is thick with sand, We mixed (*corn*) meal with it and after it settles a while strain it, and it becomes tolerably clear:;

May 29th   Came 8 miles to Fort Kearney; We here halted awhile to write letters, look at curiosities, &c. The fort is a rather shabby looking concern but contains two very good looking dwelling houses which to us who had been traveling for three weeks without seeing a house or any thing like civilization presented an appearance of a very pleasing nature [11]

Ater leaving the fort we traveled about 8 miles, up the Platte with the expectation of going on upwards of one hundred miles before finding a place to ford it; We however seen teams crossing at this place and therefore came to the determination to cross here too, as the health, as well as facilities for wood and grass is much better on the North than South side :: We are camped on the banks of the river to night, without ordinary fuel but we find plenty of buffalo chips;:

May 30th   Sabbath day.;. Intended to have lain by

---

[11] "The fort is a rather shabby looking concern, but contains a well built hospital and one handsome frame dwelling. The country around the fort is a rather barren looking plain, almost wholly destitute of timber." 1853 Revision.

to-day but after taking all matters into consideration,
we concluded that it was best to cross the river this
morning;; We found the crossing more tedious than
difficult :; The place we came through was about a
mile and a half wide, about three feet deep (*except*) in
holes where the cattle were sometimes covered for a
time almost out of sight.; It (*took*) a team just one
hour to cross it.;.[12] We find no timber on this side, (the
North) except what grows on islands   The day is clear
and very warm;..

May 31t   Traveled to-day about twenty four miles:
We are journeying up the Platte   The bottom is very
level but sometimes in our traveling to day we came
to kinds of sloughs or creeks which we would scarcely
see at all until we came onto the bank.;. These hollows
unlike others we have seen had no timber around them
We camped to-night on the margin of one of these
hollows where we get considerably better water than
that of the Platte:; We are about one mile from the
river,– on the South side, and and on the North about
three miles from us tho' it does not look to be more
than one   the bluffs are ranged along in quite a romantic manner.; We have no wood except the chips
before mentioned; which in the absence of ordinary
fuel makes a very good fire

---

12 "The Platte river, swift and swollen, didn't seem to have any banks.
We had heard of the dangers of quicksands. My father had, with the help
of his drivers, raised the beds of the wagons, so as not to dip water – oh!
the excitement – I feel it yet! When everything was in readiness, all of us
were tucked inside the wagons; my father put me, last of all, inside the back
end of the last wagon, told me to keep still and not be afraid. The loud
voices of the drivers as they yelled and whipped up the oxen, the jogging
of the wagons through the surging waters and over the quicksands, the
memory is with me yet! When they got over the river all were accounted
for but they couldn't find me. Finally I was pulled out from under the bows
nearly smothered." Etty's "Memoirs," p. 2-3.

June 1t   Traveled about 18 miles .: The weather is
exceedingly hot, making going ahead a tedious and
laborious. . occuption   Our sick folks who were all
rather better when we crossed the Platte are getting
along rather slowly but amidst all the obstacles which
seem to come across our way in the course we are
pursueing, one hope seems yet to inspire us all;– that
of one day arriving at the place of our destination:;.
Where other folks have gone *we* certainly can go; at
any rate we think so   We met a company to-day who
had started back (*to the states*) on account of sickness
and death; They buried one man yesterday, and another this morning and had come back about four miles
when we met them   They had started from Springfield
Illinois   We have suffered considerable inconvenience
this afternoon in consequence of the great scarcity of
good water; The water of the Platte being .. so mudy
and warm that it was impossible to drink it   We however (*this evening*) found an excellent spring just in
reach of where we wanted to camp and it seemed to
me that it was the best water we. had (*tasted*) since
we left St Joe. Passed four graves

June 2d   Came about 18 miles to-day :; The country
is level   We are traveling through the Platte bottom:
The weather has been remarkably hot all day but since
we stopped this evening the West wind has arisen and
blowed a perfect gale   Its fury has now partly abated
though we think a hard storm may be looked for tonight, as heavy clouds blacken the Western horizon
and we hear repeated reports of thunder, which sounds
as if they cannot be at a great distance from us

We find tolerably good water this evening by diging
near a kind of marsh or slough; We camped this eve-

ning about as far from the river as we, did last evening

June 3d   Traveled according to our guides about 19
miles :: We found the roads very sandy, in the afternoon .;. In (*one*) place the bluffs came up very near to
the river, and I ascended on horseback to the top of
highest one that we could see from the road, and there
saw, indeed a romantic spectacle.; The Platte below
me flowing on in peaceful music, intersected with
numerous islands covered with timber, when when no
other timber could be seen, The emigrants wagons
cattle and horses on the road in either direction as far
as the eye could reach, the plain below in which all
this living, mass was moving contrasted strangely with
the view on the other side of. where I was;; There
nothing could be seen but still higher ranges of bluffs
or rather sand hills, A these of these hills the ground
was in most places almost covered with a kind of flower
the seed of which exactly resembles our buck-wheat
while the flower in shape, size and color exactly resembles the common touch-me-not— — —

Some of our company killed a buffalo to-day which
considerably changed the (*regular rotine*) of our diet
at supper time; it tastes almost exactly like beef but
has a considerably courser grain

They also killed a prairie dog and brought to the
camp; They are courious looking animals, remebling
the rat, squirrel and rabbit, and look as if they might
be good eating tho' we do not like to be the first to
try them ; We camped again near the Platte; on the
margin of a little creek called Skunk creek   We last
night experienced all the realities of a Platte river
storm   The rain fell in torrents until one o'clock,
while the thunder and lightning was to some the most

terrific and to others the most sublime of any thunderstorm we had ever witnessed The tents belonging to some of our company were upset in the midst of it, the wind blowing a perfect gale, rendering it almost impossible for even the wagons to keep their places

June 4th Came about four miles to another part of Skunk creek and as the water is clear, and we had great need of resting and doing our washing we stopped to get our goods and chatels in order;. We find excellent grass; and have hauled wood from an island on the river about three miles from this place

June 5th We came about twenty miles this day; We found the roads very sandy.; About the middle of the afternoon a storm came up, and we halted, arranged our wagons beside each-other as closely as we could place them, chaind up the cattle and horses & pitched the tents and gathered a supply of fuel in about as short a time as any thing of the kind could be accomplished (At least I thought so) In about one hour the storm abated and we started on again and went on about two miles carrying the dry chips we had gathered along with us

We camped near the river,– passed four graves

June 6th. Sunday; We find that keeping the Sabbath rightly by lying by on the plains is "no go" and we accordingly started as early as usual and came about twenty-one miles:, The (*day*) is pleasant we passed six graves,:

June 7th Traveled about 16 miles:: The roads are very sandy rendering it difficult to get along;: Killed another buffalo to-day A man died last night in a train which camped opposite to us;: They buried him

this morning and when we started they had got almost
re(a)dy to move on.;. The train overtook us while
we were lying by at noon, and one of our company
who was going through without any occupation joined
them intending to drive a team in place of the man
who had died.; They are going to California We
camped this evening near Wolf springs about half a
mile from the Platte

June 8th   Made twenty (*four*) miles,; The day has
been quite warm but the South wind kept us all animated and considerably allayed the heat of the sun.;.
We found the roads very sandy in some places but in
others we found the roads excellent

We passed eight fresh graves: Hear of considirable
sickness in a great many trains.;. At one time to-day
we saw upwards of sixty teams ahead of us besides
two large droves of cattle; while behind us as far as
we could see others were moving on,;, The great cause
of dierrehea which has proved to be so fatal on the
road has been occasioned in most instances by drinking
water from holes dug in the river bank and along
marshes,:.[13] Emigrants should be very careful with
regard to this especially along this part of the road
as the ground is impregnated with alkali :; In some
places the ground is covered with this substance;; It
looks about like ashes and has considerably the same
taste only it is a great deal stronger.;. We are camped
again about one half mile from the river on the margin
of a little stream; the water is better tasted than any
we have seen for some days

We saw three buffaloes this morning; They were

---

[13] "The great cause of *emigrant Cholera* we think to be imprudence in
eating and drinking." 1853 Revision.

coming down the Platte and in a few moments after
we first seen them they turned and crossed the river
thus eluding pursuit but it gave us a fair opportunity
to see them and as they were the first I had seen they
excited my curiosity a good deal

June 9th Traveled twenty two miles ;: We started
in very good season this morning, the weather being
fine and a pleasant breeze was stirring.;. The heat of
the sun (*became*) very oppressive about noon, and continued so throughout the day until night,;; The evening seems to me to be cool enough for frost ;; We
passed Ash Hollow at three o'clock in the afternoon
and in a short time came to Castle Creek,; This stream
is about as wide as the little Blue and in some places
two feet and in others about six inches deep; The
water is clear and palatable;; The roads have been
very sandy in some places to day,;; We camped again
near the Platte; Passed eight graves

June 10th Came 18 miles; The morning was fine but
the afternoon was so very oppressive that it seemed
almost impossible to breathe About three o'clock a
black cloud arose in the west with every sign of an
approaching storm We halted and all hands went to
work to collect chips: this done we started on and drove
near two hours longer; Contrary to our expectations
and wishes the cloud passed over us but we were favored for a time with a very refreshing West wind
We passed two graves to-day Camped about one
fourth of a mile from the Platte

June 11th Traveled 18 miles:; The heat was oppres-
ive about noon almost beyond endurance:: About three
o'clock again, clouds arose in the west the same as

yesterday, and although no rain fell yet the wind blew
such a gale that it was for a short time impossible for
us to proceed:; The sand blew in clouds hiding every
thing from our sight for twenty minutes when the wind
suddenly changed and cleared the dust from the road,
which enabled us to move on ,;, We have seen the
wildest and consequently the most romantic scenery
to-day that I have seen since we started; Columns above
columns of sand and sand stone formed in massive
bluffs shaped by the hard winds of this region into
rude appearunces of images which the traveler gazes
at and is forcibly reminded of the histories of the
renowned ruins of magnificent structures of the Old
World.;..

The distances which these bluffs lie from the road
are very deceiving: This evening a difference of opinion arose among some of the company about the distance to a bluff which did not look to be one half mile
from the road:; Wishing to gratify their curiosity several of the men started to the point and upon measuring
the distance it was found to be more than two miles,;:
They carried some cedar from the bluffs for cooking
purposes which came very opportunely as no chips
could be found .;. We passed 6 graves and camped
near the Platte

June 12th   Traveled 20 miles;, At noon we for the first
time hailed the rock known by the name of "Nebraska
Court House   This huge mass looks as if it might be
the ruins of some ancient collossal edifice   It is on the
South side of the river and rises up as if (to)mock
the scenery around it with its bold and majestic front.;
It is represented as covering an area of one acre of
ground:;: After traveling a while in the afternoon we

came in sight of the long heard of and renowned Chimney Rock; It at first looked as if it were a spire pointing towards Heaven's blue dome but as we came nearer to it the spire seemed to enlarge and bear rather more the appearance of a chimney extending high above a dome shaped building

We passed five new made graves; We camped this evening on the river bank without buffalo chips and with no wood at all except a few small sticks of cedar which will answer for boiling water &c. but we made out a supper in the way of bread by eating sea-biscuits A hard storm came up about six o'clock, and although but little rain fell yet the wind blew so hard that the wagons rocked to and froe;; One of the tents got blown over and the many laughs and jests occasioned by the predicament of the inmates of the tent were left in for a few moments, made us all forget to regard the fury. of the storm;: We got everything straightened up again and all went off peacibly and well

June 13th   Sabbath Eve;: Did not go forward to day Carried some chips from the bluffs two miles off which answered for cooking purposes; the day has been quite warm but a shower about five in the evening cooled the air and we are now favored with a refreshing brezee;; Upwards of one hundred teams passed us to day;; Every one is anxious to go ahead and we amongst the rest, but to rest a day will do our cattle a great deal of good and we think will do us no harm

June 14th   Traveled about twenty four miles:. We have seen very romantic scenery all day; The Chimney rock has been in full view all day:; It is represented as being three hundred feet high but from the road we are traveling it does not appear to be more than

one hundred feet.;. Palmer in speaking of this rock
very truly says that it has the unpoetical appearance
of a hay stack with a pole extending far above its top
We are now camped in full view of Scott's bluffs,;
These bluffs derived their name from a melancholy
tradition   A traveler (*of the name*) was once taken
sick near these bluffs and becoming unable to travel
was, at his own request abandoned by his companions;
He was never after heard of but a party in passing
these bluffs some times afterwards found the bones
of a man some distance from the spot where the unfortunate person had last been seene

We passed two graves, A light shower came up this
afternoon which continueing for some time cooled the
air and made the weather quite pleasant

[Entries through June 19th are by Margaret Ann or Maggie, except
part of June 17th by Tucker. Abigail has cholera.]

June 15th 1852. We traveled I suppose about 18
miles we had very good roads mostly all day. We
passed a small creek this afternoon called spring creek.
About noon we stopped nearly opposite the "Scott
bluffs" sometimes called capital hills These hills
have a truly grand romantic appearance calculated
to fill the mind with indescribeble amazement approaching almost to sublimity. There are numerous
cedars growing uppon them, which gives them a still
more grand appearance. We came in sight of a peak
called Laramie's Peak (*in the*) afternoon whose lofty
summit appeared to reach above the clouds in the distant horizon, It is supposed that we are about 70 miles
from it. We passed seven new made graves to day and
camped about three quarters of a mile from the Platte
where we get good water and grass but no fuel of any

kind even Buffalo chips are impossible to (*obtain*) and we will be obliged to eat sea biscuits for supper,

June 16th   We came I suppose about 24 miles   we had good roads mostly excepting some mud holes which we had to cross this forenoon, We have seen considerable of water to day termed alk(*a*)li   it is considered dangerous for cattle to drink any excepting running water as all these sloughs and marshes are impregnated with this substance. The Platte is the surest resort. There are several of our company sick but we hope they are not dangerous   About ten o'clock this morning we passed a train who were busied in buriing a body of a female who had died about two hours previous to that time, They had buried her husband a week before, Little did he think that his young wife would so soon follow him, What a sad thing to leave our friends in this uninhabited country inhabited only by the red man of the forest We are camped this evening one (*half*) a mile from the Platte where we have good grass and use the water from the Platte. We passed ten new made graves to day, and heard of considerable sickness in diferent trains. Laramie's peak is distinctly in view it is the highest peak of the black hills. By crossing— to the north side we will miss the black hills intirely which will save considerable hevy roads.

June 17th 1852.   We started this morning about half past seven. We have very good roads   have stopped at noon on the banks of the Platte and intend staying here till a wagon belonging to the train overtakes us which did not start this morning as soon as the rest did there being a sick man in the wagon. We hope after we leave Platte river there will not be so much sickness. There

is an Indian trading post on the opposite side of the
river from where we have stopped.

[Rest of entry is by John Tucker Scott]

our waggon with the sick man has come up & he is
much better; we started out at 3, oclock & travelled
about six miles which brings us within 3 miles of Laramie   we are encamped on the banks of the Platte
where we have a plenty of good wood, the grass is
rather poor; we travelled about 15 miles to day

[Maggie resumes writing]

June 18th   We started early this morning   passed
Fort Laramie about 10 o'clock. Two of our company
crossed the river (*and carried some*) letters which the
company had written. We passed several indian trading posts this morning. We can see some trading posts
on the opposite side of the river, We passed three new
made graves this morning. The tribe of indians that
occupy this territory are called Sioux. They are represented as being thievish but it is thought if emigrants
use propper precaution they need fear nothing from
them, In pas(s)ing a dirty stream we met with quite
an accident, a wagon belonging to the train upset, and
surely I never saw such a mud hole as it was fortunately, there was no person in the wagon [14]   The train
moved on about two hundred yards, where we stopped
for dinner. We have very poor grass, and will stay
here no longer than we can get the unfortunate wagon
reloaded and the cattle can be rested. Most of the sick
folks are better   As we ascend the Platte the scenery
is more beautiful than any we have seen for some time,
At least we think so as we have seen no timber before
for two hundred miles and we are heartily glad to see

14 "mother's wagon." Leslie Scott, p. 270.

(*it*) once more. It is about 500. and 40 miles from Laramie to Hall according to the best information we can obtain. We find numerous beds of prickly pears enough to astonish any one in the *"States"*. We have traveled this afternoon between to ranges of black hills. (but not the principal range) The scenery is grand high ranges of hills on each side adorned with cedars and pine, while numerous wild flowers and pl(*a*)nts of evry discription (*which*) adorn the valeys below gives alike beauty and variety to the scenery, We are encamped this evening between two lofty ranges of hills where we can obtain wood but no water   we will consequently have to drive the cattle to the river which is some distance *off*   The grass is tolerably good and if we only had plenty of *"Adams ale"* we would have a delightful camping place. We have passed 4 graves in all to day and have come about (*14*) miles, The sick folks are all better,

June 19th 1852   We were camped last night 9 miles from Fort Laramie, The train moved out about 7 o'clock, came 10 miles farther where we again strike the Platte which we are all glad to see. We found several delightful springs this morning   the water was as clear as crystal, and was quite refreshing to us, The road was very hilly and rocky this morning and if I felt disposed I should call them "[   ]" [15] We are all very glad to see a change in the scenery, we were tired of the dull monotony of the *"plains."* But I think we have come to the long wished for hills at last, There is not grass enough for the cattle here. (where we have come to the Platte) and we will not stop here longer than the cattle can be waterd. and then we

---

[15] Blacked out; "young mountains."

intend going on till we can obtain the desired article
We came on about 100 yards where we found another
excellent spring, The water is as pure and appears to
be as wholesome as any in the *"States"*. Thinking it
rather uncertain when we could obtain more we thought
propper to fill the casks. which we did and came on
about two miles where we have stopped for dinner
and to give the cattle an opportunity for grazing. We
find tolerable good grass here. We are about opposite
"Laramie's peak," which is about twenty miles distant
from us, the road still continues hilly and rocky and
in consequence of this our progress is much retarded
The breeze blowing from these hills seems to inhale
us with new life and vigor, Some of the hills are three
hundred feet high and to me who had never seen a
mountain they seemed to be one continued chain

We are camped this evening near some excellent
springs which seem to gush from the rocks. We have
good grass and wood and in a word have a very good
camping place! We are surrounded on all sides by
bluffs and a great many others are encamped close
by us, The evening is pleasant and the sky is without
a cloud. Came 22 miles to day and passed four new
made graves, (*We have just heard that*) there is a
woman dying about 100 yards from us, The part of
our train who were sick are much better and improve-
ing all the time. Those who were sick in the first part
of the journey are getting healthy, It is most generally
the case if persons are sick and their health is restored
that they are much (*healthier*) than they had been
for some time.

[Abigail resumes writing]

June 20th '52   Sabbath Day:. How mysterious are the

works of an all wise and overruling Providence! We
little thought when last Sabbath's pleasant sun shed
upon us his congenial rays that when the next should
come it would find us mourning over the sickness and
death of our beloved Mother! But it has been even so;
our mother was taken about two 'o'clock this morning
with a violent dierrehea attended with cramping She
however aroused no one until daylight when everything
was done which we possibly could do to save her life;
but her constitution long impaired by disease was unable to withstand the attack and this afternoon beween
four and five o'clock her wearied spirit took its flight
and then we realized that we were bereaved indeed

A lady died last night in a train camped near us
and they this morning interred her lifeless remains and
started off without (*any*) apparent delay being occasioned by her decease

June 21t We this morning dispatched our breakfast in
silence and with sorrowful hearts prepared to pay the
last tribute of respect to the remains of the beloved
lamented dead:; She now rests in peace, beside the
lady (*before mentioned*) who died the night before;.
The place of her interment is a romantic one and one
which seems fitted for the last resting place of a lover
rural scenery such as she when in good health always
delighted in;: The grave is situated on an eminence
which overlooks a ravine intersected with (*groves of*)
small pine and cedar trees.; In about the centre of this
ravine or rather basin, there wells forth from a kind
of bank a spring of icy coldness, clear as crystal.:. In
the outskirts of this basin clusters of wild roses and
various other wild flowers grow in abundance.;: And
from an eminence where all this can be viewed at a

single glance, reposes the last earthly remains of *my mother*.:.[16]

We call the place Laramie's Point or Castle Hill We passed three new made graves and came about twenty miles   The road has been tolerably level all day, as it follows along the valley of the Platte, and we were not often disturbed by sand hills;

[Inserted by John Tucker Scott in space left probably for such a tribute. The title is printed in open block letters with no space between words]

THE GOLDE BOWL BROKEN

1   T,was midnight and he sat alone–
    The husband of the dead,
    That day the dark dust had been thrown
    Upon her buried head;
    Her orphan children round me sleep
    But in their sleep do moan
    Now bitter tears are falling fast
    I feel that I,m *alone*

2. The world is full of life and light
    But ah no world for me
    My little world once warm and bright
    Is cheerless as the sea
    Where is her sweet and kindly face
    Where is her cordial tone

---

[16] Fanny, in a Fred Lockley interview of March 21, 1925, remembered that: "We buried her wrapped in a blanket in a shallow grave by the side of the road. Father and the others heaped stones over the grave so that the coyotes and other animals might not disturb it." Etty's "Memoirs," p. 3-4; added: "We had to journey on and leave her, in a lonely grave – a feather bed as a coffin and the grave protected from the wolves by stones heaped upon it. The rolling hills were ablaze with beautiful wild roses – it was the 20th of June, and we heaped and covered mother's grave with the lovely roses, so the cruel stones were hid from view. Her grave is lost. No one was ever able to find it again."

I gaze around my dwelling place
And feel that I,m *alone*

3   The lovely wife – maternal care–
The self denying zeal–
The smile of hope that chasd despai[r]
And promised future weal
The clean bright hearth nice table spread
The charm oer all things thrown–
The sweetness in what e'er She said
All gone– I am *alone*

4   I Slept at last and then I dreamed
(Perchance her spirit woke)
A soft light *oer* my pillow gleamed
A voice in music spoke
"Forgot forgiven all neglect
Thy love recalled alone
The babes I loved o love protect
I Stille am all thine own
                Lafayette   O.T.   Jan 29th 1853

[Abigail continues]

June 22   We came twenty miles.;. The roads are very
sandy and for (*the last*) ten miles our road run over
cliffs of rock, and wound about to such a degree that
we cannot be more than ten or fifteen miles from where
we started in the morning ;; Some of the rocky cliffs
resemble rude images of men and animals, rising up
as if to mock the surrounding sterile and barren scenery.;. Rocks of immense proportions are seen on all
sides of us covered in some places with the sage brush
and a slight covering of sand, and in other places the
winds;. have blown away the sand and leaves them
for rods in a place without covering of any description

We find very poor grass this evening.:. The sage brush, prickly pear, wild pea, plum and bean, with great varieties of flowers are the principal and, I may say the whole productions of these sandy regions:, We are camped on the Platte and find but little wood, but with sage roots and what wood we have, we can get along finely in the cooking line;; The evening is quite cool   Passed five graves

June 23.   Traveled twenty five miles.; The road run over bluffs all day, and the country has had very much the appearance of what we seen yesterday

We have saeen in some places a few scrubby pines and cedars but nothing in comparison to what we seen some days ago,; We are encamped on the Platte under the shade of some cottonwood trees arranged as regularly in many places as if it had been the work of art;, The evening is quite pleasant but the sky and atmosphere portends approaching rain   Passed six graves. Poor grass

June 24   Came some five or six miles again & half past eight o'clock and finding a place of good grazing we halted and turned our cattle out upon it:; We had been there but a few moments when rain commenced falling slowly, and continued falling until one P.M. when we emerged from our over crowded wagons, despatched our dinner and resumed our journey; We traveled until dark and (*again*) found no grass, but plenty of wood and water;:, We found the roads very wet and slippery but the sand would not adhere to the wagon wheels, and in consequence of this the hauling was not very hard   We came I think about fifteen miles in the afternoon and passed two graves: Camped near the Platte

June 25   Started early and traveled until eleven A M, when we came to good grass: We halted and waited until our cattle eat as long as they would and started on again at half past one;: We had a very grand and altogether romantic view of a range of bluffs on the South side of the river;, They appeared as a city of dome shaped houses churches and every manner of public buildings the whole of which wore an imposing appearance on account of being surrounded by an impenetrable looking fortress:; Traveling a few miles further the illusion is partly dispelled but we are now opposite to it and it still wears something of the same appearanc[e] though not altogether so picturesque and complete   It is rumored that gold mines of considerable value have been discovered on the South side on a stream called Deer creek and that some three hundred teams have stopped and are digging for the precious ore;: In order to ascertain the truth of this two of our company [17] left the train on horseback this morning with the intention of crossing the Platte and going to the "diggins", They have not yet returned   We came some eightteen miles and are camped on a branch of the main river in a conttonwood grove,; Passed no new graves

June 26.   Started with the expectation of leaving the river after going three miles but we had not proceeded far before we seen that our road would not leave it until near noon;; We kept on until half past 11 o'clock when we halted in a place of poor grazing but it was the best we could obtain, as the sage brush was so thick that it was impossible for much grass to grow:; This brush together with the thorny grease

[17] Frank Gay and Robert King. Leslie Scott, p. 273-74.

wood is almost all that we can see on these sandy hills
and hollows in the shape of vegetation,;; We remained
at the place before mentioned until two P.M. when as
we then expected to take a final leave of the Platte with
no water to be found on the road until we should come
to willow springs reported to be twenty five miles off,
we filled our water casks and as we thought bade a
final adieu to the river, to which many of us have become much attached   Contrary however to our expectations in about two hours we struck it again and
traveled in sight of it most of the time until night when
(*we*) encamped for the night near its peaceful current
We came eightten miles and passed two graves;: We
find no good grass;; Mosquitoes are quite troublesome

June 27;   (*Sabbath day*) We took a new road this
morning and traveled along the Platte until near noon
when we came to a place of tolerably good grazing
when we halted and turned our cattle upon the grass,
pitched our tents eat a cold dinner and prepared to
rest until evening;: We are now opposite to the red
Buttes   These hills are the color of well burnt brick
and are about three hundred feet high

A storm came up in the afternoon, and the rain fell
where we were, very rapidly for about one hour when
it ceased and left the atmosphere quite pleasant but
the musquitoes are so troublesome and annoy us so much
that it quite hard to keep one's patience.:, While (*it
was*) raining where we are some men (*belonging*) to
a train camped near us, (*who*) crossed the river and
ascended to the top of the red Buttes informed us that
there the snow fell thick and fast for one hour while
at the same time our men who were out one and a half
miles from the camp watching the cattle, were in a hard

hail storm   The Platte river here is not one fourth as
wide as where we first struck it below fort Kearny but
it is very deep and swift and it is almost impossible
for a man to swim across it   We have heard of two
men being drowed in the act of swiming this river (*in
places*) where to look at it (*many a*) one would (*he*)
had waded much more dangerous looking streams

Late last evening the men who went to examine the
gold regions before spoken of returned and brought
some specimens of mica and from the best conclusions
they could form they beleive that gold is to be found
in abundance along that creek if it were properly ex-
plored

Ferrymen have been busy for several weks on the
other side of the river in ferrying the wagons and
emgrants across to this side   They take a loaded wagon
across for five dollars and swim the cattle;;, We came
today about eight miles and passed two graves

June 28th   Came twenty four miles:; Sixteen miles
brought us to willow Springs, three miles to Green
creek three miles further to Harpers creek and two
miles (*to Sage spring*) We get good grass tolerably
good water but no fuel but sage brush and a few buffalo chips tho. the latter are quite scarce We have
went over an uninterupted sage plain all day.;. Alkali
abounds here to a great extent and it requires great
care to to keep the cattle away from the water We
saw beds of saleratus on our right in many places:; The
marshes where this alkali abounds, have a very unpleasant and strong smell but we can pass over such a
place in one or two minutes and are not disturbed by
it until we come to the next marsh We passed nine
graves to-day.: Had a light shower in the afternoon

and the evening is quite pleasant.;, The name of this
branch is Fish run instead of Sage springs

June 29   We came twenty miles.: We struck the Sweet
water about two o'clock and about three came to Independence rock;; The Sweet water is about one hundred
feet in width;: The water is clear and palatable but
is – warmer during the day than water of the Platte;
Independence rock is an immense mass covering an
area of, I think about ten acres, and is about three hundred feet high,:. My sisters [18] and I went to the base
of the rock with the intention of climbing it but a we
had only ascended about thirty feet when a heavy hail
and wind storm arose obliging us to desist:: We then
started on after the wagons and before we reached
them they had all crossed the river except the last
wagon in the train which by hard runing we managed
to overtake   They had intended to let us wade it (it
was waist deep) to learn us not to get so far behind
the team;, I would have liked the fun of wading well
enough but did not like to get joked about being left.:.
Immediately after leaving Independence rock we came
in sight of the well known Devil's Gate five miles ahead
of us and when we came near enough we turned off
the road about one mile and halted for the night opposite to it in a bend of the river

We in company with many others paid this gate a
visit; It is indeed a sight worth seeing,: The Sweet
water passes through it, and it really seems left by providence for the river to pass through as we can see no
other place where it can find its way through the
rocks;: The cliffs of rock on either side are at least
four hundred feet in highth and on the South side

---

[18] Fanny, Maggie, and Kate according to Leslie Scott, p. 276.

almost perfectly perpendicular;; The rocks are in many places covered with names of visitors to this place a few of which were of as early date as '38 a great many were dated '50 and '51 but the majority were '52,;; We passed seven graves

June 30th (52) Came twenty two miles.; We traveled all day along the Sweet water between two ranges of rocky cliffs which in many places cannot be less than five hundred feet high though I should think they would average from three hundred fifty to four hundred feet   I went this morning to pay a farewell visit to the Devil's gate and did not overtake the wagons until 10 o'clock when I was obliged to own for once that I regreted taking such an unnecessary ramble unless I could go on horseback ;.;; We to-day passed seven graves   Two were placed tolerably near each other one bearing the inscription "Charles Botsford murdered June 28th 1852:, The murderer lies in the next grave": The other bears the inscription of "Horace Dolley hung June 29th 1852" It appears (*that the murderer*) Dolley had contracted a grudge towards Botsford with regard to some little difficulty between them– had persuaded him to accompany him in a excursion and while alone with him (*hunting*) he dealt the blow at which human(*i*)ty would at any time recoil Vengeance however quickly followed him and he was doomed to (*receive*) the the penalty which his conduct so complety deserved:; We passed a trading post this moring belonging to a Salt Lake company;; They asked $20 per. bbl. for flour $12 per. gal. for brandy and other things in proportion ;; We encamped this evening near the banks of the Sweet water between two high ledges of rock where we get sage brush for fuel but find the grass rather thin   Killed a mountain sheep this evening

July 1t 1852   Traveled eightteen miles:;– We found the roads and scenery very much like that of yesterday.:. We crossed the sweet water twice and came out on the same side we were on before in order to avoid crossing the bluffs which is next thing to an impossibility

We had to raise our wagon beds six inches by which we managed to keep our "plunder" from being damaged.:, Passed eight graves to day   Encamped in about one half mile from the river and find better grass than we have had for some days:; No timber or sage near us but chips are plenty

July 2d   We came eightteen miles::. A dispute arose among us with regard to a white substance on our left on the summit of one of the Sweet Water hills which some declared to be snow others as firmly beleived it to be a species of white granite or white gravel: To settle the dispute and satisfy their curiosity two of the company went to it and found it in reality to be snow A chain of the Wind River mountains are plainly visible (*ahead of us*) with their lofty peaks capped with everlasting snow;; The air has been quite cool all day and this evening the wind blows a perfect gale, and and (*it*) is cold enough for frost at least we would look for frost in the States if the weather were near so cold

We camped this evening on the Sweett Water   Grazing is poor, we use the sage for fuel;; Passed six graves

July 3d   Came eightteen miles:; We traveled during the forenoon along the Sweet water valley until 11 o'clock when the road forked   One was to ford the

river and the other to cross the hills,; As the fording
was bad we concluded to go over the hills and by so doing we managed to get ahead of thirty teams which
had been sending the "never failing" but very annoying dust in our faces all the morning

The distance over these hills was one and a half
miles;: During the afternoon our road was over hills
and rocks making the traveling very tedious and difficult In some places for numbers of rods a (*stretch*)
the road was slightly up hill and as perfectly smooth
and hard being composed of minute particles of sand
and gravel:, This together with the large rocks is very
hard on the cattle's feet though but few of ours have
got lame We see a great many abandoned, lame and
worn out cattle and the air is literally filled with stench
from dead oxen:;;, We passed one as often as every
half mile through the day Passed a trading post this
afternoon:: It is kept by french and half breeds with
some specimens of humanity for their wives which
plainily tells of the extent of their ambition:; They
are squaws of the most disgusting appearance imaginable paying no regard whatever to cleanliness:;, We
camped near a small stream where we get plenty of
snow to eat which in the (*Sucker*) States (*so near the
Fourth*) would be considered quite a treat;;:: We find
very poor grass and our cattle and horses are much in
want of a good feed,;. Passed four graves

July 4th   Sabbath Day.: By following a ravine about
two miles we this morning found a place of tolerably
good grazing and we herded our cattle at that place
all day.; We see a great difference (*between*) the exercises of the glorious Fourth this year and last The
weather is cold enough for snow ,; indeed from the

threatening appearance of the clouds we look for a
storm to-night and have made preparations accordingly;

July 5th   We traveled to-day about twenty miles   Last
night we were visited by a tremendous wind storm
which upset two tents, made the wagons rock from side
to side, and caused the cattle to take a stampede   We
had last evening omitted the usual custom, of tying up
our cattle around the wagons, in order to give them
time to graze.; After some difficulty and haste the
guard succeeded in bringing them to a halt without
losing any of them.;.;. We crossed the Sweet Water in
the afternoon for the last time and encamped for the
night in a ravine one half mile from the banks of the
river

We find tolerably good grass at this place and use
the wild sage for fuel–   passed four graves

July 6th   We traveled 18 miles through the Pass;; The
ascent and descent is very gradual it being impossible
to exactly determine where the culminating point is;;
The first accurate conclusion we could form was at the
Pacific Springs;, These are so called from the fact
that they are the first we see whose waters flow towards
the Pacific ocean,;, The next stream we passed was a
small one called Pacific Creek   The water here runs
West while every other stream we have passed runs
either (*East*) or South

The water in this stream is not very good though
it is not impregnated with alkali

We encamped this evenng near the Dry Sandy though
we found some standing water (*yet*) we can not obtain
grass of any description

July 7th We traveled twenty two miles;; We started at half past four o'clock without our breakfast and traveled fourteen and one half against ten o'clock when we struck the Little Sandy;: We found some rather poor grass but it was better than none;;. We got dinner over and started on at two P.M. and traveled until six when we struck the Big Sandy and halted for the night;. We here find tolerably good grass. The warter of this stream tastes exactly like that of the Little Blue,; Passed one grave;: This evening two Indians came up to our camp riding a pony;: They were of the Shoshonee or Snake tribe and were the first we had seen since leaving fort Laramie except a few at two trading posts;., They are sensible and and savage creaturs as one might wish to see

July 8th We came to-day about twenty miles; To avoid the desert of forty miles between Big Sandy and Green River we took a left hand road yesterday morining and are now in the Utah territory,: We find the roads very good They are perceptibly down hill almost continually We have been traveling all day in sight of ranges of Snow capped mountains on each side of us:; The weather is clear and cold .; We carried water from the Big Sandy this moring which answers for cooking purposes and we are now camped in sight of Green River.; We find plenty of wild oats at this place which is an excellent substitute for grass and our cattle are in need of all they can get

July 9. We traveled to-day about twenty miles By taking a right hand road we missed our way to the Green River ferry and were were piloted across to the ferry in company with several other trains by some

ferrymen   We were mistaken in thinking last evening
that we saw Green River as it proved to be a bend of
Big Sandy;.

Green River is a very swift and clear stream and is
very difficult to cross unless the crossing is skillfully
managed   They are however well prepared with two
boats (one very good one) and we were landed on this
side without any difficulty and but little delay;; We
canped for the night near the ferry;: There is a trading station here.;, Potatoes are sold here for ten cts.
per. pound, butter 25 cts. eggs 25 cts. per. doz, flour
$6 per, cwt. and other articles in proportion   We have a
fair specimen here tonight of the various occupations
of different persons in the (*world*),: Betting and playing cards is going on at one encampment, music and
dancing at another, while at a third persons are engaged singing religious hymns and psalms with apparent devotion;; Indians of the Shoshonee tribe are encamped near us in several wigwams.;. They are as
loathsome spectacles as one might wish to behold
being as filthy and as far from every appearance of
civilization as any set of dumb animals in the world

July 10th   We traveled eightten miles,;; The weather
has been quite warm the most of the day; Snow capped
mountains are in full view on our right and before us
spots of snow are seen several miles off which look like
covered wagons arranged one behind the other:; Our
road has been over hills and rocks the most of the day;:
We crossed a small stream every few miles ;; We encamped on a hill near a small run, (&) about one
fourth of a mile from our camp we find (*tolerably*)
good water in a, kind of spring;; poor grass

July 11th   Sabbath Day;; We started this morning in

good season and traveld six miles when we came to
a (*small*) stream a good spring and tolerably good
grass;,. We here halted as our cattle are much in need
of rest;;

The weather is warm in the valley though snow is
in sight on the hills not a great distance from us;:

July 12th   We came seventeen miles.;, We have
crossed hills and jolted over rocks all day making
going ahead a tedious and laborious occupation,; We
passed several bea(*u*)tiful springs and one stream
which I noticed in particular that had its source in
a mountain. near us:; It was about one foot in width
and depth with a pebly bottom and banks not more
than two feet apart covered with sage, rose bushes, and
grease wood   These banks are from four to five feet
high and the water is remarkably clear and cold   We
encamped this evening on the west side of Ham's fork
of Green River; This is a very clear stream with a
gravel bottom   We forded it without difficulty

July 13th   We came eightteen miles; The country is
exceedingly mountainous; much more so than any we
have passed over before; The day has been quite pleasant:. This morning the teams were obliged to go a
semi-circle of about two miles in order to find a practicable place for ascending a ridge known as the "Devil's Back Bone..: To save walking this distance a
number of us concluded to climb the mountain and
strike the road in advance of the train; We accordingly set out on our enterprise but found the ridge
much higher than we had anticipated:; I think it
must be seven hundred feet above the plain and we
walked about two miles from the time we struck the
base until we reached the summit;, These hills, or

rather mountains are composed of rocks and sand and have no vegetation upon them except some sickly looking sage brush and a few stinted aspen bushes in (*some*) hollows;; On their summit we found plenty of excellent looking lime-stone rock and some specimens of quartz:; After we got over this range we traveled for a few miles in a comparatively level portion of country when we again struck the mountains and did not leave them until night;; These were more beautiful in appearance than those (*had*) we seen in the morning.;. We passed through a grove of fir trees on the summit of a high peak, which awakened within us feelings of a pleasing nature, as it was the first timber (*thro. which*) we had passed which deserved the name of a grove since we left the timber six miles west of St Jo. In the afternoon we descended a very long and steep hill from whose summit we viewed the Bear River Vally Creek:; We traveled two miles without unlocking the wagon wheels and in many places the men held back the wagon in addition to having both the back wheels locked;; I walked ten miles to day;; We passed four new made graves the first we have seen since the first inst. We camped near a small stream with a tolerable good spring adjacent to it A hail storm came on about six o'clock and the females repaired to the wagons and the men to the tents, to wait till it should abate Several of us myself among the nmber being much fatigued went to sleep before the storm was over and did not wake until morning We consequently missed our supper, which would have come very opportunely when we first halted as we were quite hungry

July 14th We came eleven miles to-day when we struck Smith's fork of Bear River and halted here to

rest our cattle & do our washing; There are plenty of
Indians around us and they are troublesone enough
We cannot trust them on (*any*) account as they will
steal whatever they can lay their hands on   We keep
some one busy wat(*c*)hing them constantly   The
weather is quite warm and we have enough to do to
keep all hands briskly employed: There are mountains
all around and bunches of willows are growing close
to our camp so completely matted together that nothing can get through them: There are several trees near
us which resemble the balm of Gilead but we suppose
they are bitter cottonwood

July 15th   This day we remained in camp.: We have
been thrown into considerable excitement in consequence of a murder being committed in a train from
Wisconsin, which is now camped one (*half*) mile
from us.. (*in the trial of which the men of our train
have been called upon as jurymen*)   The murder was
committed on Hams fork of Green River, and the circumstances connected with it as near as I could learn
was as follows,:. One Daniel Olmstead was taking five
men across the plains, and it appears that they had not
lived very agreeably together as it was proved in the
trial which came off to day that the five had boasted
that they had their boss under their thumb and intended
to keep him there   It was proved that Olmstead went
out in the morning to watch his cattle telling Sherman
Dunmore ((*now*) the murdered man) to make a fire
and put on the teakettle so they could have some breakfast,; When he returned at breakfast time the other
men had finished their repast and he asked where his
breakfast was   Dunmore replied that if he wanted
any he might cook it himself.; This was the result of

much abusive language on both sides; however Olmstead prepared his breakfast himself, Dunmore threatening in the most abusive manner to whip him   Olmstead calmly replied that if he did he would not live long to brag about it   Upon this he left him and went into the tent and commenced eating his breakfast, using for the purpose a small sized butcher knife; Dunmore followed him and jumping upon him commenced beating him and endeavored to kick him in the face with his boots   Olmsted called upon the bystanders to take him off saying at the same time that he had a k(n)ife; As no one interfered he stabbed him in the lower part of the chest;: Upon this Dunmore started back and exclaimed that he was stabbed   He fell and in twenty minutes was a corpse.:, The jury after an impartial investigation of the tragical affair brought in a verdict to this effect; That the wound made by the knife of Olmsted caused the death of the said Dunmore and that the same was inflicted by the aforesaid Olmstead in self defense.:. This evening the Indians were quite numerous and rather troublesome around our camp, so much so that a young man inconsiderately, roughly ordered one who was beging him for something to eat to leave; (*the Indian*) however did not go and he seized a spider which happen to be near him and pushed him from him with it blacking his blanket which was a very white one;; This enraged him and the other Indians around him and no inducem[ent] we could offer would make them act friendly with any one and we could not get them to accept any(*thing*) which we offered them;; They soon left the camp and we feel considerable uneasiness about the final termination of this matter.;. (*See Appendix*)

[The reference and entry on page 86 of the manuscript is in darker ink]

(*A.*) We here met the famous mountaineer, Green [19] He has been among the mountains sixteen years, is apparently about forty years of age, six feet three inches in hight and muscalar in proportion.:, He is a Canadian Frenchman, was principa[1] actor in the insurrection in Canada in '36 and fled to the mountains for protection,. He has an Indian wife and nine children; dresses in buckskin and appears quite at home

July 16: We traveled twenty five miles.:. On our way this morning we met some Indians who were going to bury a man who had been thrown from his horse and got his neck broken;. They were wailing in a most piteous manner The dead man was warpt in a blanket and thrown across a pony and and Indian was riding behind him and as he passed us directed our attention to the body, and then passed by us with a heart touching wail;: We traveled through the Bear River valley in the forenoon: This valley is one of great beauty being covered with good grass with mountains behind, before and on either side in plain view with groves of fir trees noding at their tops; (*and spots of snow visible in may places*) This (*valley*) is tolerably fertile and looks as if it might be well adapted to raising wheat.; At half past two o'clock we came to two toll bridges built ac(*r*)oss a stream known as Thomas's fork of Bear River; They charged us one dollar per. wagon for crossing the two bridges.;.

[19] Not identified so far. Tucker was likewise tall, and this description is one of a man measuring someone against himself.

During the afternoon our road was over the mountains and were quite slippery in consequence of light
showers which fell at intervals during the day;; We
encamped near the Bear River and find good grass;;
The mosquitoes are troublesome in the extreme: passed
four graves

July 17 We came twenty two miles, traveling all day
in the Bear River valley;. The valley and mountains
are covered with grass and the summits of the latter
are adorned with splendid groves of fir making the
scenery beautiful.:; We passed a (*small*) stream every
few miles; The water runs very swiftly and is perfectly
clear and very cold with a pleasant taste:; A horse
(*belonging to our train*) ran away to day causing a
train ahead of us to stampede

All was consternation hurry and confusion for a few
minutes but they soon got everything straight again
and there happened to be no serious damage done.:.
We encamped near a good spring one mile from the
river on a green sward in a pleasant situation

July 18th Sabbath Day.; As wood is scarce in our
last night's camping place we concluded to move on
this morning until we could find wood water and
grass We traveled six miles and turned out of the
road and went to Bear River two miles farther where
we find good wood, grass, and use the river water which
has no unpleasant taste although it is quite warm The
day is warm and the heat of the sun quite oppressive:;
We find plenty of, black currants near the river, which
we gather and serve up and they make an excellent
substitute for green fruit;: We find good grass by
crossing the river

July 19 We traveled twenty two (*miles*) About 11 o'clock we came to the Soda Springs ;; They are a great curiosity: The first view we had was was two mounds of lime-stone rock. We drove up opposite to them and halted, when all went to work searching out curiosities; The best spring (*is*) on the margin of a small stream, It (*is*) surrounded by a natural stone wall; The water boils up about one foot from the top of the wall; it is quite cool and when when sweetened, with the addition of a little vinegar, makes a drink equal to any prepared soda in the States A short distance from these we found two other smaller springs walled in the same manner as the first one but with a very small opening at the top, The warter in these is of a reddish caste tho. one is much deeper colored than the other .; Still farther on, on the summit of a lime-stone mound, (*is*) a walled spring of the same kind of water as the first one tho warmer the water boils up on the very highest peak of this cliff and part of it runs off down the sides of the rock but the greater part of it evaporates;: This mound is full of small springs some red and some black.:. Two miles from this on the road near the river we found a still better (*soda*) spring than the others;; A half mile farther we came to the Steamboat Spring The water puffs up out of a (*reservoir in a*) solid rock When we were at the spring it puffed to the highth (*of*) one and two feet alternately but we are informed that at sun set it puffs to the highh of from six to ten feet The water is impregnated with soda the sane as the others, but is much warmer than any that we had seen before

In the afternoon we came to the Soda Pool This is a large rocky resorvoir in which the (*most of the*)

water stands until it evaporates It boils up in one small chasm and runs off a little at one place but most of the water stands in the pool.: We this afternoon saw on our left, a hollow crater which has been long extinguished but blackened rocks in many places cover the ground which plainly shows that this place has once been the scene of volcanic eruptions.:. We camped this evening near a good spring which is the source of a beautiful stream

July 20th We traveled eightteen miles, through the Bear River valley:; The scenery is beautiful and the weather delightful:; The roads were excellent with the exception of some mud holes which were rather difficult to get through

We halted at noon by one which contains water that proved to be rather unhealthy for the cattle as some of them are this evening sick;:, The grass at that place is excellent :: (We passed a trading post this afternoon.:) We have given our cattle a dose of vinegar and melasses which has the tendency to counteract the effects of the alkali and soda with which the water of this slough is impregnated We encamped in a valley covered with excellent grass, and near a creek from which we obtained some mountain trout;. The water palatable but rather warm.;, Fuel is quite scarce: We passed one grave

July 21:; We traveled but twelve miles Our cattle were so weak after their last night's sickness that we did not leave the camp of the night before until noon;; We came to a brige about two miles from our last nights camp across the before mentioned creek The proprietor wished to tax us twenty five cents per wagon to cross on it but the fording was not very difficult and we got over the creek without trouble,;. The first four miles of our road was through the valley of this creek; the last eight was over the mountains though they are not so high nor so difficult to get over as those we passed some days ago;; We passed innumerable aspen bushes which had been killed by fire;; The country is barren, producing nothing but stinted sage and aspen with a few weeds.;. Snow is plainly visible on the mountains not a great distance from the road while fir trees grow near the snow presenting a rather strange appearance ;, We encamped near a good and beautiful spring which is the source of a clear stream coursing its rapid way over a rocky bottom into "Snake or Lewis R(*i*)ver". We this day met a Mountaineer who had been in the mountains since /39– he is a native of Kentucky and the best spicimen of a backwoods man I ever saw   he appeared to be about 35 years of age & I should judge would measure six feet 3 inches in hight & weigh about 200 lbs strong & muscular in propertion   his name is *Caldwell*,[20] *"his uncle Mr Wm Caldwell was one of* (our) *nearest & most intimate neighbours in the "Sucker State"*   After inquiring with regard to his relatives and finding that we were acquainted with them he appeared much rejoiced and quite glad to see us, particularly Father whose hand he grasped in honor of old Ky, His broadcloth coat and silk neck 'kerchief contrasted strangely with his buck skin pants & moccasins; and (*his*) long, flowing hair and whiskers,;, He was mounted on an Indian pony and armed with two horse pistols, and was engaged in driving cattle   While in conversation with this mountaneer off to N.E. in the distance was plainly

---

[20] Not identified so far. Again Tucker is measuring the man against himself.

visible the three Tetons with their lofty (*snow capped*) summits reared high above all the surrounding mountains, and at the same time the three Buttes were visible in a N.W. direction from us presenting a truly romantic and poetical appearance

July 22   We traveled twenty miles this day   Our road was over the mountains all day,; We passed several springs during the day whose waters form tributaries for the stream whose source is at the head of the spring of last nights camp;; (*camped on this branch*) The weather is very warm & the country barren and sterile in the extreme

July 23d   We traveled 18 miles;;, twelve and a half miles brought us to fort Hall;;[21] A half a mile after we started in the morning we struck a sandy road, and traveled through the heavy sand for seven miles, with the dust and sand blowing so thick that it was difficult to see our way   On this part of the road there is no vegetation but sage and a very small amount of grass which is now perfectly dry; After leaving this sage plain we traveled five miles over comparatively good roads when we reached the Fort; This fort is built of sun burnt brick (adobes), It is a rather shabby looking concern, but in case of an attak from without its inmates would be tolerably well protected   It has port holes through the walls for the admission of guns,; This fort is now abandond by the goverment and is occupied by some traders;; They had flour for sale at $20 per. cwt,,: After leaving the fort we had the first view of Snake or Lewis river   There is timber enough

---

21 "Here at Fort Hall the shoes of Mary Frances, the eldest of the Scott daughters, give out, and she has to cover her feet with wrappings, as best she can, until near The Dalles in Oregon." Leslie Scott, p. 291.

on this river for farming purposes;; We in the evening
crossed the stream which rises at the spring where we
camped on the 22d; It has received numerous tributaries and where we crossed it, was about fifty feet
wide and three and four feet deep

We camped two hundred yards from the ford and
musquitoes were so thick around us while we were at
supper that it was with difficulty we finished our repast

July 24th We traveled about nineteen miles Nine
miles brought us to the crossing of the Portneth.:. This
is a clear stream about one hundred yards in wi(*d*)th
and six feet deep.:. (*with a remarkably swift current*)
We raised our wagon beds by tying ropes under them,
across the standards; by so doing we managed to keep
our goods free from damage After crossing we ascended a hill and traveled over a sand and sage plain
until night.: The road is a very bad one, being hilly
and rocky in the extreme in addition to the deep sand
and dust which blew so thick that we could scarcely
see our way,.; We camped near a spring, (*which is*)
the source of a little brook; The weather is warm, the
musquitoes annoying, and and a dead animal not far
from our (*camp*) in no way accebarates our enjoyment
We are two miles from Snake river

Owing to (*the*) carelessness of one of the drivers
the wagon in which myself and sisters were riding ran
into a deep mud hole and upset;; We were very much
frightened but fortunately did not get hurt The wagon contained chests of clothing and feather beds with
which it was heavily loaded;; There happend to be
no serious damage done; The wagon bows were all
broken;; After having been told to leave the train or

do better he took French leave of us, and we have not
seen or heard of him since [22]

July 25th   (*Sabbath*)   We remaind in camp as our
cattle were quite weak and the grass in the bottom is
good; A man died in the afternoon in a train near us,
with the mountain fever   They buried him in the
evening:, There are five other persons sick with the
same disease in the train   The weather is excessively
hot

July 26th   We traveled twenty miles:;: Five miles
brought us to the American Falls;; A melancoly oc-
currence accounts for this name.: A party of three men
were on this river in a canoe and not being aware of
their proximty to the falls went on until they were hurried along by the current and precipitated over the
falls.; All but one found a watery grave;: [23] The water
tumbles over the rocks and falls forty feet presenting

---

22 "We were very much frightened but did not get much hurt, The wagon
contained chests of clothing, and feather beds, which was the only loading,
The wagon bows were all broken, but were repaired this evening.

"Mitchell (The driver alluded to) after having been told that he must do
better or leave the train, took *'french'* leave of us and we have not seen or
heard of him since. He is a   (*'Cultis, Tilaqum'*), which being interpreted a
(*trifling fellow*)." 1853 Revision. The use of the Chinook jargon is interesting.

"One day our 'Salon Wagon', as we called the wagon that served as a
'parlor', overturned, my sister Fanny (Mrs. Mary Cook) as soon as she
could extricate herself, poked her head out of the hooded wagon and cried,
'Oh Lord, come here quick!' My uncle came running up and said, 'Jenny,
hadn't you better call on some of the company?' Etty's "Memoirs," p. 8-9.
The Uncle was Levi Caffee.

"The most serious loss is that of a small fund of money, which John Tucker
Scott has been saving to buy needed oxen. His money is going fast, from
purchases of food supplies, and he can ill afford this loss. The loss greatly
troubles him, and he orders the driver, Mitchell, to leave the train or take
a horsewhipping. Mitchell chooses to leave." Leslie Scott, p. 292.

23 This episode is narrated in Palmer's *Journal*, p. 44, whose route the Scott
party is following. Leslie Scott, p. 293.

a handsome appearance, and making a great noise,;,
We found the roads very bad; being over an sand and
sage plains   we encamped for the night on "Snake
River"
[Tucker writes the rest of the entry for this day and the beginning
for July 27th]
two miles above the mouth of Falls creek   good
grass 1 mile back on the bluff   the weather is excessively hot & the dust so dence that it is with difficulty
we can see our way,

July 27th   we resumed our journey and in ten miles
arrived at Raft River where we watered our teams &
let them run on the grass in the bottom three hours
& at 3 oclock filled our casks with water as it is 16
miles to the next stream, intending to stop at 7 oclock
& remain until morning but owing to want of proper
dis(c)ipline a part of our men with the loose stock
pushed ahead to the no small annoyance of some of
us & we were compelled to travel until midnight before we arrived at Marshy Creek & then the grass
was so poor that our cattle could obtain *none*   we
shall get out of this "snap" as quick as possible with
this for our motto "better luck next time," we made
26 miles   *Roads Rough (& rocky)*
[Abigail resumes writing]

We encamped on Marshy creek; The water is poor
and after we had halted and unyoked our cattle, we
discoved a dead horse and ox about twenty steps from
our wagons, which caused us all to feel much discon-
tented and for a few minutes a bystander would have
thought us (*certainly*) a grumbling company [24]

---

[24] "I well remember a July day's travel that extended far into the night.
The women were jolting along in the wagons (the custom in daylight was

to walk over the roughest parts of the road) in that semisomnolent state
which renders humanity, even under the most favorable circumstances, ill-
natured when required to make any exertion. The thirsty, lagging teams
were urged on by their tired drivers, in the hope of 'striking water,' from
the lack of which element the patient beasts for hours had trudged onward
with lolling tongues. The children at frequent intervals were whimpering
from thirst, intensified by the oft-repeated assurance that there was 'not a
drop of water to be had.' At length we came to a steep hill, down whose
uneven declivity the road sidled off into darkness. Two men were pushed
forward to reconnoiter, and, returning after a time, reported water and a
camping place at the base of the hill, which one Jehu declared to be 'all
fired steep.' It was deemed prudent for the women and children to get out of
the wagons and make their way to the camping place on foot, and the
night air was burdened with many plaints of somnolent wretchedness, as
the order to that effect was obeyed. The fat woman in our company was
especially energetic in resisting the order of her husband to 'come out,'
given, it must be confessed, without any attempt at the cooing and the
gentleness of tone that presumably characterized the days of his court-
ship. The angry protest of the tired woman ceased, however, with a sud-
denness that surprised her fellow travelers. Astonishment gave place to
dismay, when something like two minutes of silence were followed by muf-
fled shrieks, which seemed to come from the very bowels of the earth. They
grew more distinct as the poor woman caught her breath fully, and an
impromptu search with lanterns discovered her far down the mountain side,
hanging to a scrub juniper tree, which was the only object intervening
between her and further descent into the darkness of the nether world.
The voice of her husband had not been gentle a few minutes before, but
compared with this, when, after much tugging and straining, she was
towed into camp, which by this time had been duly located by the advance
guard, it was as a summer zephyr to a howling nor-easter. She was only
placated the next morning by the discovery that he, having left the con-
jugal couch in a huff, had made his bed in the darkness, close to the lee-
ward of what in life had been a fine gray mare, but which, being now, some
days defunct, he had mistaken in the darkness for a friendly rock. The
shout of laughter that went up at his expense was turned upon his spouse,
as he explained that the smell of sulphur had been so strong upon the night
air, when he rolled up in his blankets, that he was not able to detect any
other odor.

It was noticeable, throughout the remainder of the journey, that a suggestion from her husband that she 'take a tumble,' was sufficient to quell
a rising storm in the breast of this worthy and sorely tried woman, while
she, on her part, did not hesitate to suggest upon occasion, and with like
soothing effect, an independent bivouac as a panacea for her lord's rising
choler." Catherine in *The Oregonian*, June 17, 1890, reprinted by Leslie
Scott, p. 243-44. He identifies the couple as Martha and Levi Caffee.

July 28th   We traveled fifteen miles;: Eight miles
brought us again to Marsh creek, where we found some
tolerably good grass;; We here halted four hours, when
we started on again and during the afternoon we crossed
the creek twice   At the latter crossing there is a patch
of pretty good grass.; We traveled seven miles in the
afternoon and encamped on Snake river; We find good
grass;: This afternoon we were so fortunate as to meet
Mr Alexander Johnson, a nephew of Rev, Neill Johnson, (now in Oregon): He brought us a letter from
the latter gentleman, which contained the news that
he would meet us in the Cascade mountains with fresh
teams if he could learn that we were in need of aid:;
The day has been as usual on this river exceedingly
hot but the evening is quite pleasant;; We found the
roads much better, than those we passed over yesterday

July 29   We traveled eightten miles; Three miles
brought us to goose creek: There is grass enough here
for a small party of cattle: The water is not very good
being warm and muddy   At ten oclock we again struck
struck the river and at noon halted on its banks   We
hired a seine and caught a good quantity of fish. We
traveled along the river during the afeternoon and encamped a hundred yards from it. A wagon in the train
broke down and we stopped earlier than usual to repair
it: The roads this afternoon were *very* rough and
rocky.:. Some of the work cattle are failing very fast,.
We found the grass good this evening

I am now seated on the bank of the river upon a
ledge of rocks which form a kind of natural sofa   The
river here runs through a rocky *kanyon*   The current is remarkably swift and the water tumbles over

the rocks with a roaring noise; The scenery here is of a truly wild and romantic description   Huge piles of rock rise up in bold array around me with often a cedar nodding at their tops, Off in a northeastern direction from me a seemingless endless sage plain is situated and when I look with admiration upon this wild plain and reflect that far, far, beyond it is the home of my childhood together with dear relatives and friends whose faces I perchance may never behold again, a feeling arises in my breast of peaceful sadness which may be inagined but not described

July 30;;   This morning our broken wagon was repaired and we got ready to pack up to resume our journey when the cattle were taken to the river to drink;: One of them started to swim across and the rest immediatly followed and as the current was so swift that no person could get around them they all swam over and landed on the other side; After consulting with eachother two of the men concluded to go up to yesterday's fishing place and swim across after them;; They accordingly started but two other young men, being more ventursome than the rest concluded to swim across the swift water at this place   One of them being an expert swimer got over without difficulty but as the other one had never swam in swift water he was carried down the river by the current and drowned! It was impossible for any one to render him assistance as he floated down so fast that a man could not run (*on the bank*) and keep (*even*) with him   His name was John McDonald

He was about twenty one years of age, was going through on his own resources with another young man: They were from Mt. Sterling Brown county Illinois and had traveled with us from Missouri

The deceased was a worthy young man; and being sociable affectionate and accommodating he won the esteem of all, and was beloved by every one who knew him:. His (*untimely*) death has cast a gloom over every countenance   The young man who swam across could not drive the cattle over without assistance and the men who started to go above, to cross with horses returned to the (*camp*) when the fatal accident occurred;;; He was (*consequently*) obliged to stay there until other measures could be taken,:, Four men therefore started to the place before mentioned; two intending to swim with three horses and the other two were to return to the camp and report if they got into difficulty.;. They started across the river on the horses but they were so weak they could not swim the current and our favorite and faithful *Sukey* was drowned and came floating down the river long before the men returned;; Fortunately the men and other horses escaped with their lives but did not succeed in getting across;: They [25] hired two men from anoth[er] train to go across for thirty dollars   They went and with the assistance of the man who went over in the moring suc-

---

[25] Leslie Scott, p. 296-97, identifies some of the individuals: "The bull which led the stampede was owned by Stull Swearingen. The two men who went up to yesterday's fishing place were Robert and John Dickson (Dixon). The second time they are joined by Tucker Scott and Levi Caffee with the horses, and they loose "Sukey", escaping with their lives. The two men who got across were hired by John Tucker Scott."

The 1853 Revision provides other details of McDonald: "but the other one never having swam in so swift water was carried down with the current and precipitated over the falls and was drowned and after diligent serch we could not succed in finding his body it was impossible for any one to render him any assistance from the shore as the current carried him faster than a man could run! . . . [of the two men hired from another train] . . . they went over and with the assistance of the man who went over in the morning succeeded in driving the cattle 6 miles up river but could not get them across."

ceeded in driving the cattle into the water but they could not get them to swim across and were compeled to come over themselves and leave them until moring when they will make another effort to get them:. The man [*John Jordan*] [26] who went over in moring was so weak after he came back that he could scarcely stand;: He was in a hail storm in the afternoon with with very light clothes on and got badly bruised with hail stones

I am seated in the same place where I was when writing last evening but alas! how changed are our prospects, how (*greatly changed*) are meditations! The roaring of the river is no longer pleasant music (*to my ears*), but is a jarring discorant sound, and I startle and half rise to my feet at rustling of the leaves about me; and these huge rocks which I then looked upon with admiration, now only terrify (*me*) as I have throught several times when I would hastily glance around me that a wily Indian or a wild beast was just in readiness to destroy me, but still I love this spot as It corresponds with my feelings

July 31 :: Early this morning measures were taken for building a raft to cross the river upon, and about a half dozen men hunted some logs and carried them to the camp and were preparing to start with them up the river when *again* owing to want of proper disciplin a part of the company opposed this measure and they went back without the raft: When they got there but one (*or two*) of our company ventured across, and they hired other men to go again, with those who went before, and by paying $64.– they got them to go over

---

[26] In purple indelible pencil, in a different hand.

but when they got there they could not drive the cattle back, and a party,[27] about ten o'clock returned to the camp and corked a wagon bed placed an air (*tight*) water cask on each end and a large log at each side.;, They took this back and crossed the river in it without difficulty.;, The cattle were drove into the river again and by the greatest exertions on the part of the men they were made to swim across about dark, and at ten o'clock at night they were all drove into camp and tied up,

Our anxiety was then releived, but when we look around us, one [*John McDonald*] [28] who was with us (*when we came here*) in health and with fair prospects for a long life (*is*) not to be seen and when we we reflect that in trying to recover these cattle, he threw away his life a feeling of melancholy is visible on every countenance

August 1t Sab) We this morning found three cattle dead, having lost at this place, one horse and five head of cattle: We started early in the morning and traveled eight miles; In six miles we came to a dry branch, which contains a few puddles of standing water;; We crossed this and took a left hand road and in a short time found a good camp, the grass being much better than we have seen for a long time.; A hard shower of rain fell in the afternoon and the evening is cool

August 2d We traveled twenty miles; The roads were as usual, rocky and dusty:; The (*weather*) was more pleasant to day than any we have had before since we reached fort Hall, owing to yesterdays rain,;. We

---

[27] John Tucker Scott. Leslie Scott, p. 297.

[28] In purple indelible pencil, in a different hand.

traveled ten miles and came to Rocky creek where we
halted and by driving our cattle across the creek we
found tolerably good grass;; This morning a young
man [29] in the company packed a few clothes on an
Indian pony and started on, to Oregon City ahead of
us as he had a good pony and no particular occupation;,
He intends to buy his provisions from emigrants on the
road At noon John McDonald's partner [30] succeeded
in selling his team and buying a pony and he started
on in a short time to overtake the man who left in the
morning;; Before starting a dividen was made of (*the
money from the sale*) his effects and those of the de-
cased and the latter (*was*) placed in the care of Mr
Swearingen to refund to the father of the deceased the
first opportunity

We traveled near Rocky creek during the afternoon
and at night encamped adjacent to it in a *kanyon*.:.
We find but little grass at this place the first emigration having taken what there was

Augus 3d We traveled 17 miles.: Two miles from
last night's camp we found a quantity of dry bunch
grass:; As our cattle were very hungry we turned them
out upon it for an hour; they eat this grass very greed-
ily as it is much like (*the*) hay of the states Three
miles from this we came near Rock creek again and
found a place where with difficulty we succeeded in
getting our cattle to the water It took us one hour
to water them

We saw no grass on the road after we left this place::

---

29 "John Hancock. . . on an Indian pony. . . as he had nothing to do."
1853 Revision. Leslie Scott does not name him.

30 "John Jordan. . . John Tucker Scott aids in the trade for the pony, as
he has use for Jordan's oxen, after his recent loss of four oxen." Leslie
Scott, p. 298. Jordan's departure is omitted from the 1853 Revision.

The roads were very rough and stony: Where there are no rocks, the road is worn into *chuck* holes which it is impossible to avoid At night we came to the river bluffs and by driving our cattle down the bluffs for one mile we managed to get them to the water;: A beautiful spring gushes out out from the bank in plain sight on the other side of the river and tumbles over the rocks with a roaring noise;; These bluffs are at least one thousand feet high and are (*composed*) of basalt rock; The men packed water in kegs and buckets to the camp;. We passed a grave this forenoon
We find poor grass

August 4th We traveled about fifteen miles A ten o'clock we were favored with a very refreshing shower: The roads were very dusty until the rain fell after which the traveling was comparatively pleasant Nine miles brought us to the river again where we watered our cattle without difficulty Five miles after this we reached the river again (*and encamped*);; A warm spring branch (*empties*) into it at this place,: The river here runs very swiftly over the rocks.;; We find no grass;– nothing for our cattle but willows:;

August 5th We traveled but nine miles Four miles brought us to Salmon Falls creek This is a clear stream with a rocky bottom and is about one hundred feet wide, and two one half feet deep;; We crossed this stream and traveled one mile when we left the river bottom and went over the bluffs for three miles when when we came to Salmon Falls and encamped One mile after we came to the bluffs we found some grass which we turned our cattle out upon for three hours The roads were very hilly and the Sand six inches deep We traded with the Indians this evening

for salmon: they are the best fish I ever saw;: The
Indians will take almost anything in exchange for them
that the emigrants have to to dispose of We to day
saw several beautiful spring branches pouring over
the bluffs on the other side side of the river Some
of these have a fall (*apparently*) of four or five hundred feet

August 6th We traveled sixteen miles One mile
after leaving the falls the road again struck the bluffs
and we had very hilly and sandy r(*o*)ads until noon,;
after which we found them rather better until night
At ten o'clock we found some dry grass, and let our
cattle graze for two hours. We did not get to water
until nine P.M. when we came to the (*river*) bluffs and
encamped The distance down the bluffs to the river
is one mile. The men packed water this distance to the
camp. A light shower fell in the afternoon; We find
no grass

August 7th We traveled twelve miles: Eleven miles
brought us to the crossing of the river.[31] Emigrants
were busy ferrying in their wagon beds Grass wood
and water is much easier to obtain on the other side
than this, but a part of our company were afraid to
run the risk of crossing, and we will be compelled to
go down on this side with no better prospect for grass
than we have had for one hundred miles. We filled
our casks at the ferry and moved on one mile and
encampd We find a small quantity of dry bunch
grass at this place:. We here left one ox who was worn
out and starved!! We found good roads with the exception of a few hills

---

31 "The Frémont route, 1843, of the Preuss map, 1846, which the Scott
party has been following from Bear River, shows the two crossings of
Snake River. . ." Leslie Scott, p. 301.

August eighth. Sab. We traveled seven miles five miles brought us to the (*second*) crossing of Snake river, here are two islands which look as if they might (*have been*) covered with good grass a few days since, but it is now all eat off.: We traveled near the river two miles farther and encamped. Tolerable good grass. About noon a party of ten men and two women passed us going down the river in a boat made of a wagon bed. They were bound for the Dalles and from thence to Oregon City::

August 9th We traveled fourteen miles– eight miles of the road was through a rocky kanyon The (*traveleing*) here is very difficult and dangerous; Much more so than any before.:. In many places the wagons were held by two or three men or they would (*have*) been precipitated over the rocks into the river The last six miles was more level than before but still the traveling was quite difficult and tedious;: We saw no grass on this side of the river until (*near*) night when we encamped:: upon the river bank:. We again saw some men going down the river in a wagon bed bound for *the* City

August 10th
[Tucker begins to write]
August 10th we travelled about 8 miles this morning & arrived at the river and as the weather is verry *warm* & our cattle much in want of rest & food we concluded to remain here this afternoon as by driving our cattle up the river 2 miles there is excellent grass the weather is oppressively hot & dusty and the country all around extremely barren

Aug. 11th we travelled to day about 14 miles six brot us to Catharine creek here is good grass 8 miles

further brot us across the ridge to where the creek
empties itself into the river our present encampment
The grass is in the botton while on the uplands there
is nothing but the wild sage & wormwood   Father has
been quite sick to day but is some better this evening
& I have got the toothache gloriously

[Abigail resumes writing]

Aug 12   We traveled twenty miles.:. We came to the
river every few miles during the day and at night
encamped upon its banks: We find, no grass, willows,
or even sage brush,– nothing like vegetation is to be
seen except the thorny Grease wood and a species of
herb resembling the garden wormwood

We have seen no grass at all during the day   After
getting supper over, and allowing the cattle time to
rest we concluded to move on six and one half miles
to a small branch where we are informed by our guide
that grass could be obtained:; We accordingly drove
in the cattle and got about half of them yoked when
we discovered that several were missing: As it was
growing dark we could not find them and we were
compelled to unkoke and wait for moring when we
will resume our journey

Aug 13. We traveled fourteen miles   six and one half
to the branch before mentioned, where we found good
grass and water; we here halted for two hours   In the
afternoon we traveled about seven miles when we
turned out of the main road (*for*) near two miles to
the river.; We camped within a half mile of the river
Grass is plenty and good

[Tucker resumes writing]

the dust to day and for the last 100 miles or more
has been verry annoying   it is as light and as easily

stirred up as the dust of the summer threshing floor allmost suffocating man and beast. The country all around is extremely barren interspersed with deep Kanyons & high rocky bluffs all blackened as if by the action of fire and is doubtles of volcanic formation

Aug 14th We started this morning in good season as we had 16 miles to go and 14 of the last without grass or water we found this the hardest day on our teams of any yet travelled, we arrived here late in the evening thirsty & weary with poor grass for our cattle; here we lost another of our cattle from drinking too much water this makes 8 head we have lost out of our five teams which makes them rather light & in all probability we shall have to leave one of our waggons

Aug 15th Sabbath day we are encamped on the banks of the "Snake" the weather oppressively hot we shall remain here until morning & then resume our toilsome journey. To day 5 of our company concluded to go on by water. They accordingly fitted up two wagon beds for the purpose and launched them into the *"Snake"* they seem to answer a good purpose and if no accident befalls them they will reach the dalles in ten days or less [32] to day we lost another of our cattle by drowning!

---

[32] "The Scott family abandons the 'mother's wagon' here, because of shortage and weakness of oxen. The road along Snake River is already littered with such derelicts and abandoned furniture of advance travelers, which have been thrown away to lighten the loads. Five members of the Scott party decide to make use of the abandoned wagon bed, to float down the river to Fort Boise. They obtain another abandoned wagon bed, probably Frank Gay's, caulk them tight and launch the two in Snake River, and prepare to set forth to-morrow morning. These men will float down river to Fort Boise, fifty miles, and thence travel afoot, on account of river rapids and falls. They include John Dickson, Frank Gay, Robert King and Burns

Aug 16th   This morning we resumed our journey and
went on 7 miles to dry branch   here we found good
water to the left about one mile above the road   the
grass is rather poor   we stopped and grazed our teams
and then went on to the hot springs 5 miles further
making to days travel 12 miles   the grass is miserable
the dust very annoying & the sun oppresively hot
we lost another ox to day from eating some poisnous
herb, Our men that left us this morning in the *boats*
landed at our encampment to night in fine spirits and
highly pleased with their enterprize,

Aug 17th   Today we came but 5 miles and stopped
on the top of the bluff taking our cattle back (*two
miles*) to the (*foot of the*) mountain to grass where
there is good water but it sinks in the sand long before
it reaches the river   we carry our water for camp use
up the river bluff near half a mile which is very laborious   we find this continual travel rather wears on our
strength but we are in good spirits & *"right side up"*

[Abigail resumes writing]
Aug 18th   We traveled twelve miles., The roads in
the fornoon were quite hilly and in the afternoon very
heavy, the sand being six inches deep   At noon we
found dry grass for our cattle   The road followed the
river until we went about three miles, and it there
turned away from the river and, owing to our negli-

. . . Mary Frances Scott Cook has informed the compiler that the members
of the Scott party see many abandoned wagons and articles of household
furniture, feather beds, etc., on this part of the route, but no abandoned
food supplies. Stull Swearingen will abandon two of his three wagons on
Snake River." Leslie Scott, p. 304. Crawford Morrison was the fifth member
of the party which left by the river, according to a letter from Mag, June 7,
1853. (See Scott letter No. 12 below.)

gence in filling the casks we were without water for dinner:: We encamped on the river bank upon the first decent looking grass plot we have seen since we left Catharine creek and since we covered a dead ox we feel like enjoying ourseleves,:

The day has been warm but the evening is pleasant

Aug 19th   We came (*nine*) miles and finding some dry bunch grass we encamped to rest our stock and let them graze. Our cattle are very much jaded and many of them too nearly worn out to work:. A number of the company and two of our own family are sick; some of them dangerously so, in consequence of which we feel much discouraged.[33] We are encamped upon the river bank.. the afternoon is very coll; Light showers are falling at intervals and the western wind is quite high

Aug. 20th   We traveled twelve;; miles   The roads (*are*) very heavy and hilly and we are all very tired, as every person has to walk who is able to go alone The country around is barren in the extreme. We saw some trees this afternoon in a S. W. direction from us along the Snake river

---

[33] "A number of the company are sick; also two members of the Scott family, John Tucker Scott and William Scott. . . Harvey W. Scott and John Scott, his brother, have been sick on Snake River, and their lives have been saved by their eldest sister, Mary Frances, who has nourished them with especial care, from the food and medicinal reserves. After the death of the mother, Ann Roelofson Scott, on June 20, maternal duties have fallen to Mary Frances. She has been cooking for the twenty-seven members of the party, assisted by her sister, Margaret Ann, and her aunt, Martha Roelofson Caffee. Abigail Jane does not work in culinary duties nor in any other camp matters, her part being that of writing the diary, under the direction and aid of her father, John Tucker Scott. Fresh bread is mixed every morning, allowed to 'rise' during the day and baked every evening by Mary Frances and Margaret Ann." Leslie Scott, p. 305-06.

We encamped upon the Owyhee   This is a clear and
rapid stream with a pebly bottom;, It is (*about*) twenty
five yards in width; it rises in the Blue mountains and
runs in a nearly northern direction till it reaches the
Snake river into which it empties.; The water is clear
and palatable but is rather warm;; There are two
graves near our camp, of a recent date,;. We have seen
several graves every day for the past week but I have
beene rather negligent, and consequently took no note
of them:; Some of our folks are yet quite sick,– others
are getting better, but there are none among us who
can say they are quite well.: The warm weather and
bad water, causes dierrehea with which almost every
person is troubled

Aug. 21   We came three miles which brought us opposite to fort Boise   As this fort is on the other side
of the river I did not get a very good view of it, but
was informed that it has much the appearance of fort
Hall, but is even a poorer concern:. It was built by
the Hudson's Bay company, and was intended, more
for a recruiting, or intermediate post than as a trading
point:: It is now abandoned by that company and is
in the possession of trad(*d*)ers

They however had nothing for sale, except sugar and
tobacco; There is an island near the fort covered with
luxuriant grass, which we concluded to turn our cattle
upon for the remainder of the day; The men with the
loose stock, pushed ahead, and were out of sight when
the wagons halted; One of the company started after
them and walked on for six miles but could not overtake them and returned.;[34] They had to go fifteen

---

[34] "Levi [Caffee] . . . he returned rather out of humor." 1853 Revision.

miles to the next water without food or drink, for
the cattle or themselves We think it has learned
them a lesson

The young men who left us the 16th inst. in wagon
beds reached the fort and learning that there were
some rapids of thirteen miles in extent below the fort,
they sold their boat and for $25. and went ahead on
foot;: Emigrants are ferrying across to this side in the
boat, and paying $10[35] per. wagon for the privilege

Aug 22d Sab We came about fifteen miles which
brought us to the Malhuer or Malore as it is sometimes called;: This is a stream of ten yards in width;
it rises in the Blue Mts,[36] and runs in a southern direction for a considerable distance and then takes a north
western direction over (*a succiosion of*) sand hills,
sage plains and occasionally fertile, valleys and empties into the Snake river ;;The road to day was through
a winding ravine and is mostly down hill;. The sand
hills on either side present an extremely barren appearance. We found but little grass at the present encampment the first emigrants having taken it all:: The
water of the Malhuer is not very good but when we can
get no other, we are content to use it..[37]

August 23d We traveled about fourteen miles; Two
miles from the last night's camp brought us to the
crossing of the Malhuer; We here halted to consider
what course to pursue as the next (*good*) water is
twenty miles from this place:; One of the children[38]

---

[35] "$5. pr wagon!" 1853 Revision.

[36] "Cascade Mountains and takes a southeastern direction. . ." 1853 Revision.

[37] "the Malheur is verry warm as a number of its tributaries are branches
of Boiling springs! Our little *Willie* is verry sick." 1853 Revision.

went ahead to look for some strayed cattle and returned while we were halted and said that the road after two miles came near a branch of the creek, which appeared from the number of willows upon it to be as large as the other and principal stream: We went on and found it to be as represented, (*but*) when we came to the bed of the stream we found it dry.:. There was no alternative but to stop as it was then the heat of the day, We accordingly stopped & by digging four or five feet we found good water, for camp use, and drove the cattle back to the Malhuer to drink   We halted at this place until three o'clock when we yoked up and drove on to Sulphur springs, ten miles, and encamped   The road was through the valley of the dry branch for several miles; this valley appears fertile, being cov-

---

38 "Mrs. Palmer" – identified in pencil, or Harriet Scott McCord Palmer, or Etty. This is confirmed in 1853 revision as (*Harriet*). In her "Memoirs," p. 7-8, she described her duties and an incident not recorded in the journal: "It was my duty to keep up the loose stock in crossing the plains, and I was given charge of an old sorrel mare, who had one eye. Her name was "Shuttle-back" on account of the shape of her back. She was a big powerful animal, and when she'd get a whiff of an Indian she would kick and plunge and many a time would throw me off. One day we had traveled long in the heat, and both Shuttleback and I needed water. I was about a mile behind the train and off at the side of the road a grove of willows was growing, it looked like water might be there.

"There was! A little tributary of the Snake River; so I gladly got off the saddle that had no horn on it, and first let the mare drink. It was a steep place. The mare began to plunge and I soon saw she was in quicksand. I held on tightly to her rein, yelled with all my might, knowing there was a man behind me also driving stock. He heard me and rushed to my assistance, telling me to hold on and not be afraid; he would bring help. He rushed ahead and brought back my father and three other men, and with ropes and a long pole pried her out of the quicksand and floated her down the stream where she finally landed on her feet. I fully expected punishment but my father just picked me up, sat me down on the wet, muddy saddle, slapped the mare and said, 'now go on!' Poor old Shuttleback got lost in the Cascade mountains one night. About a year afterwards a man reported her roaming near Mt. Hood, Oregon. My father went after her and brought her back with a fine black colt he named Black Democrat."

ered with grass Leaving this bottom we struck sand hills and traveled through a *very dusty* ravine until ten o'clock when we reached the before mentioned spring and encamped.:. The evening was very pleasant and we were favored with a beautiful moonlight The water of these springs is not very palatable, it being strongly impregnated with Sulphur:

Aug 24. We traveled about ten and one half miles;. Eight miles to a dry branch two from there to Birch creek and one half mile to another (*point*) of the same where we encamped; There are several good springs at the head of this stream which is a small one, it heads near the road; The Snake river is about one mile distant from our camp; A range of mountains of great beauty is situated (*just beyond it*) ; the sun shining upon (*these mountains*) throws upon them a reddish lustre;; They appear to be covered with grass

[Tucker resumes writing although "quite sick"]

Aug 25 To day we made about 8 miles 5 miles brot us to the Kanyon on "*Snake*" which is the last place we shall see *this* river & three more brot us to Burnt River; here the country changes its appe(*a*)rance the hills are mostly covered with grass tho now it is dry yet our cattle eat it very well; Father [39] is quite sick & has been unable to to walk for the last two days, Our dear little "*Willie*" is not expected to live 12 hours as he evidently has the "*Cholera Infantum*" or Dropsy in the brain the Doctor tells us it is in vain to administer any medicine as he must surely *die* this to us is heart rending, but gods "ways are not our ways neither is his thots our thoughts"! O! may we bow

---

[39] Note that when Tucker writes he refers to himself as Father, but his daughters rarely identify him when they write.

with submission to his will   one of our young men is
also verry ill with the prevailing disease of the country *"dia(h)ree"*   we shall lay by half this day on
account of sickness   to day we lost another ox

Aug 26th   To day we came about 14 miles and con-
tray to our expectations our dear little Willie is still
alive and in about the same condition as yesturday
we have watched him incessantly for the last 96 hours
& there appears no visible change yet he evidently
grows weaker   Father is some better & has walked
all day tho he totters as he walks   *"our hope is in god"*

[Abigail resumes writing]

Aug 27th   We traveled about fifteen miles. :. The first
eight miles was along Burnt river, (*across*) which the
road passes a number of times :: The road was exceedingly mountainous all day, and sometimes rather difficult to pass over on account of sidelong ridges which
are very narrow. : The day was quite warm about noon
but the morning and evening cool as usual :: We saw
several excellent springs and beatiful spring branches. :.
We encamped in the evening in the valley of Burnt
river : This valley is covered with green grass of a luxuriant growth   The stream is lined with numerous
trees and bushes consisting of alder, birch, bitter Cottonwood, and balm of Gile(a)d; I have noticed our
common pith elder and sumac growing near this stream
in quantities   The tops of the mountains are decked
with cedar and their sides are covered with grass, tho
in the latter case, some lawless per(s)on has burned the
grass in many places to the mountain tops. Our little
Wille lingered through the day in apparently the same
condition as yesterday but he is so debilitated that he
cannot live much longer

Aug 28th   Two months and seven days this moring
since our beloved mother was called to bid this world
adieu, and the ruthless monster death not yet content
has once more entered our fold & taken in his icy grip
the treasure of our hearts! Last night our darling Wille
was called from earth, to vie with angels around the
throne of God :; He was buried to-day upon an elevated
point, one hundred and fifty feet above the plain in a
spot of sweet seclusion, where his peaceful remains will
sleep in undisturbed repose until the triunp of God
shall sound upon the last great day to awake the
slunbering millions of ea(r)th to stand before their
final judge   A beutiful cedar [40] waves its wide spread
branches (*over*) his tomb, and here beneath its shade
I have wandered in remote seclusion to be alone with
Wille and his God. and while I reflect that he is now
beyond the reach of mortal suffering, in my heart I
praise the Lord, who gave and who has taken away.;
This child has long been the hope of his parents, the
pride of his brothers & sisters:. He was four years of

---

[40] "The soil here was thin and full of rocks. My poor father, broken
hearted, had the men cut a cavity out of the solid rock that jutted out of
Burnt River Mountain, and here the darling little form was sealed beside
where the only living thing was – a little juniper tree. My brother Harvey
found it twenty years later and he peeled some of the bark off of the juniper
tree and brought it back to my father. My father had carved Willie's name
on the tree." Etty's "Memoirs," p. 5-6.

"it was the *only* tree or *shrub* in *sight* in that arid place – and – some
20 years later when uncle Harvy and Amos Cook – and your uncle William
– were going out to the *Salmon River Mines* – (*then* causing a great excitement–) – uncle Harvey *located* this spot and the little *tree* – and *found*
the *bark* on it (tho somewhat curled up) the *letters* of the *name* of *our Willie*
– and he peeled off some of these – and some of the pices of the juniper
tree" and brught them *back* to father – The very *scent* of the *sage brush* was
in the Pkge!" Etty to Wilkie Duniway, April 11, 1924.

"This tree will stand for some fifty years as a monument to the youngest
member of the Scott family, and will disappear about the year 1905." Leslie
Scott, p. 310.

age and possessed an uncommon degree of intellect a
kind disposition and agreeable manners: He often before his illness talked of dying and wanted to die and
meet his mother who doted upon him with all of a
parents fondness and hope

[Tucker writes the rest of this entry]

we shall lay by this day to recruit our cattle as they
are much jaded and in want of rest, and we too are
worn down with fatiege & long watching, and need rest.
Father is still feeble but is slowly improving; our sick
man is no better and but little hopes are entertained
of his recovery

[Abigail resumes writing]

August 29th   We traveled about fourteen miles: This
morning a heavy frost covered the ground in the valley
of our encampment; (*ice formed*) in buckets (*of water*) under the wagons one eights of an inch in thickness:; The middle of the day was excessively warm;;
The roads have been rolling but good with the exception of a few ridges and high hills;; We traveled for
two or three miles in the morning along Burnt river
in the valley;;, At noon we halted upon the north fork
of Burnt river;; This is a very small stream; the water
is clear and cold and runs very swiftly;; We pursued
this stream for some four or five miles when we turned
to the right over a mountain from the top of which
and and about two miles distant we viewed a small
run, which contains a small quantity of water   We
found a spring near the road along this branch, between two mountains in a deep ravine; where we encamped   The grazing is poor;: Our sick man is still
living but we have no hope that he will recoverer: The
evening is cold and windy

Aug 30th We came sixteen miles; Mr Clason the
young man who has been sick was still alive when we
started this morning, was so near gone that we did not
wish to remove him and as our cattle had no grass we
could not stop.;. We therefore left horses and a wagon,
a tent, and three men [41] to attend him; those of us who
left him took a farewell look and came away with
saddened hearts.;. He came from the State of Maine,
and joined us at St Joe; he was highly esteemed among
us and his melancholy fate is a cause of deep regret
to (us) all

The weather has been very cold all day The roads
very good the most of the day a few miles was quite
rocky

We came to a slough or dry branch in the Powder
river bottom where we encanped:. Since writing the
above the men who remained with Mr Clason have
returned stating that he died in one hour and a half
after we started in the morning; They buried him and
left him at four o'clock and overtook us at 9, in the
evening There are mountians all around us; some of
them appear covered with snow but we are told that it
is white clay; others are densely covered with timber,,

Aug 31 We traveled fourteen miles This morning
our cattle were much scattered and we could not find
them all until nine o'clock

We consequently started late and were obliged to
drive hard: The first four miles brought us to another
slough of Powder river which is larger than the first
one; nine miles brought us to Powder river; this is a
clear stream of ten yards in width; it's banks are orna-

---

41 "Levi Caffee, Robert King and one other man." Leslie Scott, p. 311.
"4 men" according to the 1853 Revision.

mented with willow, birch, and bitter cottonwood;
We left the river at this place and directed our course
over a rocky bluff for two and one half miles to the
river again,, where we found a good camp The valley has a very fertile appearance, and I think would
produce well

September 1t We traveled (*sixteen*) miles this day;
We at first followed along the river for one mile and
then turned across the valley crossing the river twice:,
In nine miles we came to a small slough where we got
water for our cattle; grass is good; we here halted
for two hours and then directed our course over plains
and bluffs till we reached the brow of a mountains
overlooking the Grand Round; We then descended
this mountain and ascended a (*rocky*) ridge which has
the longest and most of difficult descent of any hill
which we had yet encountered;: The dust (*would*)
blow (*for a time*) in clouds, hiding the wagons teams
and roads entirely from our view,. when a sudden contrary breath of air would clear away the dust for a
few moments enabling us for a time to proceed; The
rocks so filled the road, that any one who had not begun
to "see the elephant" would have been afraid to have
attempted the descent; When we came to the base of
the mountain we were delighted to find ourslves (*safely*)
in "Grand Round"; We were all hungry and tired, and
hastily preparing our supper, we gladly retired to rest

September 2d We traveled eight miles through the
Grand Round valley when we came to the foot of the
mountain and encamped to rest our cattle preparatory
to ascending the mountain

This valley is near ten miles in width and covered
with luxriant look(*ing*) grass; high mountains are

ranged all around it, the most of them covered with pine, balsam fir, cedar, and other trees   Grand Round river runs through the western part of the valley; it's banks are adorned with willow birch, bitter cottonwood, & alder, in the valley, and pine, cedar, balsam fir, birch and larch, where it meanders among the mountains; this stream is about four rods in width & six inches in depth   Mr Swearingen remained in the Grand Round to recruit his cattle, and our five wagons are now alone;: The indians at this place are very wealthy, they have numerous herds of horses and possess many of the luxuries of life in abundance   Contrary to our expectations we found no provisions here for sale except flour at $40 per. cwt.[42]

Sep 3d We came, I think, eleven miles; over the mountains; the scenery was delightful all day but the road was extremely hilly and rough; Eight miles from Grand Round brought us to the crossing of the Grand Round river; The descent of the mountain down to the river bottom was down the most dangerous looking place we had yet came down, but we reached the river without accident: After crossing we halted & prepared our dinner, and took a long rest, as our cattle were very tired in consequence of the very hard roads of the morning's travel   We then started over the mountains again and traveled three miles, when we came near an excellent spring and encamped having traveled through heavy timber almost all day

This is the first night we have camped in (*heavy*)

---

[42] "we were joined this evening by Mr Stevensons waggon who also concluded to go on with us they had been with us from St Jo. but separated from us this morning. Mr Stevenson is quite sick!" 1853 Revision. "The Stevenson party is still in the train." Leslie Scott, p. 313.

timber since we left *"Hundred and Two"* bottom, east of St Joe. The timber here is yellow pine and balsam fir It is worthy of note

[*we here lost another ox* inserted in pencil by Tucker.]

that in this place common conversations can be overheard at the distance of one hundred and fifty yards, and the noise of men speaking to cattle in a loud voice sounds loud enough for a savage war whoop; Sounds echo and reverberate from hill to hill, to such a degree that the noise of discharging a rifle is equal to the report of a canon and may be heard a half dozen times reverberating from mountain to mountain

September 4th   We came, I think, fourteen miles this day over the principal range of the Blue mountains, traveling all day through a densely timbered region: Eight miles brought us to an opening in the timber, in a range of mountains heading to the north; off to the left and about one fourth of a mile from the road we found good water in a deep ravine; grass was also good and our cattle fared well: We halted at this place for two hours, and then filled our water casks and started on intending if the cattle held out to reach Lee's Encampiment nine miles distant; another train was just ahead of ours and my sister [43] and myself wishing to get out of the dust, went ahead of it and walked all the afternoon, thinking that our teams were coming on; we went within one mile of Lee's Encampment when (*we*) came to good roads and stopped to ride in the wagons when they should overtake us, when we were told that our wagons had encamped two miles

[43] Catharine. Leslie Scott, p. 313. The sister sent after them is Etty. Her identity is confirmed in the 1853 Revision.

back; it was then sun-down and the road back to our camp was through heavy timber, which appears dark in dalight; we started back and met our little sister coming after us on horseback;; We went back all the way in a hard run and just before we reached the camp met a man, who seeing we were disconcerted thought he would have some fun; he told us it was three miles back to the camp, and through the darkest road he ever saw, or heard of; he went on and as we were then about ready to give up with fatigue, we almost concluded to wait till morning among the trees and then find our way back or await their coming, when we met Father who was more uneasy if possible than we, and who was quite out of patience at our ludicrous mistake at least we considered it ludicrous when we got time to laugh: In runing I wore the soles off my moccasins against the sharp stones, and blistered my feet before I got near the camp

When we got back supper was over, and we found that the cattle (were) doing much better than if they had kept on, water (was) found in a ravine (off) to the left of the road one fourth of a mile from it; Grass was was also procured in plenty

September 5th   Sabbath day; We came but five miles; about three to Lee's Encampment, a creek which now contains water standing in pools but which at certain seasons of the year is quite a stream; one fourth of a mile to the right of the road is a good spring, We again watered our cattle and came on some two miles further when we found excellent grass in the timber and three hundred yards to the left another spring, with water for the cattle near it; We encamped near the road in a heavy grove of pine

September 6th   We traveled about sixteen miles   Ten
miles was through the tinber and four & half over the
last part of the mountains to the Umatilla   While on
the sumit of the last mountain we got the first view of
the Cascade mountains west of us, while mount Hood
reared its snow crowned summit in awful granduer
high above the other mountains and appearing as a
stationary white cloud;; The valley below also presented an appearance of unparalelled beauty while far
as the eye could penetrate (*over*) the plain the country
was a rolling prairie, with no timber in sight except
that which grows along the Umatilla   We pursued
our way down to the banks of this stream and were
showed by an Indian where to water our cattle; We
found the river quite low, being about three rods in
wi(*d*)th and six inches in depth; its banks are ornamented with bitter cottonwood, birch, choke-cherry
and thorn-apple trees Choke-cherries and thorn-apples
abound in plenty and are of an excellent quality;:
pheasants [44] are also (*as*) numerous in this valley as
the prairie chickens are in the praires of *Illinois*;;
We here found the largest Indian village we had yet
seen   The inhabitants are filthy looking creatures;
they have made some attempts to cultivate the soil but
are too lazy to affect anything worth notice by it: We
traveled down the river one and a half miles and encamped; grass is very poor, the numerous herds of
Idian ponies having eaten it close to the ground

We here obtained fresh beef at 12½ cts. per. pound;
from a French trader

[*we lost another ox today* added in pencil by Tucker.]

---

[44] Grouse. 1853 Revision and Leslie Scott, p. 315.

September 7th   We traveled about eleven miles: One
of the oxen was missing in the morning and we were
detained some two hours before he could be found
We traveled near the river for five miles, when the
road turned to the left over a high, grassy plain   The
dust was extremely suffucating; in six miles we again
came to the Umatilla, crossing it twice   After crossing
we drove two hundred yards from the river and encamped; Grass was poor; We had a fine dish of pheasants for supper

September 8th   We came twenty miles this day; in one
mile after starting the road left the river and turned
to the right over a high, rolling, dusty, grassy plain
after ascending a long ridge we again came in sight
of Mt. Hood, and off to the north east we viewed
Mt. St, Helens,. Traveling over the plain for seventeen miles without water we again came to the Uma-
tillo, along which we traveled for two miles and encamped; grass is good

September 9th   We traveled about fourteen miles this
day   Four miles brought us to the Indian Agency,
which is now unoccupied by the government, here was
a new looking frame house, the sight of which animated
us all a good deal: [45] We left the river for the last time
at this place and the road took its course over a sandy
plain ten miles to Alder creek which we crossed and
encamped: This is a stream eight or ten feet in width,
with banks on each side six and seven feet in highth;
the water is excellent   Grass was good but dry

September 10th   We traveled twenty miles which

---

[45] "as it was the first we had seen since we left Fort Kerny." 1853 Revision.

brought us to Well Springs;.[46] The road was very hilly, and sometimes quite sandy; We reached the springs about sun down, There were about thirty wagons here before us and the cattle had to be watered out of buckets; a slow process when so many were wanting water   We found but little grass

September 11th   We traveled about fifteen miles this day: The roads were quite hilly but solid, the country presented much the same appearance as that of yesterday, being a rolling, grassy plain; We found no water during the day and at night encamped upon Willow Creek; Here is a trading post where very poor flour can be purchased at $40.[47] per cwt, We used our last flour for supper and were obliged to purchase at this enormous price; A man came to the creek this evening saying that he had nothing at all for his family to eat until he could purchase something: another told us (*he*) had walked forty five miles, and eaten nothing but a few grains of wheat and he could not find anything to eat anywhere. We lost an ox to-day

Willow creek is now dry except in low places: grass is good

September 12th [48]   Sabbath day; we remained in camp until three o'clock when we filled our water casks and started on over the bluffs, and encamped at nine P.M. having traveled about seven miles   The dust

---

[46] "this was a hard day on our cattle as we found no water until we arrived at the Springs." 1853 Revision.

[47] "40 cts pr lb." 1853 Revision.

[48] September 12th thru 18th, the ink is very light. Entries for September 13th, 14th, and 16th thru 18th have been traced over in stronger ink, not always with accuracy. Where possible the original text has been followed. Changes in formation of specific letters indicate that the darker tracing was the work of Tucker.

was so dense that traveleing in the night was rather dangerous as the ground was full of chuck holes which in the dust and darkness we could not see We found (*no*) good grass and but little of any description

Sept 13th Early this morning we resumed our journey and traveled until eight o'clock when we found good grass and halted to feed both ourselves and the cattle; We then marched on & about three o'clock came near a small spring at the foot of a bluff; a short distance from this we met our cousin Mr J. L. Johnson [49] from *Oregon* He was returning to meet us, and his then unexpected appearance, thrilled each kindred heart with joy

We exchanged salutations and traveled on for three miles where we struck a small stream and encamped, making this days travel about seventeen miles grass poor

September 14th We traveled twelve miles this day; the first five miles was along the stream where we encamped last night The road was through a deep rocky kanyon; we crossed the stream several times; Leaving this stream we struck John Days river, a stream of fifty yards in width and two feet deep; we followed this for one mile when we crossed the stream and– traveled along it one mile where we halted and to our inexpressible joy, met Mr Lawson Scott,[50] a

---

49 "John L. Johnson from the Willamette Valley"! 1853 Revision. "John Lawrence Johnson, Neill Johnson's eldest son, who made the journey to Oregon from Illinois, the year before, in 1851." Leslie Scott, p. 317.

50 "Lawson Scott was a son of Peter Scott, who was a brother of James Scott, who was father of John Tucker Scott." Leslie Scott, p. 247. The meetings were described by Abigail in the *Oregonian,* October 7, 1900, reprinted by Leslie Scott, p. 247: "At last, in the middle days of September, when food even for ourselves was gone, we were met at John Day River by our rela-

cousin of father's, and our cousin Foster Johnson a
brother of the young man who met us yesterday; They
were just from the Garden of the *World* and we were
all much rejoiced to meet each other, in this wild and
romantic spot our hearts were filled with gratitude to
know that these estimable young men would leave their
pleasant homes and undergo the toil and privations of
this laborious and toilsome journey and for pure friendship without expectation of pecuniary fee or reward

[Tucker resumes writing]

Sept 15th   we travelled to day about 20 miles   yesterday evening after eating our supper and watering
our cattle we filled our casks and ascended the bluff
by way of a winding rocky ravine (which by the way
was the worst piece of road we have travelled over)
and went out about 5 miles & encamped   early this
morning we resumed our journey over excellent roads
we halted about 9 oclock and got our breakfast and
grazed our cattle   the grass is good over this part of
our road. about 4 oclock this evening we reached the
Columbia River and camped on its banks; several of
our cattle got stuck fast in the quick sand and it was
with difficulty we could get them out [51]

---

tives, Lawson Scott, an immigrant of 1847, and John and Foster Johnson of
1850, who brought a quarter of beef, some flour, and one of them a bottle
of 'oh, be joyful,' thus horrifying our teetotaler crowd. It was little wonder
that a relative, whom my father was bringing to Oregon to reform him, got
gloriously tipsy, and engaged in a carnival of drunken songs; much to the
diversion of the children, to whom it was all very funny."

To this Leslie Scott added two footnotes:

"It was understood that Lawson Scott brought this liquor from the Willamette Valley.

"Levi Caffee had been addicted to drink in Illinois, and John Tucker Scott
had forbidden him to use liquor, as a condition to his coming to Oregon in
the Scott party. Levi Caffee was a son of John Tucker Scott's aunt. He also
was the husband of Martha Roelofson, sister of Ann Roelofson, John Tucker
Scott's wife."

[Abigail resumes writing]

Sep 16   Early this morning we took up our line of march and came four miles when we came to Deshutes of Falls river; this stream is about one hundred and fifty yards in width, and courses its rapid way through rocky kanyons (&) forming numerous cascades until it reaches the Columbia into which it empties.;. We got an Indian to pilot the wagons across the river and also one to take the females over in a canoe, for which service they taxed us four dollars; The ford is at the mouth of the river and a short distance below a handsome cascade. After getting all safely over we ascended a long, steep and (*somewhat*) rocky hill, when we again overlooked the Columbia river adorned on each bank with lofty bluffs of basaltic rock; Five miles from this place brought us to Five-mile-creek. While on the sumit of the last hill before reaching the creek bottom, we viewed Mt. Jefferson for the first time, Mts. Hood & St. Heleens were also in plain view;: After crossing the creek we directed our course over the rolling plain for about one mile and encamped near a sulfur spring, having made this days travel about ten miles

Sept 17th   We came eightteen miles this day   Eight miles brought us again to Five-mile-creek along which we traveled for ten miles crossing it several times, where the road turned to the left over a rolling grassy plain; we encamped upon the banks of the creek and were glad to retire to rest without our supper as night had spread his sable curtain before we reached the encampment–   We this morning sent two of the wagons by the way of the *Dalles* to be sent to *Oregon City*

---

[51] "Father got verry wet here and the wind blew so cold that he took a severe chill and then was crazey with a fever all night." 1853 Revision.

by water   Mr Stevenson also left us at this place in
order to go down the river, as he has been a long time
sick and was too weak to think of crossing the mountains [52]

Sep 18   We traveled this day about six(t)een miles;.
The road was hilly but solid; while we were halted
at noon the men who went with the wagons to the
Dalles overtook us, bringing with them Mr Stevensons
team, which father intends to take across the mountains; he also took the four horses belonging to the
same gentleman to take care of which again gives
me the privilege to ride on horseback ; a privilege
which I have not enjoyed but little since our *Sukey*
got drowned in Snake river:; We traveled all day
without water and at night encamped near a small,
warm spring bran(c)h & within one mile of Indian
or Village creek; before encamping we descended a
very steep and rocky hill

[52] "We this morning sent 2 of our wagons to the Dalles to be taken to
Portland by water we also left 1 yoke of oxen here to be herded and delivered to us in the spring if they should live through we also left our remaining mare with the same arrangement (*the mare we got the oxen died*) Mr
Stevensons folks also left us at this place in order that they might go by
water as he is so feeble that it will be out of the question for him to go
over the mountains." 1853 Revision.

"Several members leave the Scott party this morning for The Dalles, to
go to Willamette River, by easier route of the Columbia River, including
William H. Goudy and his wife, Miranda Jane Brown Goudy, and George
Stevenson, his wife, Ruth Eckler Stevenson, and their two young sons. They
take two of the six wagons of the train, which will be sent to Oregon City
by the Columbia River route. George Stevenson's team of oxen and four
horses overtake the Scott party next day, and are used by John Tucker Scott
and his family for the rest of the journey of nearly two weeks. John Tucker
Scott goes to The Dalles at this time to buy supplies, and will rejoin his
family next day. Among the articles bought by him are shoes for his daughters. 'These were the first shoes,' says Mary Frances Scott Cook (1921), 'that
I had to wear after my old pair wore out at Fort Hall.' Such things as these,
and especially food supplies, are very high-priced." Leslie Scott, p. 320.

Sep; 19th   We traveled this day about ten miles; one mile brought us to Village Creek, where we bought potatoes at the rate of $9.00 per bushel;– After crossing the creek we ascended a long and difficult hill and traveled two miles to a small stream; we here obtained two yoke of fresh cattle, sent to us from the Willamette valley, by uncle Johnson,[53] About seven miles farther brought us to another small stream, and within three miles of Barlow's gate, at the foot of the Cascade mountains; We here found a good camp

Sep 20th   We came three miles this morning and encamped near Barlow's gate.[54]

[Maggie writes the rest of the *Journal*]

a short time after encamping, clouds gathered thick upon the mountains, and a strong south wind, warned us, of an approaching storm;– we were therefore afraid to start in the mountains, and busied ourselves during the day, in washing, and preparing provisions for the remainder of the trip;– We obtained flour at, 40 cts and beef at 50 cts per pound :–

Sep 21;   This morning our apprehesions of a storm could no longer be a matter of doubt, and at nine o'clock, rain comenced slowlly falling, and continued falling at intervals until noon when the clouds broke away and strong north wind, caused us to feel once

53 "1 mile brought us to Indian village creek here we bought potatoes for $4. pr bushel. . . we travelled about 2 miles to a small stream, where we got 2 yoke of fresh oxen that Mr A. Foster Johnson brought to us from the Willamette Valley." 1853 Revision.

54 "Sept 19th . . . We have to pay at this place $5. on each wagon for the privilege of travelling over the worst road that ever was passed by wagons! Sept 20th   We came 3 miles this morning and encamped near the 'Gate' which is nothing more than a *tent* with two men sitting at the *'rceipt of custom'* to take from the way worn emigrant his last red cent under the authority of a *'Democratic'* Charter." 1853 Revision.

more at ease. I strolled out in the afternoon to the open ground, not far from camp, and watched the clouds, playing around, and receding from, Mt Hood A frish fall of snow upon its broad summit, had given it an appearance of dazzling whiteness, which contrasted strangely, with the gloomy appearance of the thickly timbered mountain around and beneath it, and presenting a spectacle unlike anything I had ever before witnessed. preparations were made during the afternoon for an early start in the morning.

Sep 22; This morning the sky was again overcast with clouds, causing us to remain all day in camp.

Sep 23; We came about 14 miles through the mountains; in ten miles we reached, the little Deshutes This is a rapid turbid stream, ten yards in width, and 18 inches deep The water is thick with white sand, bu[t] is *very* cold; Before reaching the stream we descended a long steep and rocky hill, the descent of which, was very dangrous The mountains are covereed with heavy timber, consisting of pine, cedar, fir, poplar, scrubby, white oak, bitter cottonwood &c, &c. We found no grass but the cattle fared very well upon the leaves of trees and fern.

Sep 23. [24] We traveled some twelve or fifteen miles, over an extremely rough and difficult road; We encanped below the Sumnit hill near a marshy prairie of several miles in extent, which is covered with green slough grass. The weather was cold in the moring, but moderated during the day: Mt Hood was in plain view from camp, in a north eastern direction a small stream of icy coldness rushes down from this mountain, thru a long ravine near our camp, and the cutting wind, was blowing severely from the naked summit of the great mountain

Sep 24; [25]   We traveled about twelve miles, seven brought us to the foot of Laurel Hill, and five to the crossing of Zigzag, creek; Laurel hill is an almost perpendicular desccent of two miles in extent, with three benches where the teams could stop to rest [55] The country around abounds in Laurel which gives the hill the name it bears. food for cattle was scarce and what was worse, we had *none* for ourselves, as we had been disapponted about receiving supplies.[56]

---

[55] "Then we reached Laurel Hill in the Cascade mountains. Oh, that steep road! I know it was fully a mile long. We had to chain the wagon wheels, and slide the wagons down the rutty and rocky road. My aunt Martha lost one of her remaining shoes; it rolled down the mountain side. I can hear her now as she called out in her despair, 'Oh, me shoe, me shoe! How can I ever get along?' So she wore one shoe and one moccasin the rest of the journey.

As we started down the road my father said: 'Jump on the wheel and hang on, Fanny!' It was an awfully dangerous thing to do and he didn't realize what he was telling her to do. Poor sister Margaret fell and rolled down and down. When she picked herself up Uncle Levi was there with his humor. 'Maggie, aint this the damndest place you ever saw?'

'Yes, it is!'

'Well, you swore and I am going to tell your father.' "

Etty's "Memoirs," p. 8.

"But this man was not a wee bit jolly some days later. We had toiled all day through the famous Barlow Pass, and had camped at night at the foot of Laurel Hill. My uncle, who was usually the jolliest of souls, discovered that we did not even have a cup of coffee grounds to ease the gnawing of the stomach, and I, who, with my sisters, had fed ourselves on salal berries, struck an attitude before him, and repeated his own words as he had often uttered them, when romancing over the anticipation of a famine, saying, 'ten days on half allowance and two weeks without anything to eat! Lawd, Lawd, the prospect tickles me!" The poor fellow, who was really suffering from hunger, lost control of his temper." Abigail in the *Oregonian*, October 7, 1900, reprinted by Leslie Scott, p. 247.

[56] "Food for cattle was very scarce. and what was worse we had *none* for ourselves excep coffe and that without any '*trimmings*'." 1853 Revision.

" Rations grew shorter and shorter. A real relish was prepared for one

Sept 25; [26]   this morning, one of the company,[57]
started ahead of us on horseback after provisions.
Several of the cattle got away, and we waited until ten
o'clock to find; We did not find the lost cattle, but went
ahed about eight miles with the remainder of our
teams; In company with other misfortunes, we broke a
wagon tongue a king bolt, and some loose cattle could
not travel fast enough to keep (*up*) with us. All this
time we had nothing to eat. We encanped again on the
Zigzag, where we we bought some sour flour for $15,00
which answered for our supper,

Sep 26, [27]   We traveled twelve miles, and encanped
upon the Devils backbone, near a good spring of water.
We found the lost cattle this day.

   we were met this day with supplies [58]

Sep 27th [28]   We traveled 18 miles, without accident,

---

meal by boiling an antiquated ham bone and adding to the liquid, in which
it was boiled, the few scrapings from the dough pan in which the biscuit
from our last measure of flour – which, by the way, was both musty and
sour – had been mixed. We still had coffee, and, making a huge pot of this
fragrant beverage, we gathered round the crackling camp fire – our last
in the Cascade Mountains – and, sipping the nectar from rusty cups and
eating salal berries gathered during the day, pitied folks who had no coffee."
Catherine in the *Oregonian,* June 17, 1890, reprinted by Leslie Scott, p. 245.

   "Our provisions were exhausted by this time, and for three days we had
only Salal berries, and some soup made by thickening water from flour
shaken from a remaining flour sack. My uncle Levi Caffee, who was a
great joker, looked at the poor mess and said to his wife, 'Why Ellen, aint
there a little bread or something?' 'Oh no,' she said, 'we are all starving
together!' . . . My sister, having charge of the two smaller children, and
my aunt, whose youngest was seven, saved and hid in their pockets some
biscuits they from time to time doled out to the three littlest children." Etty's
"Memoirs," p. 6.

   [57] Lawson Scott. Leslie Scott, p. 323.

   [58] "We this morning about 10 oclock met our provisions and stopped to
cook and eat our breakfast Father went back this morning to look again
for the lost cattle he found them and brought them up he was verry mutch
wearied and soon after gathering into camp took a hard chill and was crazy
a[ll] night." 1853 Revision.

reaching Mr. Fosters at the western base of the mountains We here obtained vegetables in plenty by paying enough for them; Mr Foster has a splendid farm, under good cultivation.

Sept 27th [29] We traveled twelve miles this day without accident, but did not take exactly the right road, and did not get to Oregon city as we intended.[59]

Sep 28th [30] We traveled eight miles when we reached the far famed *Oregon city* we found it to be a long, narrow town situated in a kanyon, on the Willamette river; It is half as large an Pekin Ills but is a hard looking place.[60]

We remained here fore an hour and then moved on six miles and encamped;

Sep 29th [Oct 1] We traveled twenty four miles when we reached the residence of uncle Johnson in French prairie. We found them all in good health, and well satisfied They were of course glad to see us

ACCOUNTS OF JOHN TUCKER SCOTT FOR THE TRIP TO OREGON.

In the back of the *Journal* are memorandums of accounts kept by John Tucker Scott covering the trip to Oregon. On the assumption that they were entered from the back in reverse order to the *Journal,* they are presented in that order:

---

[59] "Before we reached Oregon City my father was fortunate enough to buy 2 pounds of butter. The hungry crowd was so great that before we smaller ones had our turn at the improvised table the butter had all been eaten up. There were 6 of us smaller children who did not get a taste of butter, and the thought of that rankled in us for years! Now we can laugh over our miseries!" Etty's "Memoirs," p. 6-7.

[60] "it is a long narrow town situated in a rocky Kanyon at the falls of the Willamette river where it tumbles and 'squeezes' throug the rocks with a descent of near 40 feet making a deafening noise." 1853 Revision.

I loaned to R H.King $. 5.oo before we started
     "   "   "   1.oo at St Jo
sold R.H. King 1 oil cloth coat   5.oo
R H King is to pay me   50.oo for his fare to Oregon
City and drive team one half of his time   he is to pay 10 percent.
on the above sums from the 1st of April 1852 until paid

Receved of R. Dixon on his fare to Oregon City $50.oo
    "   "   J. Dixon   "   "   "   "   50.oo
    "   "   Sommers ————   50.oo
         J. H. Clason ————   100.oo
      G Burns ———— "   "   "   50.oo
      J L. Wafer   "   "   "   55.oo

this memorandum was copied August 28th 1852   J T Scott
   Paid John Gowdy for W. H Gowdy   41.78
   Recved a horse of W. H Gowdy   72.oo
   I paid in Missouri for oxen, Bally & Buck   70.oo
                 Poullup & Popcorn   30.oo
                 Bright & Berry   50.oo
I paid on Burnt River for oxen 2 yoke   150.oo
I have one yoke of oxen Tiger & Lion; upon this condition I pay
Mr Swearengin for them the sum of $75.oo or return him the said
oxen in Oregon City at his option

the Bill of provisions for the trip across the plains is not included
in the above [61]
crackers of Brown county   4.90
Paid for swimming oxen on Snake   23.50
Paid for flour in the Cascade mountains   3.20

     220 00
     126 56
     215.69
     149 30
      28 40
      67.90
     ————
     806.96

[61] Some final entries including summary which is at an angle are in pencil.

this memorandum was copied the 28 of August 1852

April 1st Ferriage at Peoria	+	$6.00
Knowltons Bill "	+	12.50
Wisemans " "	+	11.51
6 Sacks "	+	.60
Stove	+	4.00
camp Kettle	+	.50
April 3. Bill at Farmington	+	4.80
" Fairview	+	10.62
whip lashes	+	1.00
Bill at Lepers	+	3.50
Drowning fork	+	8.50
flour	+	3.44
medicines	+	2.00
" 11. Esq. Beams *for hay*	+	10.80
Camps–	+	8.72
Doctor Bill	+	1.50
corn	+	4.10
sugar	+	.50
Bill at Michals	+	2.95
12 Hay on road–	+	2.50
corn & Bill over night	+	4.93
corn & Molasses	+	2.65
Bill at ursa	+	3.80
articles bot at Quiny	+	6.80
Ferriage at Quiny	+	17.50
Lagrange	+	3.35
oats	+	2.00
Monticello	+	4.00
corn	+	1 60
Bill at Bowns	+	16.95
Flour at Edina	+	7.25
Bill at Monroe	+	5.00
Hay & corn	+	2.40
20. Bill at Kirksville	+	7.75
coffee & Molasus	+	2.20
corn at Kirksville	+	4.20
Dr & Tavern Bill	+	11.00
Ferriage at Chariton	+	4.75
Bill at Lefevers	+	7.50
		———
		215.67

Paid Verner for Straps & Spancels		
40 ox straps	+	9.20
17. Spancils	+	5.95
Butter of Jo Landes	+	4.62
1½ doz plates	+	1.50
Bill a Pekin for		
plates coffee mills &c	+	9.97
corn (not to be added)		1.33
Bill over night		3.60
corn meal	+	1.20
corn—	+	2.00
Hay & pasture	+	2.70
sugar	+	1.00
Sugar & Molasses	+	2.95
Sundries bot at *St Jo*	+	"89"47
toll on Indian Bridge	+	2.50
Do– "	+	1.00
corn meal	+	1.00
Ferriage at Green River	+	15.00
toll on Bridges	+	5.00
Elk skin–	+	1.50
		———
		126.56
Paid for 1 sack of flour	+	15.00
Do Do on J Days river	+	14.00
for Beef umatillo	+	2.00
Do J Days river	+	4.50
Do Dalles	+	3.55
Pork Dalles	+	6.80
flour Do–	+	15.00
Beef Do–	+	5.20
Salt & pepper	+	.80
Saleratus	+	.50
crossing J Days river	+	4.00
Flour at the gate	+	28.00
Salt & Beef– Do	+	18.75
toll at the gate	+	15.00
Bill at Fosters	+	11.85
" oregon City	+	2.25
" all night	+	4.20
		———
		149.00

Livi sold—			1.00	sold coffee on snake	3.65
Sold candles at Boise			1.00	" " at Grand round	2.50
"	"	" willow creek	9.00	at willow creek ———	7.50
"	"	J Days river	3.00	sold bacon at powder river	2.75
"		at the gate	1.50	" " at Grand round	2.50
			15.50		18.90

sold Harness at Grand round	$22.50
12 ox yokes of J. Shaw	+ 45.00
tent & fixtures———	+ 13.50
whiplashes & Buckskin at peoria	+ 3.00
Brass nobs	+ 5.60
Bill of medicines ———	+ 12.60
Mattrasses ———	+ 8.00
Flour of Dr Crawford	+ 3.20

KEY TO REFERENCES IN FOOTNOTES

1853 Revision: Abigail Jane Scott. Journal. . . revised copy sent to James Scott, July 22, 1853.

Abigail: Narrative by Abigail Jane Scott Duniway, *The Oregonian,* Oct. 7, 1900, in Leslie Scott, pp. 246-49.

Catharine: Narrative by Catharine Amanda Scott Coburn, *the Oregonian,* June 17, 1890, in Leslie Scott, pp. 237-46.

Etty's "Memoirs": Harriet Scott Palmer. *Crossing over the Great Plains by Ox-Wagons.* 9 p. [privately printed by her children ca. 1931).

Fanny . . . interview: Lockley, Fred. Impressions and Observations of the Journal Man, 3-21-25, in the *Oregon Journal.*

Leslie Scott: Compiler's Appendix, in Harvey W. Scott. *History of the Oregon Country,* Cambridge, 1924, vol. 3, pp. 232-325.

Scott Letters to Illinois and a Poem

❧ The Scott Sisters

INTRODUCTION

These letters from the five older Scott daughters are to the family in Illinois. Written from the trail and in the first year after their arrival in Oregon, they round out the story told in Abigail Jane Scott's *Journal* through marriage in 1853.

Omitted are John Tucker Scott's tender letters to his father and his public letters to the *Tazewell Mirror* published in his old market town, Pekin, Illinois. They would intrude his point of view into the writings of his daughters. Two public letters are pasted in Abigail's *Journal,* one of which is incomplete. There may have been other letters, but there are only a few scattered copies of this newspaper which are known to have survived. These are now on microfilm and have been searched. Not found was Crawford Morrison's account of boating down the Snake River to which Margaret Scott refers, or additional poetry by Abigail or other members of the family.

A major portion of these letters was sent to the grandfather, James Scott of Groveland, Illinois. They are owned by R. Edwin Browne of Independence, Missouri, who also owns the 1853 version of Abigail's *Journal* sent to James Scott. They are published with his generous permission, as are quotes from that revised *Journal* in the footnotes. Mr. Browne is a great-great grandson of James. He, his wife and friends, followed the Oregon Trail in a car with the *Journal* in hand in 1977. At the Oregon Historical Society they were referred to David Duniway, grandson of Abigail Jane Scott. The discovery of these manuscripts was a miracle.

The other letters were sent to the other grandparents, Lawrence and Mary Roelofson or their sons. They were brought to Oregon by a great-grandson, Wylie W. Rolofson when he moved west after his marriage in 1908. Wylie's grandfather had simplified the spelling of the Roelofson name. The original letters are now in the Roelofson Clan Archives currently in custody of David Duniway.

The poem by Abigail written on the Oregon trail is recorded in her *Journal* in three versions. In the John Tucker Scott *Polyglot Bible* in the Old College Hall Museum at Pacific University, there is part of a clipping pasted in which provides the finished text for the last five verses of the poem. This we have used with the generous permission of Pacific University, along with the obituary of Ann Scott and her son William, quoted in a footnote. Omitted from this publication are poems recorded in the *Journal* by Tucker and by Harvey W. Scott, the brother who grew to maturity, and a poem by Margaret Scott Fearnside to her father John Tucker Scott, preserved in manuscript and printed form in his *Polyglot Bible*.

It is possible that letters from the trail may be found for many other diarists published in this series, still in the hands of relatives in the mid-west and east. Their discovery rests upon the efforts of those who work in the field of genealogy and try to tie together the dispersed families of America and even Europe. Their discovery also rests upon the expert analysis of family papers in various eastern depositories by their catalogers and custodians.

Thanks go to John McKesson, my wife's nephew, for his help in providing missing portions of the text from the original manuscript in Mr. Browne's possession.

DAVID DUNIWAY

1: LETTER – Margaret (age 15) to Lawrence &
   Mary Roelofson

Sunday   April 18th   1852
                                  State of Missouri Lewis Co
                         In camp 30 miles from the river
Dear Grandfather, mother and all of you
It is with the greatest pleasur imaginable that I
occupy a few moments (*in*) writing to you to let you
you know how we get allong since we have undertaken
this tedious and arduous journey. We are not all well
at present   Mother I am sorry to inform you has been
very sick but she is a great eal better and we think she
will have better health after she gets over this than she
has had in a long time. Uncle Levi is very sick now
he was taken a few days ago but he is much better than
he has been and we think with care he will soon be
able to travel. William Goudy(*'s*) wife is sick also but
we hope that the trip accross the plains will do them
all good and restore them to health   "if it was'nt for
hope the heart would fail"   We have all gotten allong
very well notwithstanding   the weather has been so bad
but the main thing was to get started but it was a hard
trial to bid adieu to Illinois forever and to submit ourselves to be caried from our loved native land and to
launch ourselves uppon the unruffled bosom of the
"Great father of waters"   I looked back as long as
I could see any thing of Old Illinois and it was with
many tears that I left the boat to see my native land
no more. But It is of no use to talk about it for I have
left the home of my early childhood friends associates
and am now on my way to a distant land and must strive
to form new associations in the far distant west   we

are in as good spirits as could be expected under the existing circumstances yesterday was Saturday and we laid by to wash iron and to take care of the sick folks. we got it all done in good season. our clothes all washed and ironed and the sickfolks much better we think they will be able to travel tomorrow, we have considerable work to do   For cooking for 27! in family you must know takes considerable of work we are boarding eight men out there and we think they are all of the "right stripe" I think we will get though safely if we have no more trouble in proportion to the distance

We'ev had a tedious journey
And tiresome it is true
But lo! thus far through dangers
The Lord has brought us through

Yes thus far throug(*h*) *many* dangers he has brought us safely through and humbly do I trust he will protect us through, (*to the end*)   O! my dear Grandfather will you pray for me that I may be delivered from temptation.

Will you with me at close of day
Retire in secret prayer
And though long miles us seperate
I'll surely meet thee there

But there is one hope left us if we never meet on earth.

I hope we are the followers
Of jesus meek and mild
In heaven I hope we will be blest
With Christ the undefiled

I have such a poor chance to write I hope you will excuse me for not writing sooner a longer letter   give

my love to all the folks and tell them to be sure to write
Remember that I remain
                 your Sincere and affectionate Granddaughter
                                        Margaret A Scott
    I want you to write if you can as soon as you receive
this and direct to Oregon city

2: LETTER – Abigail (age 17) to James Scott

        Sullivan County Missouri   April 25th   1852
My Dear Grandfather
    In compliance with a promise made to you when I
last saw you, I now take my seat to address a few words
to you: We have progressed very slowly in our journey
so far on account of sickness: On the morning of the
snow storm Mother was taken with the ague which
terminated in the lung fever; We laid by several days
on her account and she had been able to travel but a
few days when uncle Caffee was taken sick with the
pleurisy which also terminated in the lung fever: He
lay four days and a half in all, entirely unable to travel
but is considerably better now: Wm Goudy's wife had
the ague both yesterday and to-day but we hope she
will get along after this without it.: You may think
from this narration that we have a very dull, disagreeable and unhappy time but I assure you the imagination of it would have been a great deal worse than the
reality has been:. We have in no case felt discouraged
and I have no doubt but that you have felt worse on
our account than *we* have:: Father has written to you
two or three times and I suppose has given you a description of our roads and expenses:: I will however

say that it is in some places impossible to get feed for
our cattle at any price: We are now paying .75 cts.
per bushel for corn and have paid in several instances
$20 per ton for hay: I would advise all persons going
this journey to go to St Josephs by water: The expenses
will be about equal each way; and the toil of going
that far by land, we are credibly informed is equal to
the toil and hardships we will have to underg[o] all
the rest of the journey::: You will probably want to
know if we regret starting; I can only speak for myself

When the mind is determined it can do almost anything   I left home with a firm determination to be
contented and I have succeeded so well that I can not
call myself anything else but happy:; I never enjoyed
myself so well before and never had as good health
before in my life: It is true that parting with home,
hone friends and hone associates is and has been a great
afflliction to me: When we were launched on the broad
majestic and unruffled bosom of the great Father of
Waters it was with feelings which no tongue can describe that I gave a fond farewell look to my native
state while a number of our company joined in singing
"Yes my native land I love thee" (*&c*) But no one
knows what he can endure until he untertakes (*it*)
and I seldom allow myself to think of home and home
friends and generally all passes pleasantly with me;
We have had very poor roads for several days– the
country is the poorest I ever saw– nothing but one continued succession of hills and hollows   The cattle begin to live pretty well upon grass

Tis the Sabbath day and we are going to have preaching this afternoon at five o'clock in our camp:. Rained
very hard last night but is quite pleasant to-day   Bob

King killed a turkey yesterday and we are preparing a splendid *pot pie;* Would'nt you like to have a share? I wish you were here to help us eat it up   Mr Swearengen has overtaken us and we begin to feel like we are among old acquaintences; We see folks going to California and Oregon every day; some are very poorly prepared for such a journey while others appear to have every thing in order:. We are fixed as well or better than any others I have seen :: I keep a journal and will send it to you when completed as I promised.

Fanny and Margaret talk of writing to you and as each will be ignorant of what the other has written, if they write anything contrary to this attribute it to difference of opinion.:.... The family join with me in sen(*d*)ing their love to you all: *Chat* and *Sonny* talk about you a great deal: Much love to every one who speaks my name in friendship:; I'll write to all when I have time: Please write often and direct to Oregon City.:. Tell granny not to forget me: May a kind providence guide you and yours in your declining years:; Goodby

Affectionately Yours
A. J. Scott

3: LETTER – Margaret to James Scott

In camp Sunday morning April 25th 1852
State of Missouri
Sullivan Co

My Dear Grandfather

In compliance with your request and very agreeable to my feelings I this beautiful Sabbath morning take my pen ito my trembling hand to adress a few lines to

you. I am sorry to inform you that we have had considerable sickness since we started and consequently
have been delayed. but we should be thankful that it
is as well with us as it is. they are much better now and
able to travel. Mother was very sick with the lung fever.
Uncle Levi has also been very sick but they are both
able to *scold* and so we think them not *dang* (*erous*)
We think when they get over this they will be more
healthly than any of the crowd. "If it was'ent for hope
the heart would break" We have all enjoyed ourselves
very well since we started at least I have and I never
saw so much pleasure in my life as I have seen since
I set out for the "garden of the world" we see new
sceenes evry evry day which has a natural tendency
to keep our thoughts from home and friends that we
have left perhaps forever let me be where I will a
thought of home will send a thrill of sorrow to my
heart time and things may change and fine spun
theories may glare arround me but you will remain
inscribed uppon my memory for time and eternity;
as a matter of course we have considerable trouble but
we will have trouble let us be where we will Father
wishes me to tell you for him that we are all *"right
side up"* that we have got a big turkey cooking for
dinner that we are going to have a church here this
afternoon in the camp!! as a minister lives just accross
the road We have got so gospel greedy that we have
invited a minister to our tent. Mr Summers wished
me to request you to tell Mr Childs that he is well
and doing well.

I am going to tell you of a pleasant walk or rather
ramble that I had a few evenings ago I we we encamped

in a pleasnt romantic place about 50 or 100 yards from
a river a beatiful little stream by the name of Chariton
I started out as soon as I could get ready as it was
about 4 oclock;   in the first place I went to the river
and gazed awhile on its smooth unruffled bosom   I
felt perfectly happy. if ever I (*felt so*)   as I stood
there I unvoluntarialy exclaimed who would not admire nature and adore nature's God   I went and (*seated myself*) by a tree and leaned my head against it and
went to sleep   I dreamed that I was at home of seeing
you and all my friends of parting with you again and
all about what you said to me when a dog came allong
and woke me up   I got up and went on the top of a
hill and surely I never saw more beautiful scenery
I wandered 'oer *hill* and *dale* till I allmost forgot it
was time to return and before I began to retrace my
steps the sun had dipped his golden orb beneath the
horrizon and before I reached the place from which
I started twilight had deepened into obscurity. But I
do not know as this will interest you. I do not know
what Jane has written, and if I contradict her please
attribute it to differance[s] of opinion. Mr. Swearingen has overtaken us and three young men so we
have a tolerably large company   They all seem in
good spirits   entertain no uneasiness on our account.
Give my love to Grandmother Mary Margaret Gusta
all my Aunts uncles and cousins   tell Granny that I
have not forgotten her   tell *Mary* and *Maggie* that I
will write to them from St Joseph's   Fanny Jenny
Mother Father and all send their love to you   J. T.
Goudy sends his love to all and particularly to Mary
and Margaret   but I must come to a close

My love to all   Remember I remain
your true sincere friend and (*affectionate*)
Grandaughter   M A Scott
        Margaret A Scott

Heaven delightful	Farewell Farewell a long
heaven that glorius	Farewell
home above in heaven	We must forever part
I'll try to be with you	To think I'v spent bright
this is my solemn	days with you
vow	Endears you to my heart
	M. A. S.
	consider the source
	Write! Write !! Write!!!

4: LETTER – Abigail to James Scott

St. Josephs Mo.   May 6th   1852
My Dear Grandfather
    It is with the greatest pleasure that I embrace the
present opportunity to write to you once more   I wrote
you on the 25th ult. (I beleive) and mailed the letter at
Trenton: Since that letter was written the folks who
were then sick have got almost well, but Mr J.B. Chamberlin a young gentleman who joined our company at
Peoria is now very sick and has been for several days
    We have got a very popular physician to attend him
and hope that he will get along: The Groveland gents
waited here for us more than a week and they are now
camped on the other side of the river waiting until
we can get an opportunity to cross:. We intended to
have gone over this morning but our cattle escaped
from the enclosure in which they were placed and went
back to "Hundred & Two" bottom and made us too

late to cross to-day: Guess we'll be fast enough for
them tomorrow morning. There is a perfect rush of
wagons to the ferry every morning and continues so
throughout the day: It is estimated that the enigration
across the plains this year will be greater by at least
one third than has ever been known before:: We have
had very heavy rains now for four nights in succession but it looks this morning as if we will have pleasant weather for a while at least   The folks are all busy
at present making their wagon sheets double as one
thickness of Osnaburgs cotten is not sufficient to keep
off heavy rains :: We have thrown away almost every
trunk we started with and oil-cloth and India rubber
carpet sacks in their stead.;. We are all very well satisfied with and get along very well about every thing
but sickness Cheerfulness beams in every countenance and all are anxious to go ahead:. Father received a letter from you yesterday but I was very
disappointed in not receiving a letter from any of you.:.
I hope to have better success some day :: Mr Wafer &
Mr Lyford got here safely with all our provisions and
everything appears to come around about right

I have written to Cousin Bell and would write to
others had I the time to spare:; But we have so much
confusion in camp and so much work to do that we
find very little time devote to writing:: And if I do
find time to write there is so much talking and laughing; which you know I always have to join that I can
think and care about little else.:. If you get the letter I mailed at Trenton (and I suppose you will) you
will receive all the information which I can think of
that would interest you.: I want to receive a dozen
letters from you at Oregon City and hope that I will

not be disappointed in getting them   I do not know
whether my friends have forgotten me or not   I think
it looks a little like hope   I did not receive but one
letter here and there were about a dozen promised
to me :: You will think this a very dull letter but I
am talking one minute and writing another and have
but little opportunity to think of anything. : I do not
know as you can read this but do the best you can and
let then let it go. :. I have but little time for compliments Give my love to all inquiring friends and share
a three fold portion yourself

Nothing More Farewell
Your Grandaughter
A. J. Scott

5: LETTER – Abigail to James Scott

Missionary Station, Nebraska Territory
May 13th 1852

My Dear Grandfather
   Father cannot find time to write you this morning
and requested me to write you a few words in his place..
We crossed the Missouri safely and with no difficulty
except a little misunderstanding between a ferryman
and some of our heard men which resulted only in a
few very hard words from the ferryman :. We are now
about thirty five miles from St. Joe. : We find the roads
so far very hard; a continual succession of hills and
hollows, but we think from what (we) can hear that
the roads will be better after this   We were obliged
to leave Mr Chamberlin at St. Joe–   heard from him
yesterday and he was getting better and thought that
if he could find an opportunity he would yet overtake

us:: Rained some last night– is cloudy this morning, but has some appearance of clearing off:. The scenery around our camp is beautiful in the extreme:. We see plenty of Indians and they are certainly the most despicable looking objects my eyes ever beheld:. Our train numbers 13 wagons:: Mr. Swearengen is in our company.:. We all get along very well and all feel satisfied and contented:.. Yesterday we passed three new made graves– emigrants who had died on the road and [   ] was truley a solemn spectacle to behold:: It is reported that there are hundreds of wagons behind us and there are hundreds before us:: We find excellent grazing for our cattle   The Missionary Station contains a few log cabins and is surrounded by an excellent and well improved farm   I am in haste and can write (*no*) more.: Inclosed I send a composition addressed to "My Grandfather" for the Mirror.:: The folks are all well and join me in sending their best compliments to you all:: Farewell for a while

Yours Affectionately
A. J. Scott

6: LETTER – Abigail to James Scott

Oregon Territory   July 18th 1852
Bear River Valley. Ten Miles (*East*) of Soda Springs
My Dear Grandfather:

As Father at present has no taste for writing, it becomes my duty to commence the (at this time painful task) of writing to you.: Since we last addressed you, the mysterious, relentless hand of Death has vis(*i*)ted, us and we are now mourning the decease of our beloved Mother! On the morning of the twentieth of

June she (*was*) taken with a violent dieriehea which
was soon followed by crampings, and in the afternoon
of the same day (being Sabbath) her immortal spirit
took its flight, as we have every reason to beleive to
fairer worlds on high; She had never been in good
health since leaving home, had never performed any
work, and indeed had most of the time remained in
the wagon; However the day before her death she
appeared much better, and walked several miles, getting much overheated :. We were traveling over a range
of the Black Hills, and she walked because the roads
were rough:: I was sick that day and, had been for
some days; and during the whole of my sickness she
had manifested the greatest concern for my recovery,
and as I afterwards learned had frequently remarked
that she did not believe I would get well; I little
thought on that last Saturday of her earthly career that
she so soon would be called from this unfriendly world!
On, Sabbath morning, (I slept that night with her)
she arose early, before I was awake, and remarked to
father that she was sick; he immediately went to pre-
scribing medicine, and two physicians passed in a short
time, both of whom were called to her assistance:: The
dierrehea was soon checked but her constitution so long
impaired by disease was unable to withstand the attack
and she began to sink and every effort to arouse her
was vain; She remarked that her destiny was fixed,
and drawing the little children to her, kissed them
affectionately and speaking of Willie, who was fondly
caressing her and calling her name in the kindest manner (*said*) "bless his little life," and when father tried
to get her to talk, she said she had a great deal to say
"but" said she "I shall die with weakness". These were

her last words; and dear Grandfather we now feel that we are bereft indeed! She had long felt willing to go at any time, and had felt for two months that she would not get through to Oregon.: But we must not repine at the ways of providence, and though this trial is hard to bear yet we have the consolation (*that*) our loss is her eternal gain. There are (*so*) many exciting scenes and themes to attract our attention that we do not now feel her loss as we would at home;: She rests in peace thirty miles this side of fort Laramie on the summit of an eminence that we have named Castle Hill;

We have had some very romantic and rather fatiguing times in crossing the mountains All hands have had to walk in ascending them; and in one place in descending a mountain we kept the hind wheels of the wagons locked for two miles, in addition to which in many places the men held the wagons back with all their force; Aunt (*Martha*) has walked ten miles in a day twice and I have done it several times without as much fatigue as in walking two miles at home;; We came to Smith's fork of Bear River and camped one day and a half to wash and iron.:. While there a train from Wisconsin came up and halted one half mile from us, who were in great trouble on account of a murder having been committed in their company the day before:: Our men were called upon to act as jurymen and after an impartial investigation of both sides of the affair they with one consent acquited the murderer :. It was clearly proved that he had killed him in self defense, but I have not time nor space to give you the particulars in detail.;. I have it all written out in my journal which in due time will be at your service:. This is the ninth case of death by violence on the route,

three of whom were executed, the others were murdered   This route is the greatest one for wrangling, dis-
cord and abuse of any other place in the world I am
certain; Tho we have had less difficulty than any other
train we hear of, but we sometimes feel a little ill-na-
tured.: The journey has been much more pleasant than
I had expected in every thing but sickness; we are now
all in better health than we have before been since we
started, and can eat anything cooked almost any way,
and about three times as much as at home:: A peice of
bacon placed between two peices of bread actually
tastes better than the best of cakes and pies at home:
I need not tell you how anxious we all are to hear from
you, but we expect to get through in five weeks when
we hope we will not be disappointed in getting letters
Father brothers and sisters join me in love to all who
care for us; Tell Granny that Jinny still remembers
her: May a kind Providence guide you and yours thro
life is the prayer of your affectionate Granddaughter
                                A. J. Scott

7: POEM – by Abigail from back of original *Jour-
    nal,* verses I to V; and from 1853 printed version
    pasted in the John Tucker Scott, *Polyglot Bible,*
    remaining five unnumbered verses:

BURNT RIVER   August 27th 1852
                         I
Far away over deserts and mountains so wild
   In our wearisome journey we've strayed
Towards a far distant land, a bright home in the West
   Where many fond hopes have been laid

II

The journey has been one of anguish and (*Woe*)
  (*Combined*) With (*some*) gladness and mirth
Yet we *little thought* when *we* started to go
    That our hopes would lie low in the earth!

III

Yet he who provideth for children of men
    Their pleasure, their grief and their woe
Has seen fit (*in*) His wisdom to enter our fold
    And call one of our number to go.

IV

A bright little darling some four years of age
    By afflictions rude grasp has been laid
On a couch of deep suffering and (*he*) *must* soon go
    Where grief will be *ever* allayed

V

I'm watching him now, in the deep midnight hour
    All nature is hushed in repose
No sound can be heard save the rivulets fall
    And the wind which most mournfully blows

"Burnt River Mountains" a beautiful range,
    Of these natural beauties of earth,
Their tops decked with cedar, their sides
      with fine grass
    Which adds to their grandeur and worth.

The wind whistles through them with sad
      mournful sound,
    And the bright silver moon's shining clear,
Causing shadows of bushes to assume frightful forms,
    Which have caused me to startle with fear.

In this wild retreat far away from our home
  I'm watching a brother most dear,
Whose eyeballs are frightfully swimming in *death,*
  And whose forehead looks glistening and clear.

Some ten weeks ago our dear Mother was called
  To bid her dear children farewell,
And Willie will meet her beyond yon bright stars,
  And together in heaven they'll dwell.

Oh! God help us all to consider that this,
  Keen afflliction is caused by thy hand!
And feeling it thus may we cheerfully yield,
  And not strive thy will to withstand.

                              ABIGAIL JANE SCOTT [1]

---

[1] "Departed this life, on the plains, about thirty miles West of Fort Laramie, on the 21st of June, 1852, Mrs. Ann Scott, consort of John Tucker Scott,
late of Tazewell county, Ill. Mrs. Scott was daughter of Mr. Lawrence
Roelofson, was born on 26th day of September 1811, in Henderson county, Ky.
She was dedicated by baptism, by Rev. James McGready, of whose congregation her parents were members. She made a profession of religion at an
early age; was married to Mr. Scott in 1830. Mrs. Scott was one of the first
members who constituted the church in Pleasant Grove, Ill., in which she
remained a member in good standing until her departure for Oregon. It was
with much reluctance that Mrs. Scott consented to leave her happy home
to emigrate to the far, far west, and often expressed great doubt of being
able to endure the fatigue of the journey. But characteristic of that amiable
disposition which belongs to a good wife, she finally consented to the wishes
of her husband, and set out accompanied by her youngest sister and her
family, fondly anticipating the happiness of joining another sister already
in Oregon, (wife of Rev. Neile Johnson) but an All-wise Sovereign who
giveth not an account of his matters had decreed that she should never see
Oregon. She was attacked with cholera, which finished its awful work in
nine short hours. She expressed in her last illness a calm confidence in the
Redeemer, and a resignation to his will. She left a husband and nine children to mourn her loss, which in this world can never be repaired.

"We might now conclude that the destroyir might be well satisfied,; but
death ever cries give, and the grave is never satisfied. Accordingly on the
27th of September, on Burnt river William Neill, youngest child of this
family, was called to follow and join his mother in heaven.

" 'Write, blessed are the dead that die in the Lord.'

"Banner of Peace and Cumberland Presbyterian, please copy."

Unidentified clipping pasted in John Tucker Scott's *Polyglot Bible.*

8: LETTER – Catharine (age 13) to James Scott

Lafayette Yamhill C O T Nov 26th 1852

Dear Grandfather it is with pleasure that I embrace this opportunity of wrighting a few lines to let you know how we are getting along and how we got along on the plains I have went through a great manny changes and difficulties, since I last saw you and I now know what I never knew before that is to be bereft of a Mothers advice we got along verry well after we started until we reached Fort Laramie but 35 miles west of this place in the black Hills we met with a great loss indeed. Mother (*who*) had been sick a great deal on the road, but we thought she was getting better) was taken verry violently with diareah about 2 oclock in the morning she did not awake anny one as she thought she would soon get over it but she continued to get worse until we became alarmed about her, we called in two physicians which done all that they could do but it did not seem to do her anny good and she (*died about*) 5 oclock in the eavning leaving us bereft indeed. There has been a great deal of sickness on the plains this season, we passed as many as 7 new made graves a day along Platte river, there is a great manny curiosities to be seen on the road Chimney rock Scotts Bluffs Independance rock and the devils gate are very great sights to anny person who had not been used to (*seeing*) them from (*there*) we got along tolerable well untill we reached Fort Hall here commences the worst part of the journey after we struck Snake river the dust was in some places knee deep and sand hot enough to roast eggs (*for*) 600 miles there is nothing to be seen but sand dust & sage plains the

wether is verry warm   we had to travel sometimes
15 (*miles*) & upwards without water when we got
to it it was not like the water at home but so warm
that we could hardly drink it. After we had travel[   ]
about 700 miles farther we met with another great
trial   our dear little Willie was taken sick with Direah
we did not think him dangerous at first but he continued to get worse   we called in a doctor who said
that he was not dangerous but gave him some medicine.
we traveled along with him a day or two   he still continued to get worse until his deasease terminated to
dropsy of the brain   he could not speak for several
days before he died but would take a cup and hold
it out for water was the only sign(*s*) he would make,
after nine days sickness he died leaving us in a wild
desart place to mourn over him   he is buried on the
side of a hill under a lone cedar tree on Burnt river.
From this place we went down into Grand round valley   this is a better looking place than we had seen
for a long time. it was filled with Indians and wigwams, we came along with but little difficulty to the
Dalles of the *Columbia*   here or at John days river
John Johnson Foster Johnson and Lawson Scott met
us with fresh teems to cross the mountains with   we
started in the mountains just at the right time to miss
the storms   we had to do without provision 2 days in
the mountain   we reached the Wilamette valley september 27   I have written evry thing I can think of
and a very long letter so I must close   Give my love
to Mary and Margret and all the rest of them.

(*Yours affectionately*)

Catharine A Scott

To (*Aunt Gusther,* write write soon)

9: LETTER – Harriet (age 11) to James Scott

Lafayette Yamhill Co. O. T. Nov 26th 1852
Dear Grandfather it is with pleasure that I take
this opportunity to write you a few lines to let you
know that we get along very well a very small part
of the journey I enjoyed very well but the greater part
of it is very tiresome and hard to get along I seen a
great many curiosities on the road it was a very grand
sight indeed for any person that is not used to it there
are in some places sand and dust which are hot enough
to roast eggs and is very ennoying indeed I am sorry
to tell you that old Flower died on Snake river *she
did not tare our dresses* any on the road we have got
a Cow that is a great deal like her she cost seventy six
dollars but she is not such a good looking cow as old
flower was old Suckey got drowned in snake river
we lost a great deal of our property on the road. we got
here with seven yoke of cattle I rode on horse back
most of the way but I got very tired of it there was
some places on the road that is almost Impossible to
travel we reached Oregon city on the 30th (*Sep*)
makeing our journey six months long I like Oregon
what I have seen of it very well but not so well as
old succordom every thing here is new and strange
to me and does not seem like home. I cannot be runing
about in the grass lot and pasture and rolling down
the Corn (*in*) the crib I cannot be a running to Grand-
fathers with the news papers as I used to do nothing
seems like home here to me it keeps a continiual rain
here in the winters and is very dull and gloomy the
Chat has got her thimbol that you gave her and she
thinks a great deal of it She says that we left Grand-

father and (frisky ann) at home   we have got your
likeness and it does me a great deal of good to look
at it. it looks very natureal indeed   tell Mary and
Margaret Davis that they mus write soon   tell Tommy
that he must not forget to write to me but I must
bring my letter to a close

yours Affectionately
H. L. S. From Duck

10: LETTER – Harriet to Mary Augusta Brown

Lafayette yamHill Co O. T. Nov 26   1852
To Augusta
   Dear Cousin it is with a high degree of pleasure
that I take my pen in hand to let you know that we are
all well at present   I am going to school at this winter   I like the school very well   we are living (*in*)
Lafayette Yamhill Co   this is a very beautiful part
of the country   I like Oregon what I have seen of it
very well but it does not seem like home. Fanny and
Jane are sewing for the stores   they are makeing panta-
loons and Flannel shirts   the get two dollars for panta-
loons and five bits for flannel shirts   I have seen a
great many curiosities and changes since (*I*) last saw
you   old Sucky got drowned in Snake river   I rode
on horse back most of the way but it was very tiresome work   it ride in the hot sun but I had better
Come to Close   give my love to Aunt poly and grandmother and write soon

Yours Affectionately
H. L. Scott
to
Mary Augusta Brown

11 : LETTER – Margaret Scott (age 16)
   to Lawrence Roelofson

April 1st 1853
Lafayette   Yamhill   Co. O. T.
My Dear Grandfather
   One year ago – to day my dear friend, I left the
home of my early childhood, and bid farewell to my,
friends and associates, for the purpose of hunting me a
home in the far distant "west"   O! how many changes
some of which have been of a sad and some of a joyful
nature, have taken place in one short– year. O! how I
love to think of by gone days, and be assured when I
am thinking of the past I do not forget the happy hours
that I have spent bene(a)th your roof– I can think of
them with a degree of pleasure, more easily imagind
than discribed and can call them the happiest period
of my life. I imagine I can see the rude puncheon floor
scrubbed so white and clean with the marks of Grand-
mother('s) crut(c)hes all over it, and fancy I see you
sitting under the willow (*tree*) by the gate making
baskets and axe handles, singing in a tremulous voice
some good old fashioned hymn such "*as*"
   Tho' painful at present it will cease before long,
   And then O! how pleasent the conquerer's song
While I stood regarding you both with silent wonder,
watching you do your work, as I could not see the
necessity of Grandmother being so particular with her
milk covers and crocks, although she was constantly
telling how very bad the rats were in the "*milk house*"
Then I could not see why you never got tired of singing those old fashioned *hymns*. But as these reflections
may not be altogether agreeable to you, I will change
the subject and not (*do*) the same as throw the next

page away. I wrote to you last in the bear river valey
when but a short distance from fort Hall, and from
what was in a letter written to aunt Martha from uncle
Tom I suppose you recieved it, None of us have recieved a single sylable from any of you, and (*the*)
reason why we cannot tell. you surely have not forgotten us intirely. But if you have forgotten me, remember when you recieve this token of my regard for you,
that while the warm life blood flows through my veins
I will never forget you. I will now try to give you a
faint outline discription of the journey. We crossed
the misourie river at St. Jo the 10th of may, and after
a tedious and toilsome jour(*ne*)y of six months we we
reached Oregon city, the the last day of september,
The journey from the misourie river to fort Hall is
quite pleasant in comparison with the part of it between fort Hall and Oregon city, I am sure I can give
you no Idea of the many trials and privations the emigrant has to go through with, for you would be certain
to think me exagerating, Auunt Martha and us has
walked eighteen or twenty miles many a day, and
stopped and got suppur for 25 or thirty persons, But
I suppose you are impatient to learn what we are doing
and where we are   we are still living in Lafayette and
expect to remain during this Spring and summer, We
have rented a large *tavern* or boarding house,[2] and
have a great deal of work to do, I suppose this will

---

2 "We settled at Lafayette. Father ran a hotel there, owned by Amos Cook,
called the Temperance house. Among our boarders I remember best Judge
M. P. Deady, Judge Boise and David Logan. Lafayette was the county seat,
and these men came there on legal business. Father ran the hotel till his
girls married. Not being able then to get good help he went out of the hotel
business. . ." Fanny interview by Fred Lockley, Mar 21, 1925.

"The advertisement of the Oregon Temperance House appears in con-
secutive issues of *The Oregonian,* early in 1853." Leslie Scott, p. 233.

surprise you, but it is very profitable business in this country, as board and lodgeing is eight dollars per week. I will now tell you somthing which I expect will surprise you, Father was married on the 15th of last month to a widow lady by the name of Stevenson,[3] She has two little boys, 4 and 6 years of age, she came from Danville Illinois, and traveled through in our train, she lost her husband on the road, We get allong very well together as yet and I think we always will, But allthough the living has taken the place of the dead the image of my sainted Mother will never be erased from my mind. I suppose you would like to know how we like the country climate, &c &c well I like it much than I did when I first came here, the hills and valleys have been clothed in green for the last two months, The farmers done the most of their plowing, in the month of February, The timber here is mostly fir and pine, The face of the country is hilly and mountainous and from allmost any part of the Willianette valey there is two or three ranges of mountains visible. There is indeed some very beautiful country here more beautiful in many instances than I had anticipated. Some of the scenery is truly grand, and sublime, at least it looks so to me but perhaps if you should see it you would think diffarently and call me a silly romantic *girl* who needed sadly some silver headed *sage* to control the whims of my *brain,* Aunt Martha and uncle Levi are living a short distance from Champoig and when we heard from them last they were all well, uncle Neills folks have all been sick last winter but they are mostly better now, He,

---

3 "MARRIED: In Salem, O. T., by the Rev. Mr. Pearce, Mr. JOHN TUCKER SCOTT, of Lafayette, to Mrs RUTH STEVENSON, of Salem." *Tazewell Weekly Mirror,* Pekin, Ill, May 20, 1853. vol. 5, no. 45.

will preach in this town next wendesday night and then Mary Ann is coming to spend a week with us. I must soon bring this tedious epistle to a close, Give my best love to Grand Mother Aunt Hannah Uncle Tom Uncle Bill Aunt Eliza and all who have any love for me, I w(r)ote to uncle Tom a few weeks since and tell him I shall await the arival of his letter with much anxiety   Father brothers and sisters join me in (*sending*) love to you all,   if you cannot answer this letter I hope you will get some one to answer it for you. Remember I remain your true friend and affectionate

Granddaughter
Margaret, A Scott

There's a magical tie to the land of our home
Which the heart cannot break tho' the footstep may
   roam
Be that land where it may at the of the pole
It still holds the magnet that draws back the soul
It is loved by the freeman   'tis loved by the brave
It is dear to the wanderd more dear to the knave
Ask of any the spot that they love best on earth
They will answer with pride 'tis the land of my birth

My country I love thee tho' freely I rove
To the land of the west and the lofty pine grove
Yet warmly my bosom would welcome the gale
To bear me away with the homeward bound sail
My country I love thee and O! may'st thou have
The last throb of my heart e'er 'tis cold in the grave
May'st thou yeild me a grave in thine own dasied
   earth
And my ashes repose in the land of my birth.

M. A. S.

12: LETTER – Margaret to James Scott

Lafayette Yam,Hill. Co. O. T. June 7th 1853
My Dear Grandfather
With feelings that defy discription I once more
embrace an opportunity of writing to you, Father recieved a letter from you last night which was a source
of great joy to us all. O! Grandfather if I could only
see you to day if I could only, enjoy the blessed prive-
ledge of conversing with you face to face, I think I
should be happy up to my capability of enjoying happiness. could I but be allowed to take one more ramble
through those dear old woods where I have spent the
brightest days of my existence, If I could but recall
again my early friends and companians, I do not think
that this lovely sabbath day I should feel so discon-
solate, here I am almost unconciously pouring my
thought into the ears of my old Grandfather, who
has long since ceased to think of youthful fancies, but
I trust you will look over my whimss and remember
you was young once,
I have been to church, to day and heard, a methodist
minister preach, a very good sermon, we have preaching here almost evry sabbath, but I am sorry to state
that it seems to do but little good. This is decidedly
an easier country to make a living in than Illinois,
and I can truly say I like it very much, We have had
delightful weather since the last of december, the days
are getting to be quite warm here but the evenings and
mornings, are quite cool and pleasant, You was mistaken about the winter being so very severe, true, we
had, what is a rare occurence a *"big"* snow storm –
but was but few cattle or stock of any kind died in
consequence, as they subsisted chiefly on browse, and

some of the oregonians emptied their straw bed for
their cattle   some of their cattle in the storm by driving them to far to get food for them, if we had, let
them take care of themselves they without doubt would
have lived through it. You wished to know what became of the boys that started through with us, Bob.,
King, Frank. Gay, Mitchell and Burns, are at Milwaukie. John and Robert Dixon are at Oregon, city,
Jeff Vandervort is in Portland, Bill Goudy is on the
french prairrie teaching school, his, wife died at the
foot of the Cascades, Uncle Neills folks are keeping is
child Uncle Levi's folks are living at Champaig an
are doing well I believe, Mr. Swearingen's folks are
living not far from Salem, The name of the young man
that got drowened in Snake river trying to recover
the cattle was John– Mc.Donald he was from, Mt
Sterling Brown County Illinois, was coming through
in our train, The name of the young man that died
about the time Willie did was, John. H. Clason. he
joined our train at St, Joe, was from Maine, and was
much Respected by all the company, We left, Swearingen at the Grand, round valey at the foot of the blue
mountains as he wanted to stay there several days to
recruit is teams, The blue mountains are hard on teams
to cross but they are so beautiful that a person can not
help being delighted with the scenery, Just before leaving this range and a shot time before we descend into
the valey of the Umatilla, river, we beheld for the first
time the cascade range of mountains, they are truly
a grand and magnificent sight. M't. Hood the loftiest
of these, ap(p)ears with its snow capped summit like
a white cloud rising far above all sarrounding objects,
Lawson, Scott, John and Foster Johnson met us on

John days river, but a short distance from the Dalles
of the Columbia, They brought us some fresh cattle
which of course were very acceptable to us   We were
without provision in the cascade mountains several
days which was not very pleasant We [   ] had
seen the *"Elephant"* before we got there but it is the
cream of the whole route, we slipped through, the
cascade mountains between two storms, Crawaford
Morrison I see from the Taz, *Mirror* told a snake
story with regard to him and twenty other persons
starting down the *(snake)* river in wagon beds, there
was but five of them started and none them were lost,
they did not go but 40 or fifty miles in them, and sold
the beds at fort Boise, for ferry boats they then
started on the main road on foot, you know he stated
that the Struck out through an uninhabited region,
without any road, I think him and John Handcock
had better call *"it half a day and go a fishing"* If we
had crossed snake river at the Salmon falls I do not
think we would have lost any of our stock, as the grass
is so much,better on the north side, Jenny is away teaching school in cincinatti, her school will be out in five
weeks, You have doubtless heard that Pa is married
and who he married before this time   I will only
say that we like the lady very much and she is as kind
to us as our own mother,could be, We are keeping a
hotel at present and are doing very well, This is a
flourishing little town. it contains eight stores, I am
sitting in a curious place to write it is by the garret
window, when, I look out I can see a range of mountains called the coast range   they are a beautiful sight
O! Grandfather I wish you were here this evening, O!
can it be possible that I will never see you again, The

chat was greatly delighed with your letter, she is going
to chool   she is a great deal taller than she used to be
and learns, very fast, She looks at your likeness evry
day and expreses a wish to see you, Jerry is the most
mischiefous fellow you ever seen   I must bring this
to a close, Pa will write before long to you so I will
not tell you all, Give my best love to Grandma, and
tell her this is intended for her as much as for you,
tell Agusta, Aunt Polly, Mary and Margaret, Martha,
Jane, Acquilla, Bell, John and all the rest that we
have not forgotten them and that ain't half we never
will, John T, Goudy is at work on the french prairrie,
      I remain yours in friendship, truth and love
                        Mag, A. Scott
              Adieu, Adieu

13: LETTER – Mary Frances (age 20)
     to James Scott [combined with above]

My Dear Grand father
    After reading your kind letter last night I could
not rest contented any longer without writing to you
and as Mag, has left a small space in her letter I will
endeavor to write a few lines to my dear Grand father,
And although we are far sepparated and I may never
again behold your face yet you will ever remain as
dear to me as when I enjoyed your (*company*) daily
in my childhood days   Ah. me if I could only recall
those pleasant days by far the most (*happy*) days of
my life, But why talk thus, your likeness is a source
of great enjoyment to us all   it looks as natural (*as*)
life   the *Chat* says she promised Grand father that she
would go back and and see him and she means to do

it yet when she get to be a woman   she often speaks of you and of the manny times that her and Willie ran to meet you at the big *elm tree* with newspapers in their hands   O! Grand father if I could only see you this pleasant afternoon my happiness could better be imagined than described   We have but little time to devote to writing haveing so much work to do   But we look forward to better times   But do write to us soon   your letters afford us so much pleasure   Give my love to Grand Ma and all enquiring friends and use a large portion yourself

Your Affectionate Grand daughter
Mary F Scott

Lawson Scott and his Wife are here I know you would like her she is such an agreable woman, the family all join me in much love to you all enough from Fanny I will write you a long letter as soon as I can

14: LETTER – Margaret to James Scott

Lafayette, Yam Hill. Co.: O.T. August 17th "53, My, Dearly, Beloved, Grandfather

It is with feelings of a peculiar character that, I endeavor to, form a few imperfect ideas into the shape of a letter, I beg your indulgence my, dear Grandfather, for my brain is in a perfect whirl of bewilderment," *a poor excuse is better than none,"* you know   You perhaps would like to know what, has made me feel as I do, well, I will tell you and then I do not think you can blame me, for feelings of a curious nature, Jenny, and Fanny are *both* married! gone and left me at last, Jenny was married, two (*weeks*) ago yesterday, and Fanny stepped off the, *"stage of action"* yesterday

evening at four o'clock So you percieve I am left alone,
Now do you wonder that I am rather confused, taking
all things into, consideration, you know it is not a very
easy matter to lose two sisters at the same time, Jenny's
"ole man's" name is Benjaman Duniway, Fanny, *"toth-
er half's"*, name is Amos, Cook, so you see that, Jenny
has Dun i way ("Done away") with the name of,
Scott, and Fan has gotten above her business and taken,,
A. Cook. Uncle Neill married Fan and aunt Martha
and uncle Levi were to the wedding, J. T. Gowdy,
John and Foster Johnson were here also. We had a
Grand *"Shiveree"* last, night, and as Mr. Cook did
not give them, any money to buy, whiskey, I expect
they will give it to him to night, Fanny will live, just
accross the Yam Hill river, one half a mile from this
town, Jenny lives *(twenty)* five miles from here, I
think they have both got very good kind of men, Pa's
health is not very good and has not , been for some time,
I wrote to you some time since, and have as yet recieved no answer, I can look.over it tho' as long as it
is Grandfather, When you write, please inform us how
Aunt Louvisa's are getting along and where they are
we have heard nothing from them for a long time, Your
likeness is lying on the stand before me, it does look
"so" natural, When I gaize on the likenesses of any
of our friends it is impossible to discribe my feelings,
In one instant, my whole *(past)* life rushes upon my
almost frensied mind, and, although such scenes are
past and gone forever from my sight, I can but think
of them *"with a quivering lip and throbing brow*
Many persons may say it is folly, and deem me weak
but under such circumstances it is impossible to control my feelings, Pa is going to write to you before very

long. We have not recieved but three letters from you
yet I suppose you will get the journal before this reaches you as it is now on the way, When you read that you
can see for yourself what we had to undergo on our
tedious and toilsome journey, Well, I expect we will
get so completely westernized in a short time that we
will forget all our hardships, When we came here last
fall I could not endure the sight of a fir tree, although
almost evry person pronounced them somthing extra,
but it almost turned my stomach (*to look a them*) I
had become so much disgusted with evrything pertain-
ing to "Oregon"   But now I can look at them and call
them beautiful and forget that they are entire strangers
to me, but let me be placed in any circumstances whatever whether I be basking in the sunshine of prosperity, or enduring the chilling blasts of adversity yet the
fond remembrance of my dear Grandfather will ever
remain engraven on the tablet of my memory to be
erased only by the cold hand of death, I am truly sorry
that society is in the bad state that it is at present, But
who can expect any thing better where religion is so
little cared for,
"*Religion*" what treasure untold
Resides in that heavenly,word,"
Without, this it is impossible for society to be in a
good, state,
    Aug 19th   I seat my self this morning for the pur-
pose of finishing my letter, This morning is quite cool,
and cloudy, and occasionaly we have a light shower.
Pa is quite sick this morning he has been unwell for
some time and the "*Shiveree*" company kept him awake
last night. There is certainly a great set of "*gentry*"
about this town. I do not think they can be beat for

mischief anywhere always having fun at some person's
expence, We have 12 boarders now which keeps us all
busy   We intend to stay here a few weeks longer, Pa
made arangements to leave here a week ago, but the
man disappointed him on account of some of his family being sick. Where we will go to after leaving this
place is more than I can say, in all probability we will
rent a house in town to stay in until spring, as it is too
late to do much on a claim before winter sets in   We
have not heard of any of the boys that came through
with us, with the exception of Bob King   for a long
time he is still at Milwaukie   He has been sick for
some time, but is now better and able to work, The
last we heard of Frank Gay he was, there too, Lem,
Lawson and Jim Scott live but a Short distance from
here on their claims, Aunt Nancy is well and intends
to go to Calafornia next month to live with her daughter Artemesia who married a man by the name of Grif-
fith, Aunt Nancy was here at Fanny's wedding. she
has not been well satisfied since uncle Peter died, We
had quite a number of young ladies in town last winter
and Spring. but a great many of them have gone into
the country or are married off so but a few are left to
associate with me, Th chat often talks about you and
wants to see you very much, Give my best love to
Grandma Aunts *uncle's* and cousins, Write immediately   all send their love to you, With the warmest
wishes for your future prosperity and happiness I will
close by declaring myself your sincere friend and affectionate Grandaughter, Margaret, A. Scott

Journal of a Journey Over the Rocky Mountains

℘ Polly Coon

INTRODUCTION

The bottom line question for the historical researcher is, "Where is the original document?" It is only second best to have to use a typewritten copy made by someone else; however, sometimes there is no alternative. From experience we have found that much of the copying has been done very carelessly.

In the case of Polly Coon's "Journal," the first the editor learned of it was in a letter from Phillip S. Price of Escondido, California. He wrote on October 29, 1979, that he had heard me on the radio. He wrote, "We have a daily journal or diary written by great grandmother while she trekked west from Wisconsin to Oregon." He and I have become good friends by phone and correspondence since that letter. His copy of the diary is a typescript.

In early December, 1984, I called him to ask if there was a family member who was into genealogy or family history who might aid me in identifying those persons mentioned in the journal. As a result I wrote to Mrs. Margaret Reeves of Jacksonville, Florida, for such information. She promptly answered my request in a long letter. The most significant sentence in her letter read, "It might be interesting to you to see the original." She indicated that it was in the hands of Mrs. Gladys Foss of Portland, Oregon.

A telephone call opened another door. The next day we held the diary in our hands. Sure enough, the typescript was not accurate when compared with the original, which is

written in a miniscule hand and perfectly straight lines in
a tiny book only 2½ x 4 x ½ inches. A study of the handwriting reveals it to be done with the Enoch Noyes method
as demonstrated in his *System of Practical Penmanship,*
written in the early 1830s.[1] Polly's handwriting teacher had
undoubtedly been her father, whose specialty was penmanship.

Polly Coon crossed the plains with the "Crandall train." [2]
Her parents, Paul and Sally Crandall, were the principal
organizers of the group which made the long journey together.

Paul Crandall and Sally Stillman had been married on
April 24, 1824, in Alfred, Alleghany County, New York,
the locale of Alfred University, still a viable institution of
higher learning. He was a farmer and also a teacher.

Typical of the movement of American families, the Cran-
dalls traveled west in 1838 to Lima, Rock County, Wisconsin, where they lived until the much longer western trek
to Oregon in 1852. Paul Crandall was chosen to be a member of the Wisconsin constitutional convention in 1847 and
thus was dubbed one of the "Fathers of Wisconsin." After
Wisconsin obtained statehood in 1848 he served in the Leg-
islative Assembly for one term.[3]

---

[1] P. W. Filby, Peabody Institute Library, *Calligraphy & Handwriting*
(Caledonia, N. Y., 1963), pp. 33, 35.

[2] Principal sources for the Crandall family are as follows: Delia M. Coon,
"Paul Crandall–1852," pp. 220-27, in Sarah Hunt Steeves, *Book of Remembrance of Marion County Pioneers* (Portland, Oregon, 1927); detailed letter
from Margaret M. Reeves, family historian, Jacksonville, Florida; "Names
of those who crossed the plains in 1850-52," typescript attached to typewritten
diary in the hands of Phillip S. Price, Escondido, California; Robert H.
Down; *A History of the Silverton Country* (Portland, Oregon, 1926); Delia
M. Coon, *History of early Pioneer Families of Hood River,* mimeographed
(n.p., n.d.) pp. 215-17; "Hon. Thomas R. Coon," in *Illustrated History of
Central Oregon* (Spokane, Wa., 1905), pp. 290-91; "Hon. Thomas Ray Coon,"
in Charles H. Carey, *Biographical History of Oregon* (Chicago, 1922), Vol.
II, pp. 653, 655; United States Census Office, 8th Census, 1860, Oregon; "Descendants of Eld. John Crandall," detailed genealogical history of the Crandall family, a typescript in hands of Mrs. Gladys Foss, Portland, Or.

Paul and Sally Crandall had eight living children (out of
12) when they decided to move on to Oregon.

Polly Lavinia was the oldest, born on November 24,
1825. She grew up in a family dedicated to learning and
culture. Descendants even today tell of a family memory
that "Aunt Polly" had a beautiful voice and loved to sing,
accompanied by her father on the flute. After attending
Alfred University, though for how long we don't know,
she became a school teacher. Because her mother was a
semi-invalid, Polly spent much time caring for her younger
brothers and sisters.

On January 1, 1845, she and Thomas Lewis Coon, also
a teacher, were married. When the family started west in
1852, Thomas was already in Oregon. He had crossed the
trail to California with Polly's brother, Clark Crandall,
and several other men. Today the family has a typed copy
of his "Notes of a Tour to California," written in 1850.
He seems to have been seeking a healthier place to live.
The men got to California; then he and Clark decided to
go north to Oregon. Thomas took up 320 acres of land as
a donation land claim on the exact location of what later
became the town of Silverton in Marion County some 15
miles east-north-east of Salem, the territorial capital.[4]

Thomas wrote in his "Notes" of how hard it was to
leave his family in 1850: "On the 17th day of March, having completed the necessary arrangements, took leave of
my little family consisting of a very worthy and amiable
wife and a sweet interesting girl of four years of age, and
a very large circle of relatives and kind and warm-hearted
friends."

The four-year-old was Cornelia Evelyn Coon, b. March
10, 1846. In 1852, at age six, she accompanied her mother
to Oregon, there to be reunited with her father.

---

[3] A. Tenney and David Atwood, *Memorial Record of the Fathers of Wisconsin* (Madison, Wisconsin, 1880), pp. 23, 202-3, 372.

[4] *Genealogical Material in Oregon Donation Land Claims*, II (Portland,
Or., 1959), Claim #3941.

Life in Oregon was not to prove easy for the Coon family. The father, Thomas Lewis Coon, died on January 10, 1854. The land claim record contains a note saying, "Town of Silverton is laid out upon premises and much has been sold in town lots & for other purposes." [5] Upon the death of her husband, Polly Coon had the claim surveyed into lots and sold them off to form the center of the new town. She named the community Silverton because it was on the banks of Silver Creek.[6] Silverton residents today find that their property records list as the first owner Polly Coon. The Silverton post office was established on July 6, 1855. There is a street named for the town's founder, but misspelled "Koon Street."

A second child was born on March 4, 1854, and named Thomas for his father. The child's second name was Ray, in honor of one of Polly's brothers.[7] Over the following years Polly taught school at Silverton, Salem, and several other Oregon and Washington communities.

On September 27, 1855, she and Stephen Price, a carpenter and millwright, were married. He built a "handsome frame house on the homestead." [8] In January, 1861, they moved to Salem. They had one son, Eugene Crandall Price, who was born in Silverton on August 10, 1856.[9]

In later years Hood River, right on the south bank of the Columbia River, became their home. That is where both Stephen and Polly died, he on September 25, 1896, and she on October 22, 1898, at age 73. The Portland *Oregonian*

---

[5] *Ibid.*

[6] Lewis A. McArthur, *Oregon Geographic Names,* 5th Ed. (Portland, Or., 1982), p. 674.

[7] *Illustrated History of Central Oregon, op. cit.,* pp. 290-91, also *Biographical History of Oregon,* pp. 653, 655. Thomas Ray Coon followed the footsteps of both parents and became a lifelong school teacher. He also was an original promoter of fruit growing in the Hood River Valley. He was mayor of Hood River for a time.

[8] Coon, *History of Early Pioneer Families, op cit.,* p. 217.

[9] This was the ancestor of Phillip S. Price of Escondido, California, who brought the Coon journal to our attention.

noted her death with the following brief obituary: "Hood River, Or., Oct. 24—Mrs. Polly Price, mother of Hon. T. R. Coon, was buried here today. Interment was in Idlewild cemetery."

Other children of Paul and Sally Crandall who made the overland journey to Oregon were as follows:

William Ray Crandall, age 19, called Ray in the diary. He turned back to Wisconsin early on and crossed over to California in 1853-1854, stopping over the winter in Salt Lake City. His wife was Jane (Huyack). Their son, Burton, died during that winter. They later went to Oregon.

Daniel Webster Crandall, age 17. Just before leaving Lima he and a teenage girl named Jane were married. We know nothing more about her. She died in what is now southern Idaho on August 21.

Phoebe G. Crandall, age 15. In Oregon she married Isaac Geer on December 25, 1853. She died in 1857.

Amanda Crandall, age 12. She married John Hutton at Silverton and died soon afterward in 1859, leaving one child, Ida.

Luke S. Crandall, age 9. He grew up in Oregon, but spent his adult life in Colorado.

Emily Jane Belle Crandall, age 5. She was married to Henry Crawford on July 22, 1864. Her granddaughter today is Mrs. Margaret M. Reeves of Jacksonville, Florida, who supplied much helpful information about the family.

                                        Kenneth L. Holmes

THE JOURNAL OF POLLY LAVINIA COON

March 29th 1852. Started from the town of Lima Rock Co. Wis. on our long contemplated journey to seek a home on the Pacific coast, in the territory of Oregon   came to Milton & staid 2 days with our friends there, when after bidding many a tearful adieu, we started on the 2d of April, plodding our way over frozen ground, with a chilling cold wind. Passed through Janesville to the town of Plymouth where we struck our camp for the first time, & found that we had truly left all comfort behind at least as far as the weather is concerned. But all are in health & spirits seeming determined to manufacture as much comfort as possible from what material we have. Bro Ray is with us is going as far as the Mississippi. The boys after supper struck up the violin when some young Ladies living near came into camp & feeling that music was soul elevating, could not resist the impulse to "Trip the light fantasic toe" over the seared & frozen grass.

April 3d   Traveled today 8 miles very uncomfortably the weather continuing very chilling cold   stopped at 1 o'clock in the town of Plymouth. Mr. A Goodrich [1] here joined us. Our company consisting now of Mr. Goodrich's Co. composed of 4 men – Dr. Stillman's 3,[2] Aunt Charlotte's 4 [3] and our own family composed of eleven young & old, in all 22 persons with 5 wagons & 54 head of cattle & 1 horse   Some complaints are made of bad colds & all look rather chilly – some what

---

[1] This was Anson Goodrich. We know nothing about him but his name. Polly Coon says below on July 29 that "Mr G goes with us to Oregon to go to Cal in the Spring."

[2] "Dr. Stillman's 3" would have been Dr. Clark Stillman, his wife, and their son, Thomas B. Stillman. Clark Stillman was the brother of Sally, Paul Crandall's wife.

[3] These would have been Charlotte Palmiter Stillman, whose husband, Henry, had gone to California in 1849. She had two children with her, Eunice Ann and Jay. The fourth member of her party was her brother, Henry Palmiter, who drove the wagon. There was another in her party, Jonathan Palmiter, her cousin.

I suppose the effect of bad weather and the feelings of sadness which will creep over one as they leave home and friends for a long time perhaps forever.

April 4th Traveled today 10 miles Last night about 2 inches of snow fell which makes the traveling very unpleasant. Put up about 3 o'clock. Received several visitors after supper Then we spread hay on the snow and made our beds in the tent for the first time found it much better than we expected.

April 5th Made 15 miles – passed through Monroe into Viola. Weather pleasant but snow melting made travelling bad. notwithstanding the mud I have walked 2 miles today. About 1 o'clock at night a drunken man came into our camp on horseback hallooing & swearing – affording some sport and not a little disgust, till getting tired of being disturbed the men arose and drove him & his horse away by dint of a club. His name he said was "Bill Jones" or a "perfect Bill"

April 6th Made 10 miles through mud & water I find camp life quite fatiguing There are so many in our family who are unable to work that those who are able are rather over burdened But we hope for better times and I find a great support in the cheering reflection that each mile lessens the distance between myself & my long absent husband.

April 8th All are well & in excellent spirits We traveled yesterday 16 miles and camped on a vast prarie in Lafayette Co [Iowa] where nothing but land & sky were to be seen save one little log house. But to make up the absence of other interesting matter we found a wedding party assembled in the aforesaid "log house" The "old Man" came up and gave us all an invite to

attend the dance in the evening. We all went down but
none of us joined in the exercises but Ray & Stillman.
They reported to have had a very fine time and staid
till morning the others returning at 9 o'clock   We
have tonight a beautiful camping ground near the line
between G[r]ant & Lafayette [counties] pleasant
weather but still wet under foot.

April 9th   Rained all day consequently we have laid
by – improving the time in doing some baking. At
night the ground being very wet we were obilged to
take shelter in the house

April 10th   Reached the Mississippi at Eagle Ferry
2 miles above Dubuque   found a number of teams
in wait to go over

11th   After being delayed all day in getting all crossed
over we at length reached Dubuque. We made a few
purchases & excited not a little curiosity nor a few remarks from the good people of the city by our "Bloomer Dresses." [4] Left this town about 3 o'clock passing
out some 2 miles through the deepest mud & worst
roads I ever saw   Camped in a field & got about half
enough poor hay for which the Man charged 30 cts
per yoke. I record this as a demonstration of the depth
of heartlessness to which the human heart is capable
of arriving.

April 12th   Our brother Ray left us this morning – It
was with deep regret and tearful eyes we left him to
plod on alone towards his home. We feel sad that we
leave him behind but hope another year will bring
him to Oregon   This after noon it is quite pleasant

---

[4] For a discussion of "Bloomer Dresses" see volume IV of this series,
"Introduction," pp. [12]-15.

except the chilling winds which sweep furiously across
the endless praries of the state of Iowa. All well and
judging from the talking & laughing we hear from
the adjoining tent all are in good spirits The roads
continue very bad otherwise we get along very finely.

15th Passed through the village of Cascade –

17th Crossed the Wanpsipinicon [Wapsipinicon] over
the ruins of an old bridge but passed over safely.

19th Passed through Marion Here it is determined
by our company to lay by a week or 10 days till grass
appears We are now camped in a beautiful grove, all
well but Charlotte who has taken several days ago with
an intermittant fever and inflamation of the Lungs. We
are 3 miles from Marion & 6 from Cedar Rapids.

May 1st After lying by 2 weeks we have once more
started out. Charlotte has had a run of Lung fever but
is better. Some others are complaining. We have crossed
Cedar river at the Rapids. Saw several Indians painted
& ornamented in true savage style. Have camped tonight on the prarie west of Cedar river.

May 2nd Last night a very hard rain accompanied
by thunder & wind came upon us and morning found
us rather a dreary company but we succeeded in getting some breakfast after which we picked up & started
on – a constant succession of bad sloughs made the travelling very difficult A man came to the road & told
us how to avoid a very deep slough – the Dr Pa & myself went according to his direction & came over but
Goodrich Stillman & Haywood [5] came through – Goodrich being heavy loaded got stuck & was obliged to

---

[5] Mr. and Mrs. Ben Haywood were old Lima friends.

unload & back over his load a distance of 30 rods –
after being detained here a couple of hours moved on
& camped near Scotch Grove having made only 8 miles
Stoped about 6 o'clock.

3rd May   Put up today at 2 o'clock on the same endless
Prarie which we have traveled on ever since leaving
Cedar river – several of the teams have got into the
Sloughs today. 3 days ago we were joined by some more
Lima friends – Mr Kinney [6] & Mr & Mrs Haywood –
one of their Co having shipped around to the Bluffs –
we have now 6 teams and near 70 head of cattle – Some
are complaining yet of bad colds but all in good spirits
– and excellent appetites. We have tonight found some
good grass in a large ravine & our cattle eat eagerly.

May 4th   After leaving our camp this morning we
met a runner from the Iowa River directing us to a
new ferry just established saying the road is better.
We followed him & came up in time to witness a most
distressing scene   Some Emigrants had arrived at the
ferry before us & had crossed over one wagon & part
of the family   In attempting to go over with 3 yoke
of oxen without having them chained to the boat they
backed off & sunk the boat drowning three men one of
the emigrants sons aged 16 and two of the ferrymen   A
4th man succeeded in swiming out. The boat was a
miserable one & a good deal of indignation was felt at
the imposition on the public. One of the ferrymen leaves
a wife – the other a widowed Mother. I have never felt
more sympathy for any distress than for the emigrants,

---

[6] Mr. and Mrs. Giles Kinney. She was Delilah, sister of Ben Haywood.
According to the 1850 Federal Census of Wisconsin they were both in their
early forties. They had with them two children, Rosetta, age 10, and Antional,
a 7-year-old boy. Kinney was a farmer.

who stood on the bank and saw one of their number
sink in the rapid water without being able to render
any assistance A Father, Mother, brothers & sisters
bewailing their loss What a brittle thread has life
and how uncertain that another moment is ours. We
turned back came 2½ miles to the lower ferry at Marengo [Iowa] but the wind rising we are compelled
to lay by till it goes down There are now 16 wagons
in sight waiting, with men women & children.

May 6th We have at length got crossed over the Iowa
river after having lain on its banks one day & night –
and have made 10 miles. Had a hard shower this morning which has made the roads very slippery. Passed
a number of camping grounds today – many of the
emigrants have stripped the bark from the elms near
the road & written their names thereon – Among them
I noticed Mr Perry [7] from Milton Wisc. We have left
part of our company tonight – L. Palmeter [8] & Haywood – about 1 mile back they refusing to go any farther after having traveled the long distance of 10 miles!
Have only made about 11 miles today. The roads have
been very bad indeed. It has rained some today & a
fair prospect for considerable more.

May 7th Morning – Last night was one of a continu-
ous storm of thunder and rain – I confess I felt a little fear being among tall timber & where the wind not
a long time ago has prostrated many of the trees – there
are several trees in sight also which have been struck
with lightning.

---

[7] Not identified.

[8] There were two Palmiters with the party: Henry, Aunt Charlotte's
brother, and Jonathan, her cousin. Perhaps Polly Coon meant the latter, but
inadvertently wrote the wrong letter.

p m   It has been very warm and showery & very fatiguing – many deep sloughs   Made about 20 miles the most of the distance prarie   All are completely tired out tonight & Pa & Webster much worse – we feel rather dispirited but hope for better times.

May 8th   Camped on a prarie having taken in some wood at the last grove   Made 15 miles today very easily – the sick ones some better.

9th   Beautiful weather today & pretty good roads & here made the long drive of 18 miles. We have great cause to night for thankfulness   our sick ones are improving & notwithstanding a little lowering in the sky of our future we are glad that all are as well as we are

  This morning we all got a fright which I have not yet got over. Samuel [9] in attempting to put a cup in the wagon while the team was moving – slipped & fell under the wheel both wheels running over him – all supposed him either killed or very much injured – but no bones were broken and except bruises & soreness he feels quite well tonight. Crossed Skunk river today.

10th   Reached the Des Moisne about noon   crossed this river by ferry – in about 80 rods crossed the Raccoon river & camped half a mile from the shore in a miserable hole   We have found nothing but slough water for some time – we camped to night near a good well – but the owner having a little too much of the swines nature for a specimen of humanity refused to let us draw water from it & we cooked from a pond of lizards, snakes & tadpoles.

11th   Traveled near 16 miles & camped again on a large Prarie near a beautiful spring which we consider

9 Samuel L. Coon was half-brother of Polly's husband, Thomas L. Coon.

a great treat   After getting our tents pitched & supper
nearly in readiness a heavy thunder shower struck us
& we were nearly drenched but succeeded in keeping
our beds tolerable dry.

12th   Made 16 miles today   again night finds us on
a large Prarie 3 or 4 miles from a town called Winterset   All express a great dissatisfaction at the state of
Iowa or at least that part of it which we have just passed
through   The Des Moisne Country is by far the best
of any part & even there seems a destitution of means
and enterprise. The first thing we met tonight after
camping was a Rattlesnake not 2 feet from our tent
which made some of us start

13th   Reached Middle River at Walauah [Wiota?].
Made 23 miles all Prarie & charming road. We have
found a great number of very large snakes mostly
killed – one was 7 feet long by measurment

14th   Our road is all Prarie again today & 15 miles
more tomorrow – traveled 20 miles & camped early
upon the banks of a beautiful brook winding its lonely
way across this large Prarie.

15th   Left Camp before 7 this morning & traveled 20
miles   Rested at noon on the bank of Nottaway [Nod-
away] creek. Passed 2 graves this afternoon & for a
few days back have seen a number of dead horses &
oxen   We hear dubious stories from the Frontier of
all kinds but do not credit more than half we hear

16th   Another hard storm visited last night & closed
up with almost freezing weather   a hard wind chilling cold has blown all day – we have made 18 mile –
crossed the Nishnabotna creek, the east fork, also Indian Creek – camped again on the wide prarie & found

ourselves for the first time in a long time seperate from other companies no other being in sight.

17th   Crossed the west branch of Nishnabotna. this evening Mr McGraw [10] one of Haywoods Co who has been around by the River Came out to meet them & brings discouraging news as to the prospect of crossing the Missouri also for getting an outfit at the bluffs, the emigration is so very large. we all feel a little damped in spirits

18th   Arrived at Kanesville   procured our fitout & after being detained about 3 days came down to the Missouri & lay one night on its banks   The next morning took the Steamboat ferry & crossed driving out some 3 miles to a lake where we staid 24 hours, packing & repairing & forming our train   Since leaving there we have traveled in Co with hundreds of teams in sight   Immediately after leaving our camp at the Lake we came to a small creek where the Indians had thrown in a few brush & logs & were taking toll a dime a piece for one team.

26th [25th?]   Crossed over the Elk Horn a branch of the Platte   While there waiting to be ferried a child died aged 3 years of Typhus fever – We have seen a number of graves along the road

26th   Made about 18 miles today. About noon struck the Platte and now commences our journey along its winding course. I have been sick 3 days of a Diareah also Webster has been sick of the same. Samuel has had the same fever that the others have had but seems now much better

---

[10] There were several McGraws in early Pacific Northwest history. So far we have been unable to identify this one.

27th. Reached Shell Creek & camped about a mile west. At this Creek it is reported that some of the emigrants before us had refused to pay the Indians the toll they exacted for crossing a small bridge & consequently a difficulty ensued. It was said that several Indians were killed The Indian Agent came out before us and settled the difficulty. The Indians have every appearance of friendship they swarmed into our camp in great numbers trying to trade. Nearly all of them had money – they wished very much to buy corn to plant Our folks bought a very nice Buffalo robe nicely ornamented on the inside. gave them some clothing which they seem very anxious to possess, & some bread 27th Crossed the Loup Fork of the Platte It is a beautiful country around this stream paid 3 dollars per wagon & swum the cattle

28th We have all felt much distressed today at witnessing a scene truly heartrending. About noon we came by a Camp where yesterday all were well & today one man was buried – another dying & still another sick. The disease was Diareah which they had not medicine to check & the result was death The man that was buried left a young wife to either return through a savage country or go on alone and heart-broken Many of our Company are complaining but none very sick.

June 1st Crossed over from the Loup Fork valley to the valley of the Platte It has been a very hot dusty day and we have made about 25 miles in consequence of not finding water. The last 5 miles was a deep sand and Bluffy road. The cattle were near melted when we stopped about dusk near a pond of water which they rushed into with great eagerness but could not

drink it. Our Company were all nearly exhausted with
fatigue hunger & thirst. We had neither wood or water,
but Goodrich had a few sticks of wood & a little water
in his wagon & he kindly gave us some for tea which
with a little hard bread was all our supper. There was
hundreds around us & hundreds passed on travelling
in the night to reach water which was some 10 or 12
miles distant. We started the next morning about eight
traveled a few miles till we found some water for cooking breakfast. Here we found a great many doing the
same. There were two graves here near where we break-
fasted. One of them was a man laid on the ground &
the dirt heaped over him the other was a woman
who had died 2 days before.

2nd   At night came within a half mile of the Platte
& camped for a day to do some washing &c   About
half an hour after we camped one of the celebrated
Platte river storms came upon us & lasted nearly all
night – The wind blowing from nearly every point of
the compass. I never witnessed any thing of a storm
before   Some of the tents were blown down & those
that were not required 2 or 3 men to hold them all
night. Those that slept in the wagons were nearly as
bad off. It seemed every moment that they must blow
over – Dr S's wagon cover was entirely blown off, &
his provisions much wet and damaged.

3rd   Found our mess very much dejected with their
nights watching and drenching but consoled themselves
that they had seen some of the *Elephant*.[11] Every thing

---

11 The dangers of the overland trail were summed up in this term, "seeing
the Elephant." See especially John Phillip Reid, *Law for the Elephant* (San
Marino, Calif. 1980). See also Peter Tamony, " 'To See the Elephant'," *Pacific
Historian,* XII, Winter, 1968, pp. 23-29. The Arthur H. Clark Co. published

being wet we concluded to tarry 2 days & dry & repair
& wash.

4th   All are nearly ready again for a move in the morning. Some others have been sick but are better   4 wagons more have joined us   we are now 14 wagons &
over 30 men.   A boy died today in a camp near us
of Diareah.

[June] 5th   Started out & in about 3 miles crossed
Wood Creek   Among the camps on this creek there
was much sickness & 5 had died since yesterday   Dr S.
visited them & gave them medicine   Camped at night
on the plains near a well of quite good water   had
some light showers of rain which has cooled the air.

6th   Made 38 miles since yesterday morning. A man
died last night in a camp near us. We have passed 12
or 13 graves today which have been made within 3 or
4 days. The disease is all the Diareah or Cholera which
is almost sure to prove fatal if not checked immediately   Very many of the victims to this disease have
no medicine & no preparation for sickness which seems
to be the height of presumption. Our Company have
nearly all had a touch but are all better tonight. Yesterday we met the U. S. mail carried in 3 ox teams,
also a small Company from Salt Lake which had come
out it is said to escort the Mormon trains.

12th   We are now about a days drive over half way
to Fort Laramie from Kanesville. Our family are tolerably well except a debilitated feeling which is a
general complaint among the most healthy of the Emi-

James Mason Hutchings' Journal in 1980, entitled *Seeking the Elephant*, 1849.
One more reference: J. Rea, "Seeing the Elephant," *Western Folklore*,
XXVIII, No. 1, Jan. 1969, pp. 21-26.

grants. The sickness has abated somewhat in its fatality but many are sick yet. Mr Wells [12] and Mr Peak [13] have been very sick but are a little better this morning   I feel very feeble but otherwise am quite well.

May [June] 18th   Passed the "Lone tree" & a storm arising we stoped about 3 miles above the tree at the Express Station opposite "Ash Hollow" & raised our tents in great haste preparing every thing for a severe storm but contrary to our expectations it did not reach us – it veered around on every side & about one mile below us on the south side of the Platte the Bluffs were white with hail which had not disappeared the next morning when we left. Some emigrants who were out in the storm said some of the hail stones were as large as a hens egg.

20th   We were obliged to rest for a sick man – The weather is extremely warm – A Co of Oregonians passed us today 60 days from Oregon bound for the States. They left the Willamette valley the 18th of April. Several women & children were among them. They had packed all the way to Independence Rock where they bought a wagon for the family.

21st   We have camped nearly opposite "Court House" rock & have a splendid view of Chimney Rock about 12 miles distant. We now travel from 18 to 20 miles per day

---

12 According to Oregon donation land claim records, there were four men named Wells who arrived in Oregon in the autumn of 1852. Probably this one was William Wells, who came from Johnston, Wisconsin, and arrived in Oregon on October 3, 1852. He and his wife, Cynthia Jane, settled in Benton County, some miles south of Salem. Genealogical Forum of Portland, *Genealogical Material in Oregon Donation Land Claims* (Portland, 1959), II, Claim No. 3168.

13 Mr. Peak or Peck turned off to California.

[June] 22nd   Passed "Chimney Rock" about noon. The scenery about & above this noted rock is very romantic – We have had a little rain today but have traveled about 25 miles – We find but a few graves now – We stoped today noon near one which had been made but a few moments before. But as far as we can learn the sickness has pretty much disappeared.

23rd   Noon. Camped in excellent feed opposite the "Trading Post" at "Scotts Bluffs". We are yet 50 miles according to the guide from Ft. Laramie   are nearly over the long stretch without wood – we have brought wood in bags – which with the help of Buffalo Chips or (Bois de Vach)[14] has lasted till now, we have just enough to get our supper tonight – It is singular that on the north side of the Platte here is not a vestige of a tree in sight – save one "Lone Tree" for 200 miles & yet on the South side there is an abundance of Cedar fastened in the rock Bluffs & some Cottonwood. But the feed for cattle to all appearance is much better on the N. side

23   Reached timber again

24th   Reached Ft Laramie & camped opposite the Laramie river mouth.

25th   At Noon Left Camp and began our journey at the Upper Platte

26th   Reached the "Black Hills" & were 3 days in getting through them. We found a very rough & romantic road seeming more pleasant from the contrast beween them & the vast plain we had for so long been travelling over

---

14 *Bois de Vache* is the French term for buffalo chips.

29th   We stopped to noon near the river where were 3 graves which a tree in the neighborhood stated were the graves of a Man Woman & boy who were found near there with their throats cut from ear to ear, the cause or the perpratrators of so bad a deed were unknown

30th   It seems that we are in a fated region – we had not recovered from the shock we felt from learning of the murder above stated when we passed a company from which 2 men had just been drowned in trying to swim their cattle over the river, nor had we ceased to talk about this before we came to a grove of trees where a man had just been hung by his Co for shooting his brotherinlaw   It seems that there are some demon spirits near us & the reflection is not very pleasing.

July 1st   We have laid over today to rest our teams preparatory to entering upon a long stretch where we expect to get very poor feed. Tonight we learn that another man was found murdered near where the others were found   We also learn that 3 more men were drowned in getting their cattle back & one horse was yet left which they could not get. Our Co are all well except Ma who is rather unwell.

4th July   We reached the upper Ferry about 8 o'clock & took in water for the last time from the noted Platte river. Here we leave the river & pass over to the Sweetwater. We made for Spring Creek 30 miles distant from our camp   reached there a little after dark.

5th   Did not leave "Spring Creek" till noon as the grass was poor & they thought best to let the cattle eat pretty well before starting   When the cattle men drove up it was found that one of our oxen, old "Nig" was missing – an immediate search commenced in every direction. Mr Goodrich took a horse & went on ahead to see if he had not followed some other train, but every effort as yet proved useless in finding him.

6th July   Camped ½ mile from "Rock Independence" among a multitude of people. We all visited the rock after tea   traversed it over & around & enjoyed the excursion very much. Some one had put up a banner the 4th & it still fluttered in the breeze a happy heart cheering symbol of "American Freedom" to the many weary toiling emigrants.

7th   Started quite early & got on the road ahead of the great crowd around us, made 22 miles, & Camped on the Sweet Water. I paid a short visit as we passed to the celebrated "Devils Gate" but had not time to climb to the summit of the rocks   It is truly a sublime curiosity I plucked a few flowers from among the rocks & hastened on having to travel 2 or 3 miles to overtake my teams to pay for my visit to the "Gate"   We are again surrounded by camps   it is estimated that there are 500 people around in a short distance.

9th   We left our camp very early & crossed the 2nd & 3rd ford of Sweetwater   An accident here happened which obliged us to turn into camp again having only traveled 2 miles. The Dr's team rushed in to the 3rd crossing before the drivers were ready & running up on to the bank turned over the wagon into the middle of the river. The Dr jumped out & tried to hold up the wagon but could not & it crushed him down under it draging him a rod under water. He was hurt considerable – his medicine chest was overturned & nearly everything which was valuable floated off down stream

& was lost. His provisions were all wet and some lost
– but the loss of the medicine was the worst of anything.
Charlotte was very sick this morning and on the whole
it is a good thing that we were obliged to stop. She
is better tonight

10th July   Have made 24 miles today   Passed over the
ice springs a noon   have camped on the river bank at
the 7th crossing of the "Sweetwater"   We have been
out and gathered a fine lot of the nicest large Gooseberries I ever saw. They make excellent Sauce. We
passed 2 or 3 days ago another grave of a murdered
man – the murderer was buried near.

11h   We have only made 10 miles today & finding
some excellent grass 3 or 4 miles from the road it was
determined to stop & let them fill. We are camped near
a trading station & near a large camping ground which
2 or 3 days ago was occupied by about 2000 Indians
of the Snake & Crow tribe. They have now gone to
Green river. We have a beautiful camping ground on
the bank of the S. Water. Clumps of willows thickly
tangled with goosebery & wild Rose whose perfume
is sweet as "Home" are scattered along its banks. On
every side are camped the busy bustling emigrants with
their thousand cattle   Near us nipping the soft grass is
a flock of sheep & were it not for the lofty snow capped
mountain peaks which soar aloft towards the blue heav-
ens on either side one could almost fancy himself back
among the scenes of childhood   How different will
be the scene in a few weeks – Where now are moving
daily thousands of white people will be heard nothing
but the sound of the savage tongue & the quiet hills
which now are speckled with horses oxen & cows will

soon be deserted by all save the wild animals of the country.

[July] 12th   Made about 18 miles & were obliged to go about 4 miles from the road to get grass – found excellent feed & a beautiful camp   I visited a snow bank today about 3 feet deep

13th   Passed over the summit on "South Pass" & camped 2 miles west of "Pacific Springs" on Pacific Creek near an Indian Village. I took tea today at noon, made of melted Snow from a large Snow bank –

14th   Camped among the Sage hills & Sand on the little Sandy river   Plenty of water willows & Gooseberries were the only saving qualities of this camp We make excellent pies of these berries.

16th   Only traveled to the "Big Sandy" & camped upon its banks as we have a long drive before us tomorrow through a region barren of grass   We have been visited by many Indians today   traded some with them, hard bread for Moccasins & beads   They seem perfectly friendly & kind. our fears of Indians have all disappeared

17th   Crossed Green river last night & camped ½ mile from it

[July] 18th   Made 18 miles & camped early near a nice creek but on a sage desert   Some of the Co are having a touch of Mountain Fever but it seems very mild.

20 & 21st   Our road has been for two days over steep hills & rugged descents – very difficult & dangerous for wagons & very fatiguing to those who travel them. Reached Bear river valley tonight & camped one half

mile from Smiths fork   Were visited by some Indians
of the darkest hue of any I have every seen

22nd   Camped about 10 o'clock on Bear river for the
purpose of lying over a few days to rest our cattle who
are very much jaded   Mr. Fleming [15] one of our Co
lost a very nice ox last night – Our Co are again in
pretty good health but some are very much inclined
to turn & go to Calefornia & probably some will do so.

26th   Left our camp on bear river very much recruited
both ourselves & teams, & passed on to Thomas' Fork

[July] 28th   Reached "Soda or Beer Springs" &
camped near them. Several of us visited them. They
are a great curiosity.

29th   Made 22 miles today. Passed the junction of
Calefornia & Fort Hall roads & here we left some of
our Company who are going to Calafornia   Mr D.
Burrows, Mr Webs & Mr Peak – also a part of Mr
Goodrich's Co – Mr Peck Mr Palmiter & Hemphil
[Hemphis?] with the wagon go on to try Calefornia
while Mr G [oodrich] goes with us to Oregon to go
to Cal in the Spring. Camped tonight on a small creek.

31st   Crossed the "dividing ridge" between Bear river
& Lewis river valley   here we found a new kind of
fruit called "Bartle Berries" [16]

Aug 1st   Came down on to Lewis river valley   A
little after noon we were obliged to camp as one of Mr
Goodrich's oxen was sick – The animal died in a few

---

[15] This name was also spelled with two m's. There was a Henry Flemming
who settled on a claim in Clackamas County, having arrived in Oregon on
October 16, 1852. Genealogical Forum, *op. cit.,* I, Claim No. 1904. (Portland, n.d.)

[16] "Bartle Berries" were whortleberries.

minutes after we camped of the Murrain,[17] a disease
which seems to be prevalent & in almost every instance
fatal. In the afternoon about 500 Indians passed us with
as many ponies. They discovered the ox which had died
a little while before – pouncing upon it & dancing
a while they got a knife & cut & carried away every
vestige of it & so hungry were some of the young indians
that they ate the inards

2nd   Passed Fort Hall & Port Neaf river

3rd   Passed the great "American Falls". I with several others went down to the shore & climbed upon the
rocks which jutted out over the foaming waters looking
down some 30 feet   The Falls are much more interesting than I had expected   We camped one mile & a
half below on the side hill among the sage and sand
Near the Falls were 2 spouting springs a few rods from
the shore spouting up between some rocks which were
nearly on a level with the road. The water most beautiful. The Guard who herded the cattle in the hills
some 2 or 3 miles back found some hot springs

4th   Our road lay along the river whose shores are
very rocky with bold high banks, surrounding scenery
quite romantic.

5th   Traveled about 27 miles over sandy rocky sage
plains very hard road & no water   afternoon – reached
a spring after dark where we camped. Stillman has had
2 sick oxen but both better. Mr Preston found one of
his oxen sick this morning & before noon he died. We
have counted over 40 dead animals today near the
road. Met some packers one month from Oregon who

---

17 "Murrain or "bloody murrain" was anthrax. See introduction to this
volume.

tell us we are in advance of most of the emigration.

8th   Laid by on Snake river   This is one of the most singular rivers in the world being for miles enclosed by a perpendicular ledge of rocks & the thirsty animals are obliged to toil for miles together in the heat & dust with the sound of water in their ears & neither man or beast able to get a drop. While here Charlotte had another ox taken sick & one that had been sick a day or two died & she was obliged to leave two.

[August] 12th   Since leaving our camp on the 8th which we thought was unpleasant as could possibly be, we have found our travelling & camping grows worse every day, dry deep dust to travel in & what is worse, we find ourselves every night so far from water that we can hardly get enough to do our cooking   Dr Weber has been sick for several days of a Diareah & today traveling has been very bad for him so that we are obliged to stop at noon over a ledge of rocks some where near a thousand feet high & nearly a mile from the river. Our cattle are just able to creep down the ledge to water & grass

13th   Dr Weber grew worse after stoping, medicine had no effect & about 1 o'clock at night he died. Our Co for the first time have the sad duty to perform of burying one of their number. Jane is also quite sick of a Diareah but we hope not dangerous   Samuel does not improve much. the weather is so very hot & dusty that very many are complaining & the dust is the greatest hardship to endure we have found on our whole journey. But we hope for better times.

16th   Passed some of the most beautiful cascades I ever saw on the opposite side of the river. They fell from large springs near the top of the bank where it was nearly one hundred feet high   Jane continues sick & much worse. We only made about 3 miles to Salmon Falls where the most of the emigration was crossing the river for better grass   Our Co decided to cross consequently camped but in the worst place I ever saw the dust being very deep & the crowd of teams kept it constantly flying. We were surrounded too by Carrion which made it very uncomfortable   Jane still grows worse & we fear we cannot travel with her.

17th   Our Co commenced crossing – having stretched a rope across the river & coupled two wagon boxes together, towed over the cattle first & then carried our wagons, luggage & people   We got over quite early with the sick ones in order to make them as comfortable as possible

18th   Jane is worse & unable to travel – the rest of the Co being very impatient left us & went on – Dr Maxon [18] staying behind to attend to Jane – towards night we came out to a creek 2 miles & camped

19th   Jane seemed better & we made about ten miles

20th   Were obliged to make 14 miles to find water   In the afternoon Jane grew worse but still we have not thought her dangerous   The Dr does every thing he can but seems undecided about her disease

21st   found Jane still worse in the morning   a severe distress siezes her in her chest & shoulders   Thought

---

[18] Polly Coon spells his name "Maxson" on August 24th. The only Oregon reference to a medical doctor with this name is a series of advertisements for Dr. G. Maxon in the *Oregon Statesman* of Salem. There was an ad that denoted him as a "physician" that ran from October 10, 1864 to November 20, 1865.

it not best to start till she should be better hoping a days rest might benefit her but the pain continued to increase till about 3 o'clock a change seemed to take place & in a few moments she breathed her last – thus a deep affliction has fallen upon us as well as the thousand others who have felt the stroke on this road.

22nd   We were obliged to perform the sad task of burying our own dead   We laid Jane in her narrow home by moonlight last night after which we ate our silent supper by the same light & went to our beds. We have made about 20 miles today

23rd   Traveled 18 miles & suffered very much for water   the weather being very hot but at night found a beautiful spring of cold water & camped early on a nice plot of grass   many large camps around us

24th   Left camp early about 8 o'clock   met Mr Norton [19] on a return for Dr Maxson as Mr Luce was sick The Muscatine [Iowa] people had left them & Coats [20] & Clayton as they said they could not be delayed by sickness. We overtook them at night   found Mr L. better. We have passed a hot spring today which to me is quite a curiosity.

---

[19] Thomas H. Norton, age 27, and his wife, Emeline, age 22, with their two sons, Joseph, 4, and Silas, 2, came from Pike County, Illinois. They settled on Donation Land Claim #5063 near Silverton. Genealogical Forum, II, *op. cit.* Robert H. Down, in *A History of the Silverton Country* (Portland 1926), says that Thomas was born in Rutland Co., Vermont. He and Emeline met and were married in Pike County on Nov. 26, 1846. They settled on 320 acres near "Grassy Pond" on October 25, 1852.

[20] The Oregon land records list a single man, John Coats, an Englishman, born in 1804, who arrived in Oregon on October 2, 1852. He settled in Douglas County in the Roseburg area on Claim #873. His son, Thomas J. Coats, and his wife, Carolyn, who arrived over the trail the same day, were his neighbors, on Claim #784. They had started their overland journey in Fond du Lac County, Wisconsin. Genealogical Forum, *op. cit.,* III (Portland, Or., 1962).

25th   Made only 12 miles and camped on Charlottes creek [21] as it is 18 miles to the next creek and our cattle seem to much jaded to travel that far today   [THE END].

EPILOGUE

Some Coon/Crandall Family Memories, by Delia M. Coon, as published in Sarah Hunt Steeves, *Book of Remembrance of Marion County Pioneers* (Portland, 1927).

The parents of Paul Crandall, Silas and Rebecca (Beebe) Crandall, were living at Waterford, Connecticut, on September 2, 1802, at the time of his birth. The home was known as the "Beebe House" and was on a tract of land purchased by an ancestor of both. . .

There were six sons and two daughters in the family of Silas and Rebecca Crandall, and Paul was the sixth child. The father, Silas Crandall, in partnership with his brothers owned a fishing smack, called "Lucy," and was absent from home much of the time fishing for cod. At these times the mother and sons carried on the work of the farm, Henry, born in 1797, being the main dependence.

In the war with Great Britain in 1812 the "Lucy" was shot to pieces in Long Island Sound by a British man-of-war.

Other sources of revenue being necessary to supply the needs of the family, the father and older sons found work in mills at weaving, while Paul attended school at Boston, Massachusetts, securing superior educational advantages. He was skillful with his pen and taught classes in penmanship. . .

In the fall of 1823 the family of Silas Crandall, including the married son Henry, moved to Western New York, settling in Alleghany county, where a colony of Seventh-day Baptist people had already located. The town of Alfred Center became an important point and a college was established there. Henry and Paul secured land and began improvements; the land was heavily timbered and the work slow and arduous.

---

[21] Larry Jones of the Idaho State Historical Society, Boise, says this is probably present Canyon Creek, northwest of Mountain Home, Idaho. Letter of February 1, 1985.

On April 9, 1824, Paul was married to Sally Stillman, a resident of that locality. She was third child and only daughter of Luke and Phebe (Greene) Stillman and was born January 5, 1809. . . For nearly sixteen years Paul Crandall toiled on his farm, seeking a livelihood. Sons and daughters came to them, some passing away in infancy. The mother, always frail, was unable to withstand the toil and care incident to her strenuous life and became a confirmed invalid, and most of the household duties fell upon Polly, the eldest daughter, assisted by her father and brothers. In spite of these handicaps the older children obtained a good education at Alfred Center College, enforced no doubt by the father's advice and influence.

In 1837 a financial depression was general throughout the country, at the same time the newly opened section adjacent to the Great Lakes was attracting attention. Early in 1838 Henry Crandall, James Pierce and Hon. Joseph Goodrich made a tour of investigation through southern Wisconsin and were so well pleased that Mr. Goodrich purchased the land where the town of Milton now stands and Henry Crandall secured land one mile west, where the town of Milton Junction is located. This was in July and they spent about one month in working on their claims; then Henry Crandall returned to Alfred Center, closed up his business and with two lumber wagons each wagon drawn by four horses, started with his family and household goods for Wisconsin. They were thirty-four days on the road and reached their destination, without accident or sickness, on November 16. For six weeks they lived in a small frame house which Mr. Goodrich had built on his place, while Henry Crandall and sons erected a double log house on the Crandall claim, into which the family moved just after Christmas.

Paul Crandall was anxious to join his brother, but, lacking the means, secured a houseboat and with his family floated down the Ohio River, securing work from the settlements and towns along the river. Their boat was anchored at Marietta, Ohio, about the time the presidential campaign was at its peak, and the merits of Harrison and Tyler were loudly proclaimed. One of the songs, "Tippecanoe and Tyler Too," was extremely popular. Paul Crandall was an expert player on the flute and Polly had a strong, sweet voice, so their services were in demand as long as the campaign lasted. To Polly the experience always remained a happy memory of her youthful days.

Soon after the election of Harrison and Tyler, Paul Crandall and his family embarked on a river steamer and joined their relatives in Wisconsin. Land was secured and a home established amid pleasant surroundings. Polly became one of the early teachers in that locality. On January 1, 1845, she was married to Thomas Lewis Coon, a teacher of ability and a member of a well known family.

Paul Crandall was sent as a delegate from Polk county to a convention, to formulate the constitution of Wisconsin and is known as one of the "Fathers of Wisconsin."

In 1849 Henry Stillman, brother of Mrs. Paul Crandall, went to Oregon in search of a home, his wife and children remained in Wisconsin. Thomas L. Coon had been failing in health, and in 1850, in company with Clarke P. Crandall (his brother-in-law) and D. Sherwood, Wm. P. Bentley, and Charles White, they made up a party of five and started across the plains as they supposed for California. Their outfit consisted of two covered wagons of the lightest kind, drawn by horses, two horses to each wagon and an extra horse for each man, except the drivers.

They started March 17. From Fort Laramie, Thomas Coon wrote back in May, saying that "his health was better than it had been in many months and that his appetite was enormous."

They changed their minds about the mines of California and came on to Oregon. In Marion county, east of Salem, they found land which pleased them. Clarke took a homestead, while Thomas Coon selected land further north on Silver Creek.

In adjusting the lines between the land of James Brown (an earlier settler) and the land selected by Thomas Coon, Mr. Brown voluntarily moved his lines over, so that Mr. Coon could have a certain desirable building site. This is an illustration of the neighborly kindness existing among the early pioneers.

Henry Stillman had selected a piece of land east of Oregon City and soon word was sent to the families back in Wisconsin to come to their new homes waiting for them in Oregon, but it was not until March, 1852, that the start was made from Wisconsin.

Paul and Sally Crandall had eight living children. Polly, their eldest was only waiting for her husband's call; Clarke was already in Oregon and sending for them; Ray was married but was postponing the trip until 1853. Webster, eighteen years of age, was their main dependence, but was in love with a young and homeless orphan girl. They were too young to talk of marriage and he was unwilling to go without her. In this dilemma Mr. and Mrs. Crandall advised a wedding and Webster and Jane were married and started across the plains on their honeymoon. The other children were Phebe, fifteen; Amanda, thirteen; Emily, five; and Luke, nine. Polly Coon had one daughter, Cornelia, aged six, and her husband's brother, Samuel, aged fourteen years, who drove her wagon.

On March 29, 1852, Paul Crandall with his family of eleven persons, started from their home in Lima. They reached Plymouth on April 3, where they were joined by Mrs. Henry Stillman (commonly known as Aunt Charlotte) and her two children, Eunice, aged thirteen, and Jay, aged nine. Mrs. Stillman's brother, Henry Palmiter, was the driver for her wagon. In another wagon was Dr. Clarke Stillman, a brother of Mrs. Paul Crandall, with his son Tom, and J. Palmiter, a cousin of Henry Palmiter. Anson Goodrich, with three other men, completed their company.

There were five wagons, twenty-two people, fifty-six head of cattle and one horse. The weather was stormy and cold, with some snow, and traveling very difficult.

[Here we omit key entries from the diary of Polly Coon, printed in the "Journal."]

Thus ends the diary of Mrs. Polly Coon, written on the plains in 1852. Many of their cattle had perished and those that remained were weak from lack of food and slowly climbed up the steep slopes of the Blue mountains. A messenger reached the Willamette Valley, and Henry Stillman and Clarke Crandall came to their relief with horses loaded with provisions. There was happiness in camp and tears of joy were shed at their arrival. The Cascade mountains were still ahead but the end was in sight and the fear of famine had fled. With fresh courage they conquered Laurel hill [on the Barlow trail around Mt. Hood] and came into the Willamette Valley. Mounted on a horse, Polly Coon and her daughter reached the home of James Brown (now Silverton) and found the husband and father awaiting their arrival, too ill to go out with the relief party to welcome them, but overjoyed to have them near him again.

When Paul Crandall and family started across the plains in 1852, his wife was an invalid and occupied a bed in the wagon. Doctors and sanitariums had failed to cure her and her case was considered hopeless. The outdoor life wrought a miraculous change. A gentle riding horse, a family pet, had been brought along and on her back "Grandma Crandall" rode many miles, gaining strength all the time.

Cornelia and Emily shared the pleasures of horseback riding and "Old Sally," the horse, was an important member of the train.

Paul Crandall secured land adjoining that taken by his son Clarke. A comfortable log cabin and outbuildings for the stock were soon completed. Most of the cattle had perished on the way but a few of the faithful oxen remained and they helped to break the ground and start farming operations. The Davenports were neighbors on the south and Mrs. Davenport and Mrs. Crandall became inseparable companions and leaders in neighborhood work. Mrs. Crandall, instead of being an invalid, became a very successful and popular nurse and Dr. Davenport relied upon her skill for assistance in difficult cases.

Thomas L. Coon taught the neighborhood school until failing health forbade. He passed away on January 10, 1854, at his home in Silverton. Mrs. Coon went to her mother's home, and there on March 4, 1854, a son was born, who received the name of Thomas Ray Coon.

A few weeks later Mrs. Coon, with her two children, returned to her home on Silver creek. She sold a few lots from her claim and in filing the plat was asked for a name for the plat and gave the name of Silverton from the creek which flowed through the place; in this manner Silverton received its name. A postoffice was established the same year at that place and was known as the Silverton postoffice.

In the summer of 1854 Mrs. Coon taught the neighborhood school, leaving her son in the care of her mother, Mrs. Paul Crandall.

Ray Crandall, with wife and child, arrived during the season. They had left Wisconsin in 1853 but had been delayed by sickness and spent the winter in Utah, where they had buried one child.

Clarke Crandall was elected to the Oregon legislature of the session of 1854, and about that time was married to Miss Eliza Dunbar, daughter of Hon. Rice Dunbar, a pioneer of 1846.

On September 27, 1855, Mrs. Polly Coon was married to Stephen Price, a millwright, who had built the Smith & Barger grist mill at Silverton. It was about this time that Paul Crandall taught the

Silverton school and in 1856 built a new and substantial residence on their claim, to replace the log cabin of earlier days.

At this time the Crandall home was known as "Mt. Ida" and was a center for many neighborhood gatherings, which included both old and young. . .

In January, 1861, Mr. and Mrs. Stephen Price moved from Silverton to Salem to give the children better school advantages. Cornelia and Thomas entered the Old Oregon Institute. In March the entire family came down with the measles and Mrs. Paul Crandall came from her home at Mt. Ida to care for them. She nursed them through their sickness and then contracted the disease herself. She had not the strength to resist its ravages and went into decline, dying in May, 1861.

The Mt. Ida home was broken up. Luke was only 17 and he and Webster went to the mines. Webster came back several years later but Luke never returned, although he lived many years and for a long time kept up a correspondence with his father, promising that he would come home soon.

Paul Crandall sold his home, and with his daughter Emily, fourteen years of age, and Ida Hutton, his granddaughter, three and one half years of age, went to Salem and made his home with his oldest daughter, Mrs. Price. . .

His death occured at his daughter's home, south of Salem, January 9, 1889.

"A History of our Journey"

ℒ Martha S. Read

INTRODUCTION

The contrast between the diary that follows and the previous one is quite marked. The Polly Coon journal is filled with names of persons: first names for family members; surnames for others. They are often quite difficult or impossible to identify. The Martha Read diary records few names; however, she often describes geographical features, animals, and wild flowers. She kept in extraordinary detail records of graves — compiling a total of 246. She wrote down each day also the number of "dead beasts," and her diary becomes an extraordinary historical record of the deaths of cattle along the trail. We have discussed this matter in the introduction to this volume.

Martha Stone Thompson was born in Princeton, Massachusetts, on June 21, 1811.[1] She and Clifton Kittridge Read (b. August 26, 1813) of Chenango County, New York, were married in that locale on January 1, 1835. Two children, Clifton Kittridge Read, Jr., (b. February 13, 1836), and Lucy M. Read (b. June 13, 1837) were New Yorkers by birth. New York to Illinois was this frontier family's first move west. A third child, Lydia Mariah Read, was born on October 28, 1843, in Marengo, Illinois. The second long distance move is described in the following diary and commented upon in the two letters. By 1852 the childrens' ages were Clifton, 16, Lucy, 15, and Lydia, 9.

---

[1] The family information was provided by Mrs. Daraleen Wade, of Salem, Oregon, the family historian. This includes the abstract to the Donation Land Claim.

Martha always refers to her husband, Clifton, as "Mr. Read." The only one of the children she ever mentions in her diary is Lydia, who with her mother, was very sick with "mountain fever" in late September.

When the Reads got to the Willamette Valley, they settled on a claim in rolling country south of Salem, the territorial capital. The two nearest towns were Aumsville and Turner, four miles apart. In the letter from Oregon here published she wrote that they had settled on a claim "9 miles from Salem," which is exactly right. Their claim to the federal land reads as follows:

Clifton K. Read of Marion County in the Territory of Oregon, being first duly sworn, says that he is a white male settler on the public lands in Oregon; and that he arrived in Oregon on the 16th day of Oct 1852, and is above the age of eighteen years on the 1st day of December, 1850; that he is a native born citizen of the United States, and that he was born in Chenango County New York in the year 1813 that he has personally resided upon and cultivated that part of the public land in Oregon particularly described in notification on number 2174 hereunto annexed, continuously from the 1st day of November 1852 to the 25th day of April 1853. And he further says that he is intermarried with Martha S. Read his wife and that he was legally married to her on the 1st day of January 1835, in Chenango Co New York. Subscribed and sworn to before me, in Oregon City this 25th day of April 1835.   Clifton K. Read

Martha Read was an active member of the Disciples of Christ (Christian) Church and became a pioneer supporter of the Mill Creek Church of Christ. They met in a little country schoolhouse one mile southeast of Aumsville, about four miles east of their claim. The successor to that church is now located in Aumsville.[2]

---

[2] Pamphlet in Oregon State Library, H. C. Porter, *The Mill Creek Church of Christ, now Aumsville Church of Christ.* There is no date or place of publication. However, Martha Read was still alive: "Mrs. Read of Aumsville, who has been a regular and faithful attendant of this congregation

The Read claim occupied the land on which now stands
Cascade Union High School, which serves a large area of
southern Marion County.

Clifton Read, Sr., died on October 20, 1875, on the home
place. Martha Stone Read lived on until April 1, 1891. Her
obituary appeared as follows in the Salem *Oregon Statesman* on April 2:

> DIED – Read, at the home of her son-in-law, W. H. Darby, in
> the Waldo Hills, on the morning of Wednesday, April 1, 1891,
> of old age, Mrs. M. S. Read, in her 80th year.
>
> Deceased was one of Oregon's pioneer women, having crossed
> the plains with her husband in 1852, and locating on a donation
> land claim near Turner. She leaves two daughters, nineteen
> grandchildren, and one great grandchild. The funeral will be
> conducted at Aumsville today at 2 o'clock.

We are grateful to Daraleen Wade of Salem, Oregon, for
giving us access to these never-before published letters and
diary. The letters are in manuscript form, and the diary
is a typescript. We agree with Mrs. Wade that the typed
manuscript is a fair copy, having compared spelling and
writing constructions in detail. Mrs. Wade has been most
helpful, and, as family historian, has given us permission
for publication.

KENNETH L. HOLMES

FIRST LETTER OF MARTHA S. READ to
Lorinda Sheldon, Norwich, Chenango Co.,
N.Y., April 16, 1852.

Beloved sister   I have seated myself for the purpose of
writing a few lines to you to inform you that we are
all well as usual excepting I am pretty much tired out

ever since her baptism in 1855, and is now assisting in bearing burdens of
the church from which much younger members are willing to shirk."

a fixing for California   we expect to start next monday
which will be the 19   there is a great many a going
from these parts and a great many families that we are
acquainted with   the roads are quite bad here now
we have had a very backward spring but we think it
will do to start by monday   we are a going with two
waggons one span of horses three yoke of cattle two
cows   we take a tent with us and a small stove and
things for our comfort as far as we can but be *assured*
it looks like a great undertaking to me but Clifton was
bound to go and I thought I would go rather than stay
here alone with the children   I spoke about going
there to stay with you but Clifton thought it want best
he thought we had better all hang together and then we
should not be a worrying about each other   I hope
to live to see the day to come back and live among
you but life is uncertain   I have one thing to comfort
me   I know that I have the same God to protect
me a going to California that I have here   I dont
know but I shall be called next for it seems as though
our family were a dropping of fast   O Lorinda you
cannot think how I felt when I heard of the death of
another brother [1] near and dear to me and it grieved
me still more to think he had been dead so long and
I had not heard of his death   I feel sometimes as
though you had all forgotten me but still I know it
is not so for I know I am negligent about writing but
it is not because I do not think of you. I think your
children are a marrying of[f] in a hurry   tell Lydia [2]
I think she made herself an old woman pretty young

---

[1] This was probably William C. Thompson.

[2] Lydia Sheldon, daughter of Lorinda and Benjamin Sheldon, Martha's
sister and brother-in-law.

but if she is suited that is enough   you wrote that
sister Lydias [3] health was very poor   I hope that she
will live to enjoy herself better than she does now
tell her that I think a great about her since her girls
left her but I hope they will be good to her and help
her all they can   tell her I should like to have a few
lines from her to have looked upon and known that
it was her hands that done it   tell brother Ward [4] as
he is all the brother we have now I hope he will not
work so hard to get rich as to shorten his days   tell
him to remember his absent sister   tell sister Mary [5]
I often think of the happy hours I spent with her when
I was there   tell Sister Sally [6] I think a great deal
about her since she has been so lonely but I am glad
to hear that Hiram [7] is filling his fathers place   I
hope the children will all be good to her   tell aunt
Martha [8] I would give much to see her. I must stop
writing for it is late at night and I feel as though I
required rest   tell Helen [9] Lucy wanted to write but
she had not time   she and the rest of the children
sends their best respects to all of their cousins   we
are a going to send you a bill of the things we leave
if we never live to get back   I want some of you to
come and get them and divide them amongst you
I am a going to send you and sister Lydia a card in
remembrance   So I must bid you good by   Farewell

---

[3] "Sister Lydia" was another sister of Martha's, Lydia (Thompson) Sherwood.

[4] James Ward Thompson was Martha's youngest brother.

[5] Mary Thompson was Ward's wife.

[6] "Sister Sally" was William C. Thompson's widow.

[7] Hiram was probably the son of William C. and Sally Thompson.

[8] "Aunt Martha" was Martha Stone, aunt of the Thompson children, their
mother's sister.

[9] Helen was Aunt Martha's daughter.

sisters   Farewell   brothers   All beloved ones fare
thee well

Martha S Read to Lorinda Sheldon   Marengo
Apr the 16 1852

THE DIARY

Started for California April the 16 [19], 1852 [from
Marengo, Illinois].

April 16 [19]   Traveled as far as Belvedere [Belvi-
dere], ten miles. Found bad going, crossed two streams.
The weather close.

April 20.   Traveled as far as Milford 15 miles. Passed
through a small town called Cherry Valley. The weather cloudy in the forenoon rain in the afternoon

Apr 21.   Traveled 12 miles to a small town called
Sagesville [Daysville]. Crossed a broad river. Found
hard travel. The weather cloudy but sultry.

Apr. 22.   Traveled 17 miles through a prairie country. Found very good roads most of the way. Passed
through Dickson [Dixon] on Rock River. Had good
weather quite warm in the afternoon.

Apr. 23.   Traveled 21 miles down the east side of
Rock River. Found very good roads most of the way.
Weather good but cold.

April 24.   Traveled 17 miles, still kept down the river. Passed through two small towns, Prophetstown and
Cortland. Found some hard traveling. Weather rainy
in the morning, cloudy and cool the rest of the day.
Campt out at night for the first time.

Apr. 25.   Laid by over Sunday in our tent. Found it
cold and unpleasant.

Mon. Apr. 26.   Traveled 15 miles down Rock River.
Crossed at Wilson's ferry in a small boat propelled by
ropes. Went two miles, campt for night. Found very
good roads. The weather clear and cool.

Tues. Apr. 27.   Traveled 6 miles. Came to Moline
[Illinois] on the Mississippi. Crossed in a steam ferry
boat, the stream being a quarter of a mile acrost, then
went 3 miles down the river to Davenport [Iowa],
campt a little out of town. Found good roads most of
the way. Weather good; quite warm during the afternoon.

April 28.   Traveled 15 miles acrost the plane. Came to
hickory grove [Allen's Grove], campt for the night.
Found some bad roads through the day. Weather clear
and quite warm. Passed two Indians on their ponies
in the afternoon.

Thurs. Apr. 29.   Traveled 23 miles. Crossed one plain
10 miles without any inhabitants. Found a rolling prairie and bad mud holes in the hollers. Campt within
one mile of Tipton. Travel bad after dark. Crossed
one bad stream; bridge gone. Weather clear and cool.

Fri. Apr. 30.   Passed through Tipton. Traveled 12
miles to Cedar River. Could not cross untill next morning on account of the wind. Found a very unsettled
country. Lack stores. Weather clear, very windy.

Sat. May 1.   Crossed the [Cedar] river in a ferry
boat; went 5 miles. Laid by to wash. Found a river
of soft water. Weather fine through day but hard thunder showers through the night. Found it very unpleasant.

Sund. May 2.   Traveled 12 miles to Iowa City. Crossed
the Iowa River in a ferry boat. Campt just the other

side. Found bad roads and rough section of country with the largest kinds of snakes. Weather rainy in the morning, cloudy and cool the rest of the day.

Mon. May 3. Traveled 13 miles found the country more level but plenty of bad slues. Weather very good but cool and windy.

Tues May 4. Traveled 18 miles, most of the way acrost a high prairie. Found better going. Passed a place called Maringo [Marengo, Iowa]. On the opposite side of it there were three men drowned today a ferrying the Iowa River at Maringo [Marengo]. One of them were an immigrant. I believe a rope broke before their wagon got onto the boat which caused it to sink. Some of our men saw a panther but could not kill it. Campt near Bear Creek. We were obliged to turn our teams out for the first time for pickings; at best it is not very good but hay is not to be had. Grain is getting to be scarce and dear. Corn is worth 50 cts. and oats 40 cts. Very thinly settled through this state so far. Don't like the counry so far as we have traveled. Weather clear and quite warm but windy.

Wend. May 5. Traveled 12 miles across a rolling prairie; found bad going in the hollers. Rained most of the day. Stopt before night near a grove. Turned out cattle out on a marsh, feed very shy. John Poyer overtook us tonight. Weather rainy fore part of the day, cleared off toward night.

Thurs. May 6. Traveled 10 miles passed through [unreadable] grove. Found very bad roads. Then came to a large [unreadable] stopt early on account of rain. Weather cloudy in the forenoon, rain in the afternon, hard thunder showers in the night. Our horses broke away in the night, found them about two miles from camp.

Fri. May 7. Traveled 15 miles acrost a prairie 15 miles long. Found it very rolling with bad slus in the hollers. Crossed Bear Creek again, found bad crossing. Weather clear and quite warm. Campt for the night in sugar grove.

Sat May 8. Traveled 18 miles most of the way rolling prairie, found bad slus in the hollers. Crossed Little Skunk River. Weather cloudy with some sprinkles of rain, quite cool.

Sund. May 9. Traveled 5 miles to get feed for our teams. Passed through a small town called Newton. Passed through a small grove, crossed a small stream. Weather clear and quite warm. Mr. Wikes' and Mr. Battle's and John Rover's teams traveled on and left us today. We thought best to rest our teams.

Mon May 10. Traveled 22 miles, mostly prairie with now and then a small grove of timber. After going 5 miles we crossed Skunk River. In a few miles we crossed Indian Creek, after that we crossed Snake Creek. Found good roads. Campt in a small grove. Weather quite warm, cloudy, rained considerable durring the night.

Tues. May 11. Traveled 18 miles. After traveling 7 miles we crossed Des Moines River in a ferry boat and in a short distance we crossed Raccon River at a town called Raccon Forks. We then saw a very steep hill, then a piece of timber. The rest of our days travel was acrost an unsettled prairie. We campt on the prairie. Weather warm and pleasant untill just at night we had a thundershower.

Wdns. May 12. Traveled 20 miles. After traveling about a mile we crossed a small stream called North River. Found quite thick timber on the river. We found mostly prairie with now and then a grove of timber. Found but few settlers here and these are mostly around the groves. Found very good roads excepting in the timber. Overtook Mr. Wickes' and Mr. Battle's teams tonight. Campt in a grove near a house. Found very good water. Grass is short yet. Grain is scare and dear. Oats 75cts. Corn about the same but little at that. Weather cloudy and warm, rained some through the night.

Thurs. May 13. Traveled as near as we could judge about 15 miles. After traveling 5 miles we came to a small town called Winterset. After that we came onto a prairie about 18 miles acrost looking westward. This prairie is rolling but no standing water in the hollers to speak of. We had to go south a piece from the road to camp in order to find water, and then the men had to go about a mile back from the road to get wood. Found good roads today. Saw one dead ox and one horse by the road. Weather clear and warm.

Fri May 14. Traveled 23 miles. After going a few miles we came to a stream called Middle [Raccoon] River, found a little timber. Then came onto another large prairie 35 or 40 miles acrost. Found water quite plentiful. Found good roads. Campt on the prairie again. Weather clear but very windy.

Sat May 15. Traveled 25 miles. After traveling about 18 miles came to South [Raccoon] River. Found bad crossing, no bridge. Found one dead horse in the stream supposed to have been killed a crossing. Saw four other ones through the day. Found good roads. Saw a good many elk horns. Weather clear and quite warm, thundershowers in the evening.

Sun. May 16.   Traveled 20 miles mostly all prairie. After 13 miles came to a place called Indian Town. Found a beautiful grove of timber plenty of Maple. Crossed two streams above this grove within a mile and a half of each other. One called East Botany [Nishnabotna] River. Was told there were about 30 settlers about this grove. Found the handsomest section of country we have seen in Iowa. Came onto another prairie 15 miles acrost. Found good roads, rolling prairie all through these sections of the country. Weather cloudy and cold and very windy which made is very unpleasant traveling. Campt on the prairie. Found it very cold, had quite a frost.

Mon. May 17.   Traveled 20 miles. Passed through two or three handsome groves of timber. Found quite a number of settlers about the groves. Crossed the West Botany River in a ferry boat. Near one of these groves

Tues. May 18.   Traveled 25 miles. Mostly prairie very uneven with now and then a grove of timber. Found very good roads. Campt within 6 miles of a town called Council Bluffs or Kingsville [Kanesville]. Was visited by several Indians. Gave them something to eat, found no trouble. Pleasant weather but windy.

Wdns. May 19.   Traveled 6 miles to Kingsville, stopt awhile. Found quite a town but all log buildings fronted with siding. Inhabitants mostly Mormons, a pretty hard set. Traveled on 4 miles to the river, campt there, found bad muddy water. Weather clear and quite warm.

Thurs. May 20.   Laid by and washed some. Could

not cross the river untill tomorrow. Had a good many Indians visit us, fed them and sent them off, had no trouble with them. Weather pleasant and quite warm.

Fri. May 21   Crossed the river about 2 miles below here in a steam boat, had to pay $14. Find a hard set all along here. One man drowned in trying to cross this river in a small boat and swim his cattle after. Crossing the river we went about 2 miles and campt. Rained all day and most of the night, found it very unpleasant. Several Indians visited us again, appeared very friendly. We can soon get rid of them by giving them something to eat.

Sat. May 22.   Laid by to rest our teams   one of our company had an ox chased out of the drove by an Indian train on their ponies while 2 of our men were watching them where they were feeding. They rode right into the drove and selected and run it about 4 miles and into the water and shot three arrows into him. Our men had no horse nor firearms, they ran back to camp and got their guns and took our horses and put after them. They hired three Indians of another tribe to [go] with them   They soon persued them so close that they left the ox. They found him pretty badly hurt but they think he will be able to follow in a day or two. Several have had their cattle stole. There is the common amount of Indian trouble. Weather rainy in the forenoon, cleared off in the afternoon

Sun. May 23.   Laid by again today   was visited by a number of Indians, had no trouble, they are called Omahaws. They are more civilized as they have a missionary amoung them to teach them. Weather clear and pleasant.

Mon. May 24. Traveled 12 miles found a very uneven section of country with now and then a small
grove. Saw only 5 Indians through the day. Passed
one immigrants grave burried yesterday, J. B. Morris
from Indiana. Campt a little off the road. Found a
small stream of very good water found very good feed
for our teams. Weather clear and warm.

Tues. May 25 Traveled 15 miles, kept in sight of the
Missouri River most all day. Found rolling prairie
most of the way. Saw some timber up from the road.
Campt about half a mile from the road found water
and feed for our teams and some wood. Weather cloudy
and quite warm with some sprinkles of rain

Wnds. May 26. Traveled 11 miles, came to Elkhorn
River, crossed ourselves and wagons in a ferry boat and
swam our cattle. Passed another immigrant grave today, T. B. did not state where he was from.
Saw quite a number of Indians at the river. We went
3 miles after crossing the river, campt near a small
stream. Found some willows for wood. Weather warm
and pleasant through the day. Had a thunder-shower
just at night.

Thurs. May 27. Traveled as near as we could judge
about 20 miles throught a level section of country.
Came in sight of the Platte River. Followed the river
up saw three elk passed several Indians, appeared
friendly. Found good roads, went about half a mile
from the road to camp on the banks of the river. Found
first rate feed for our teams in some places it is knee
high. Weather clear and warm.

Fri. May 28. Traveled 20 miles, followed the Platte
River up. We were surrounded by Indians all day.

We crossed a small stream over a bridge that they
pretended to claim and wanted pay for crossing, but
we were told they did not build it. They made some
threats because we would not pay them, but did not
dare attempt any thing, there were so many along.
There were about 50 wagons in sight. This tribe is
called Pawnees, they are called very hostile tribe. We
passed another immigrant's grave today, M. Galland
from Illinois. We campt about half a mile from the
road near a small stream. Found grass knee high of
the best kind. Find quantity of wild onions along on
these bottoms which we gather and eat. They resemble our set onions only they are tougher. Weather clear
and warm through the day and rained a little in the
evening. The mosquitos were so thick they had like to
have devoured us and our teams

Sat. May 29.   Traveled about 18 miles   Campt near
a river called Loop [Loup] Fork where we found a
ferry boat but think of keeping up the river to a fording place about 20 miles which we are told is just as
near. We passed another immigrant's grave today.
Burried last night with inflation in the bowels. Name
was Sheever, from Wisconsin, his family were with
him. They will keep on. Found good roads and a level
country excepting we had one bad slu to cross. Saw
no Indians today. Weather warm and pleasant.

Sun May 30.   Traveled 15 miles to get better feed
for our teams. Passed two more graves, one a young
woman aged 18 the other 9, died of cholera it was
supposed. Both of one family, named Morris. Saw
another, a man named Lewis from Illinois. Saw one
dead ox. Crossed a small stream called Looking Glass

Creek. Campt near Loop Fork River. The mosquitos had like to have eaten us up. Weather warm and pleasant.

Mon. May 31. Laid by to wash. Found plenty of feed and water for our teams. Had another siege with the mosquitos at night. Weather pleasant but very warm.

Tues. June 1. Traveled 20 miles crossed a stream called Cedar Creek, crossed another small stream, name not known, and then crossed a large branch of the Loop Fork River. Saw another dead ox. Saw the remains of two large Indian towns and the embankment where the Soos and the Pawnees had a fight and the Soos drove the Pawnees out and burned their towns. Campt near the river. Found very good feed for our teams and not quite so many mosquitos. Warm and pleasant weather and very dusty.

Wdns. June 2. Traveled 15 miles, after going 2 miles we forded the Loop Fork River, found a good fording. Left this river and struck for the Platte again. Passed four emmigrant's graves, all from Illinois. Supposed they died with cholera. Passed another man that was taken with cholera today campt on the plains not far from the road near a slu. Weather pleasant but very warm, hard thunder showers in the night.

Thurs. June 3. Traveled 29 miles, found an uneven section of country and very sandy which made hard traveling after the rain. Saw 2 dead horses. Saw some Buffalow at a distance. A woman died tonight near us with the cholera. Campt tonight where we found neither wood nor water. Weather clear and quite cool.

Fri June 4. Traveled 17 miles, crossed one small stream, found it rather bad crossing. Found some bad slues. Saw three more immigrant's graves today. Two more died tonight near where we campt. They are all taken with a disorder. Some think it is cholera and some think it is not. Campt near wood creek, found a good well of water, but rather poor feed for our teams. Weather pleasant but quite cool

Sat. June 5. Traveled a couple of miles or so and were not a going to find any more wood for 200 miles. We drove to the creek and stopped to wash and cook up some victuals for the trip. Weather clear and warm in the forenoon but bad thundershowers in the afternoon.

Sun June 6. Laid by again. Went to see Mr. Mansfield's folks about 2 miles from us. Found him sick. Had a sick woman in our company. Weather warm and pleasant.

Mon. June 7 Traveled 12 miles to a point of timber that forms an island on the Platte. Passed 11 graves today which makes it rather gloomy. We are told this is the sickliest part of the journey. Weather cold and windy. We stopped this morning to bury one woman out of our company. She had had diarrhea. We had a prayer and a hymn sung. The men made a bark coffin so that she was burried very decent. We are told that there are about 70 graves on Wood Creek. There are several returning on account of sickness.

Tues. June 8. Traveled 22 miles to Willow Creek. Traveled today through the alcali country saw 8 graves and came past 2 that were not burried. There are a good many burried back from the road that we do not find. Very good feed for our teams and plenty of wood and water as yet. Weather pleasant and cool.

Wdns. June 9. Traveled 20 miles, crossed Elm Creek and Buffalow Creek. Passed 12 graves. Campt on the bank of the river. Weather warm and very dusty traveling but we have cool nights.

Thurs. June 10. Traveled 10 miles. Laid by in the afternoon on account of sickness. Burried another woman out of our company tonight, a young man is not expected to live. They are all taken with a diarreah. The physicians think it is not the proper cholera but the next thing to it. We passed 6 graves today. Weather warm but rather windy.

Fri. June 11 Traveled 15 miles acrost the plains. Kept in sight of the river. Found no good water; all alcali, suffered for drink. Saw a number of buffalo at a distance. Campt near the river again. Weather warm and dry, dusty traveling.

Sat. June 12 Traveled 20 miles. Found a good spring of water a little sulphury. Traveled through very deep sand some parts of the way. Saw 8 graves today. Campt near a small stream found some wood here but poor feed. Weather clear and warm, very dusty.

Sun. June 13 Traveled 25 miles found 2 more springs of good water crossed a stream called Carron Creek. Passes 8 graves saw some large grey wolves. Campt tonight a little of[f] the road near a small stream. Weather clear and quite warm, but dusty traveling.

Mon June 14. Laid by to wash an[d] cook for a 200 mile trip without wood. We were told we had come to the last timber a week ago, but by looking at the guide it was not so. But now we have now got to depend on buffalo chips. Weather pleasant but cloudy through the day untill toward night it rained hard untill into the night.

Tues. June 15. Traveled 21 miles found it rather hard traveling in the forenoon, crossed two small streams, one called Bluff Fork Creek. Passed 12 graves today. Campt near the river. Weather rainy in the forenoon but cleared off in the afternoon.

Wdns. June 16. Traveled 22 miles, a good deal of the way over sandy bluffs. Found it hard going where the bluffs run close to the river. We find bluffs all the way but we travel most of the way between them and the river. We crossed quite a number of small streams that run from springs in the bluffs. Saw 11 graves today. Campt tonight near the river on a little brook, found very good water. Had to burn buffalo chips. Found very good feed for our teams. Weather pleasant and quite warm.

Thurs. June 17. Traveled 20 miles. Traveled close to the river most of the day, found it sandy traveling a good share of the way. Crossed several small streams today. Saw the Cedar Bluffs on the south side of the river. Saw 4 graves today. Campt close to the river tonight. Weather clear and pleasant through the day but rained hard just at night so that our buffalo chips got very wet.

Fri. June 18. Traveled 18 miles today found wet heavy traveling most of the way, we traveled through the bluffs some part of the way, found deep sand most of the way, the bluffs are north of the river. Crossed several small creeks. Saw seven graves today. We see wolves every day most of them are the large grey ones. Campt near the river tonight. Found very good feed for our teams weather warm and pleasant.

Sat. June 19. Traveled 20 miles found some hard traveling through the sand. Found a good deal of alcali today. Crossed 2 creeks. Saw 2 graves today. Weather warm and pleasant. We have cool nights.

Sun. June 20. Laid by today. Weather quite warm but pleasant.

Mon. June 21. Traveled 20 miles, kept near the river all day. For a couple of miles we had to travel through the bluffs they run so near the river. Find very hard traveling when we have to go through bluffs, is very deep sand. We crossed 2 streams today. Saw 7 graves. Campt near the river. Found poor feed for our teams. Weather pleasant and cool.

Tues. June 22. Traveled 23 miles today. Found good feed for our teams Weather pleasant and cool. found very good roads excepting a short distance we had to travel over the bluffs. Found no water today. Had to go about a mile and a half out of way to get to river to camp. Found no buffalo chips tonight. Had a few with us that we took along. Saw some large rocks on the south side of the river. Saw one called Court House Rock and another called Chimney Rock. They are great curiositys to look at. Saw 3 graves today.

Wnds. June 23. Traveled 20 miles today. Found very good roads but rather sandy. This section of country is all sandy soil and where the bluffs run near the river we find deep sand. We find numerous kinds of flowers. A great many of them resemble our tame flowers such as: fox glove, lark spur, rose moss, China oyster, wax flower, and in some places the ground is covered with prickley pear with a beautiful large yellow bloom on them. We have not much to attract our attention but flowers, and the bluffs in some places are quite a curiosity. Some of them are composed of rotten stone. We saw one today acrost the river that resembled a light house in form. They are all shapes and sizes. Saw one grave too. We are told we are getting through the sickliest part of our journey. We find plenty of alcali yet but much standing water where it is, so that our teams have not got any to hurt them yet. It dries down and leaves a bad smell where it is. We campt about half a mile from the road on the river. Found very good feed for our teams but no buffalo chips. Our men go onto an island in the river and got some brush so that we got along very well for fire. Weather cloudy and cool. A great many cattle are giving out by being fed sorrel. We saw three dead ones today and three that were left alone.

Thurs   June 24. Traveled 20 miles. Found good roads most of the way   passed one large slue   found very strong alcali. We have to watch our teams very close. We use river water for ourselves and teams altogether, and that is muddy nasty water, but the phisicians say it is the healthiest water we can get. Saw another dead creature today. Saw 8 graves. Weather cloudy and cool with some rain. Campt near the river about half a mile from the road. Found some brush to burn tonight. Some burn wild sage but we have not had occasion to burn it yet.

Fri   June 25. Taveled 16 miles   found good roads

but a sandy barren section of country. Found no water except river saw another dead creature passed 3 graves. Campt near the river about half a mile from the road. Found very good feed for our teams and plenty of dry wood. Weather clear and pleasant in the forenoon but signs of rain in the afternoon.

Sat. June 26. Traveled 15 miles after traveling about 6 miles we came to the fort on the opposite side of the river. Here we found a barren looking country and plenty of Indians. We found a very rough section of country the rest of our days travel. We campt off the road quite a piece, near the river. Found plenty of wood. Weather clear and pleasant. Saw 4 graves.

Sun June 27. Laid by to rest. Found rather poor feed. Weather warm and pleasant.

Mon. June 28. Traveled about 18 miles through a very mountainous section of country. Found steep hills and very stony. Found no water for our teams untill the middle of the afternoon, then we came to the river. We found 2 springs for ourselves to drink through the day. Campt on a hill found poor feed and no water but plenty of dry wood. Weather warm and pleasant.

Tues. June 29. Traveled as near as we could judge about 18 miles. Found an uneven country but not quite so mountainous and stony, found no water through the day excepting a small stream that run from a spring where we got drink for ourselves found another spring for our cattle. Just before we campt we came to a creek where we got water for the night. Campt on a high hill found rather better feed for our teams. Saw 4 graves today. Weather warm and pleasant untill toward night we had a little rain.

Wdns. June 30.   Traveled about 18 miles. Still found
an uneven country in the forenoon, struck the river in
the afternoon found it more level but dry barren
country. Found no water untill we struck the river.
Found rather better feed. Weather clear and warm
but cool nights.

Thurs July 1 Traveled as near as we could judge
about 20 miles through a very rough uneven country.
Found a good many large stone near the hills. Came
to the river at noon got water for our teams but no
feed. Then we had to travel till dark before we struck
the river again and there found no feed to speak of.
Saw 3 graves. 2 dead creatures. Weather warm and
pleasant. We were met by 15 Indians today well armed
which gave us something of a start. They paraded
themselves across the road ahead of us and would not
give the road. They wanted we should give them something but we did not. There were about 17 wagons
along at the time. We turned out and went on and left
them. Some [of] them followed us a piece and that
was the last we saw of them.

Fri July 2.   Traveled 15 miles. Found a level road
today but very dusty. We traveled near the river all
day. Saw 2 graves and one dead creature and 1 that
was left alive. Campt near the river. Found poor feed
but plenty of wood and water. Weather warm and
pleasant but we have cool nights.

Sat July 3   Traveled about 15 miles. Some part of the
way we traveled on the river bottoms and the rest of
the way over high bluffs. Found deep sand, which made
hard traveling. Campt near the river. Found some very
good feed tonight for our teams. Weather warm and
pleasant   dry dusty traveling.

Sun   July the 4   Laid by today. Cooked the best we
had to celebrate the day. Had some buffalo meat for
the first time. Found it very good eating. We feel thankful that we are spared to celebrate another American
Independence Day here in these lonesome wilds where
there is so much sickness and death. Weather warm
and pleasant but very windy.

Tues. July 5   Laid by in the forenoon a waiting for
the Marengo Company. Traveled 10 miles in the afternoon. Campt near the river to night. Warm and pleasant but windy.

Wedns   July 7   Laid by again in the forenoon on
account of our cattle. They got scart last night by some
horses that broke loose from another camp and came
among our cattle and horses and set them all to running. Our cattle went back about 10 miles and some of
the horses went 4 or 5 miles. After getting our cattle
back we traveled about 10 miles. Campt on the river
Weather rained some in the forenoon pleasant in the
after noon but quite cool. Saw one grave and 1 dead
horse and one dead ox

Thurs   July 8   Traveled 20 miles to get water. Passed
the ferry   went 23 miles   from there where we found
nothing but strong alkali water. Some of the way we
found hard hills and deep sand. Campt near a spring.
Found nothing but sage brush last night and to night
to cook   We find wild [currants?] along here in some
places which make very good sauce   Saw two dead
creatures and one grave. Weather pleasant but quite
cool.

Fri   July 9   Traveled 14 about 14 miles [*sic*]   Found
some hard hills and deep sand   Arrived Willow Creek

to day   Campt on Fish Creek   Campt about a mile and a half from the road. Saw 4 graves to day and six dead creatures. Weather pleasant but cool.

Sat   July 10   Traveled 14 miles. Came to Sweet Water creek   passed Saleratus springs. It was quite a curiosity to see it. The Saleratus was baked all over the top of the water. We saved what we wanted of it. We stopt at Independence Rock near Sweet Water and went on to it. It was a great curiosity to see it and a real job to get on and off of it. After viewing the rock we heard of some first rate feed back 3 or 4 miles and we went there to lay over Sunday. Saw one dead creature. Campt near the creek. Weather warm and pleasant.

Sun   July 11   Laid by today. Found plenty of feed and water but no wood. Had to burn buffalo chips. Weather rained some through the day but most part of the day warm and pleasant. Had a light shower in the night.

Mon   July 12   Traveled 18 miles to day keeping up the Sweet Water River. After traveling 6 or 8 miles from Independence Rock we came to the Devil's gate. This is a large rock with a deep passage of water running through it. Some say the rocks are 400 feet high. It is a complete ledge of rock on one side of us all the way now. I suppose it is the commencement of the Rocky Mountains. We passed two trading establishments to day. Crossed to the Sweet Water River. Saw 3 graves, saw 3 dead creatures. Campt close to the river. Found very good feed for our teams and some dry wood. This river is clear good water. Weather clear and pleasant excepting a light shower just at night.

Tues July 13 Traveled about 18 miles. Found a great deal of deep sand to day saw a grave and 7 dead cattle and 1 horse. Campt close to the river. Found very good feed for our teams but no wood but buffalo chips. Weather pleasant but cool except a light sprinkle of rain.

Wedns July 14 Traveled 34 miles. Found a very crooked road. We crossed the river 4 times winding around between the bluffs still keeping near the river. After traveling this distance we found we were not a going to get any more water for about 20 miles. We here left the road and kept up the river about 2 miles and campt. Found first rate feed for our teams. Saw 2 graves today and 8 dead creatures. Weather warm and pleasant through the day but quite cold at night.

Thurs July 15 Traveled 22 miles through an alchaly section of country finding no good water. We took water and grass with us for our teams from the river. After we struck the river we kept up the river 2 or 3 miles. Crossed it three times in going that distance. Saw 1 grave to day and 17 dead cattle and 1 horse. It is supposed they drank alchaly water which caused their death or most of them. Campt on the river again to night Drove our cattle acrost the river. Found very good food for this barren country. Weather warm and pleasant.

Fri July 16 Traveled 20 miles over rough stony hills a good share of the way. Found no feed untill night. We came to the river again. Drove our cattle about 4 miles before they found good feed. Saw 7 graves and 7 dead cattle. Weather warm and pleasant untill just at night we had a shower.

Sat July 17 Laid by to recruit our teams. Found good feed up the river near the mountains. On the north side of the mountains they found quite thick ice and near by they found strawberries. Weather warm and pleasant most of the day excepting a light shower.

Sun July 18 Laid by in the forenoon, traveled 8 miles in the afternoon. Crossed the Sweet Water again and came to it again to night for the last time. Saw 3 graves and 4 dead catle. Found good feed for our teams to night by driving them about 3 miles. Weather pleasand but rather cool.

Mon July 19 Traveled 17 miles. We are now in the midst of the mountains. We are a traveling on very high ground but it is nothing to what I expected to see. We crossed the Sweet Water again this morning and traveled over to Pacific Springs. Campt 2 or 3 miles below the springs on a small run that proceded from the springs. Found poor water and poor feed and no wood but sage brush. Saw 3 graves to day and 10 dead cattle. Weather pleasant but cool.

Tues July 20 Traveled 10 miles to Little Sandy then followed the stream up about 4 miles of from the road to find feed and found but little, then there is little grows here but wild sage. We have not seen much else for about 100 miles on the road. If we find feed we have to go off from the road quite a piece. Saw 1 grave to day and 10 dead creatures. Weather warm and pleasant.

Wedns July 21 Traveled 7 miles to Big Sandy then kept up the stream 8 miles to find feed. Found good feed by keeping up the stream but it took us off from the main road about 4 miles. Found a very rough road through the wild sage to get on to the main road again. Saw one dead creature to day. Weather warm and pleasant.

Thurs July 22   Laid by to recruit our teams, mowed grass and filled our cans with water for a 40 mile trip without water and not much feed. Mr. Read taken sick this morning with the mountain fever. Weather warm and pleasant.

Fri July 23   Traveled 25 miles over some very steep hills. Mr. Read pretty sick to day. Saw 4 dead cattle. Campt on a high hill. Gave our cattle part of the grass and water we brought along. Weather warm and pleasant, we still have cool nights.

Sat July 24   Traveled the west part of the dessert which was about 17 miles. Came to Green River. Crossed in a ferry boat. Paid 20 shillings a wagon and swam our cattle. After crossing we went about 4 miles up the river and then drove our cattle 2 miles farther. Found good feed and a settlement of Snake Indians but they were very friendly. Saw 11 dead cattle today. The cattle, a good many of them die with the hollow horn. Ours have all had it. We came very near losing one. Some of the cattle get so much alchaly it kills them and some die from the want of good care. Mr. Read a little better today but very weak. Weather warm and pleasant.

Sun July 25   Laid by again for our cattle to fill up. Found an excellent spring of water running right out from the mountain. We were visited by a number of Indians but they did not want to beg and appeared very friendly. Mr. Read about the same to day. Weather quite warm through the day and pleasant.

Mon   July 26   Traveled 4 miles back to the main road on the river then traveled 10 miles to a branch of Green River. Kept up the stream about 2 miles and campt. Found rather poor feed. Found a very mountainous road to day. Saw a number of Indians to night. They had a village near where we campt. Bought some berries and fish of them. They were very friendly. They are the Snake Indians. Saw 5 dead cattle to day. Weather warm and pleasant.

Tues   July 27   Traveled 18 miles still keeping over the mountains. Came to a good spring of water at noon. Found some very hard hills. Campt near a small run that proceded from a spring. Found good water, not very good feed. Burnt sage brush as usual. Saw 1 grave and 7 dead creatures to day. Weather warm and pleasant.

Wedns   July 28   Traveled 15 miles to Hams Forks of Green River. Found a very mountainous country to day. Passed 2 or 3 little runs of water and one good spring. Saw 9 dead cattle. Found pretty good feed for our teams and plenty of good water and dry willows to burn. Weather warm and pleasant except some sprinkles of rain.

Thurs   July 29   Traveled 28 miles to Grass Creek. Found some tremendous hard hills to day. Passed through a small grove of timber composed of poplar and balsam. Crossed a small stream called Stone [?] Creek. Found a good spring. Saw 5 graves and 14 dead cattle and 2 horses. Weather warm and pleasant.

Fri   July 30   Traveled 15 miles to Bear River. Had a better [unreadable] not so mountainous. Crossed 2 branches of Bear River to day. Found another spring.

We passed another Indian village. Campt on Bear River. Found good feed and willows to burn and fish in the stream. Saw 6 dead cattle to day. Weather warm and pleasant in the forenoon. Had a very heavy thunder in the afternoon.

Sat J 31 Traveled 10 miles. Found first rate feed and laid by. Found a plenty of fish in Bear River. Some of them were salmon trout. We also found a good many currants which made good sauce. Saw a few Indians here. We crossed Bear River to day on a toll bridge. Found Noah Brimhall there a trading. We also crossed another small stream. Found a good spring to day and another where we campt. Saw 5 dead cattle to day. Weather warm and pleasant untill just at night we had another thunder shower.

Sun Aug 1. Laid by to day. Had plenty of feed for our teams and water of the best kind and plenty of sage brush to burn. Weather warm and pleasant untill just at night we had another shower.

Mon Aug 2 Traveled 20 miles. Found very good road with the exception of one pretty hard hill. Crossed several fine brooks. Campt on one. Found a good spring close by and very good fuel and a plenty of dry willows to burn. Saw 1 grave to day and 8 dead cattle. Passed through swarms of flying ants and large flies which were very troublesome. Weather warm and pleasant.

Tues Aug 3 Traveled about 18 miles. Found very good roads. Crossed several small brooks, found another good spring. Campt on Bear River again. Drove about a mile from the road. Drove our cattle acrost the river. Found very good feed, had dry willows to burn, caught some more fish and picked some more currants. Saw 7 dead cattle to day. Weather warm and pleasant.

Wedns Aug 4 Traveled 8 miles. Came to Soda Springs. laid by the rest of the day. Here is quite a curiosity. The water boils right up out of high rocks in some places and it boils out of the level ground quite [unreadable] high. The water is not so strong but what a person can drink it very well. Here we find a large tribe of Indians and a trading post. The Indians did not trouble us any but I suppose they would steal if they could get a chance but we watched them close. There were about 30 wagons campt here for the night. Warm and pleasant with the exception of a light shower. Saw 1 grave to day and 5 dead cattle and 1 horse. Campt on the river again. Found rather poor feed, had dry pine to burn.

Thurs Aug 5 Traveled 22 miles. Found very good roads. Part of the day was rather hilly. Crossed 2 or 3 small streams that run from springs. We find a plenty of good springs through here. Saw a few Indians to day. Saw 1 dead creature and one dead horse. Campt on a small stream. Found good feed and dry pine to burn. Weather more cool but pleasant.

Fri Aug. 6 Traveled about 20 miles to day. Found a very mountainous country and some of the way pretty rough. Found good springs again with fine little streams running from them. Found a new kind of berries which resemble huckleberries only are as large again. They are very sweet and very plenty along. The Indians pick a great many of them and want to sell them to the emigrants but we can pick for ourselves. We campt on a small stream near an Indian village. Found very good feed and plenty of dry poplar to burn. We picked two or three quarts of berries to night. Saw 7 dead cattle. Weather good with the exception of a shower in the afternoon.

Sat   Aug 7.   Traveled 15 miles. Found very good roads but rather hilly. We crossed several small streams to day. Found good water. Saw 5 dead cattle to day. Campt on a small stream. Found very good feed. Weather quite warm.

Sun   Aug 8.   Traveled about 5 miles, laid by, found good feed for our teams. Saw quite a company of Indians pass on their ponies. Weather good.

Mon   Aug 9   Got up before daylight and went to the old fort [Fort Hall] and laid by for the day. Found [unreadable] best feed and the remains of an old fort. Found very good buildings, good rooms with good fireplace in them and furniture. Found one good large stove which we used to cook in. Found a good yard for our cattle. This fort, we hear, has been deserted about 3 years. We washed and cooked and had fine times in our houses. Weather very warm and mosquitoes a plenty.

Tues   Aug 10   Traveled 14 miles Came [to] the trading post at Fort Hall. here we stopt and bought flour. Paid 15 dollars a hundred. Saw but few Indians. Here is a small place. There are but four white men here at present. After traveling about 4 miles farther we crossed Fort [unreadable] River. Found the water pretty deep so that it ran into our wagon boxes. Saw some more Indians here. Saw 5 dead creatures to day. Campt on the banks of this river. Found very good feed. Burnt sage brush. Weather pleasant but very warm.

Wedns Aug 11 Traveled 15 miles, came to Snake River and campt. Found rather poor feed, burnt dry willows. Found hard traveling through deep sand and had some hard hills. Found another good spring through the day and another where we campt. Saw 20 head of dead cattle to day. Some of them we supposed were killed by drinking poison water. Weather warm and pleasant but very dusty.

Thurs Aug 12 Traveled 18 miles. Found deep sand again and some very steep hills. Passed some falls in the river which was quite a curiosity. The water tumbled over the rocks quite a distance. We crossed 3 small streams through the day which run very rapid. We campt on the last one we crossed. Found very good feed on the hills. We got some dry cedar on the hills for wood. Saw 10 dead cattle and two dead horses and 2 graves. Weather quite warm and pleasant but very dusty traveling.

Fri Aug 13 Traveled 8 miles to a creek; laid by the rest of the day. Found very dusty traveling and rough roads. Saw 5 dead cattle today. Weather quite warm but pleasant.

Sat Aug. 14 Laid by again to rest our lame cattle. Found very good feed and water. Burnt sage brush. Washed and cooked. Weather warm and pleasant.

Sun Aug 15 Traveled 15 miles to Flag Creek. Found no water through the day and very rough road. Found very good feed and plenty of water and dry willows to burn. Saw 1 grave to day and 18 dead cattle and 2 horses. Weather warm and pleasant and still dusty traveling.

Mon   Aug 16   Traveled 12 miles to the river. Found
no water on the road. Found very good feed and dry
willows to burn. Saw 7 dead cattle and 3 horses to day.
Warm and Pleasant.

Tues   Aug 17   Traveled 24 miles to day. Came to
the river again but found no feed. Went 12 miles farther to Rock Creek. Campt here but found little feed.
Had a very stony hard road today. Found myself sick
for two or three days past which made it hard for me
to travel. Saw 17 dead cattle to day. Weather warm and
pleasant.

Wedns   Aug 18   Traveled 12 miles to day to another
creek. Found pretty good feed and laid by the rest of
the day to give our teams a chance to eat. Found a
pretty rough road to day. Saw 4 dead cattle to day and
2 graves. Weather more cool to day but pleasant.

Thurs   Aug 19   Traveled 18 miles to Rock Creek.
Found rather poor feed and a very steep place to get
water, Burnt sage brush. Found a tremendous rough
road and very dusty. Saw 9 dead cattle and 3 horses.
Weather cool, had considerable thunder and some rain.

Fri   Aug 20   Traveled 16 miles, found no water and
very rough roads, stones without number and the rest
deep sand and sage brush. Saw 30 dead cattle today.
They drop right down dead in the road. Some are tired
and some diseased. Weather cool and pleasant.

Sat   Aug 21   Traveled 14 miles to Salmon Creek,
here we campt. Found but little feed. Had hard roads
to day, hills, stones, and deep sand. Saw 19 dead cattle,
1 grave. Weather warm and pleasant.

Sun   Aug 22   Laid by to day. Found a small patch
of feed on the hills. Weather quite warm and pleasant.

Mon   Aug 23   Traveled 10 miles. After traveling 4 miles we came to the river. We gave them 6 dollars to take our wagon acrost and 2 more to tow our cattle and horses acrost. Here we bought some very large salmon trout of the Indians which were splendid eating. Saw 12 dead cattle to day. After crossing the river we came to a spring in about a mile and good feed. Stopt and [unreadable] our teams and then went 6 miles to a creek, found an abundance of feed. Saw 7 dead cattle. Weather warm and pleasant.

Tues   Aug 24   Traveled 19 miles to another creek. Crossed a creek after going 6 miles. Found first rate feed all through the day. Found a rough stony road and some hard hills to day. Saw 10 dead cattle and 1 grave. Weather quite warm but we still have cool nights.

Wedns   Aug 25   Traveled 14 miles. Came to a creek in about 10 miles then we followed the creek down about 4 miles and campt. Found good feed. Our wood through here is principally sage brush, some dry willow. We found a pretty hilly, stony road to day most of the way. Saw 5 dead cattle to day. Weather very warm but pleasant. We have very dusty roads all through here.

Thurs   Aug 26   Traveled about 14 miles. Found some very hard stony hills to climb. Found no water through the day. One of our horses gave out before night. Campt on a small creek. Found a good spring of water here. Saw 8 graves here and 7 dead cattle through the day. Weather very warm but pleasant.

Fri   Aug 27   Traveled 14 miles this morning. We had to leave some of our things in consequence of our horses giving out and one ox being lame. We crossed a small run of water to day noon. Saw 5 dead cattle to day and 2 graves. There is a great deal of sickness along the road now. Campt to night near spring. Found very good [unreadable] this country. It looks like frost bitten [unreadable] in Illinois but the cattle eat it first rate. It is dry on account of having no rain to speak of. Weather cool and pleasant.

Sat   28   Traveled 8 miles. Came to small creek that ran from a spring. Laid by in the afternoon to wash. Found good water and pretty good feed. Saw 4 dead cattle today. Weather cool and pleasant.

Sun   Aug 29   Laid by in the forenoon. Traveled 4 miles to a creek then traveled 18 miles to water again. Traveled untill 12 o'clock at night. Found very stony road part of the way, the rest of the way found good road. Saw 11 dead cattle, 2 graves. Weather cool and pleasant.

Mon   Aug 30   Traveled 6 miles to a creek then 11 miles to another creek where we campt. Found a very uneven road but smooth to day Found very good feed to night but poor water. Dry willow for wood. Our fire wood all through is either dry willow or sage brush. Saw 2 graves and 5 dead cattle. Weather quite cold but pleasant.

Tues   A 31   Traveled 14 miles, came to Boice River. Found a pretty mountainous country and some stone with a plenty of sand as usual. Campt on the river. Found very good water and a plenty of feed and dry willows for wood. Saw 3 dead cattle to day. Weather cool and pleasant.

Wed   Sept 1   Traveled 14 miles, campt near the river again. Found a plenty of grass but not a very good kind. Found level road to day but very dusty. Saw 1 grave and 7 dead cattle to day. Weather very warm through the day but cold at night, frost in some places. The Indians campt near us to night, bought some fish of them.

Thurs Sept 2 Traveled 14 miles. Kept down the Boice River all day crossed it just at night. Found good crossing. Found a level road to day but very sandy. Saw 2 graves and 4 dead cattle. Campt near the river. Found very good feed and water and a plenty of dry willows and sage brush to burn. Weather very warm through the day but another cold night.

Friday 3 Traveled about 14 miles. Followed the river down. Found a level smooth road but tremendous dusty. Campt near the river. Found very good feed and a plenty of water and dry willows for wood. Saw 1 grave and 1 dead creature. Weather very warm.

Sat Sept 4 Traveled 3 miles, came to the river, crossed back on the other side on a ferry boat. Gave 5 dollars. After crossing we traveled 15 miles before we came to water. Traveled untill after dark, came to a creek. Found rather poor feed. Saw 17 dead cattle and 3 graves. Weather very warm and dusty traveling.

Sun Sept 5 Traveled 3 miles down the creek then went 12 miles to the sulphur springs. Our teams drank the water very well. Campt ½ mile from the spring. Found pretty good grass. Found a level road to day but deep sand as usual. Saw 10 dead cattle to day. Weather very warm and some few sprinkles of rain with thunder.

Mon Sept 6 Traveled 8 miles to a creek. Had to stop with an ox that had traveled lame about 400 miles. To day he gave out. Saw 9 dead cattle. Weather very warm.

Tues Sept 7 Laid by to day. Found ourselves most all sick from the effects of drinking sulphur water. It seemed to effect [unreadable] our teams. Weather very warm again to day.

Mon Sept 13 Just found myself [un]able to write since the last date. We have laid by ever since excepting we moved 3 miles to the river to get better water. Found plenty of feed. The Indians have visited us every day and brought us fish. They appear perfectly friendly. We have had very warm days ever since we stopt here. To day we have had a few sprinkles of rain. There is an immense sight of sickness on the road. Lydia is getting sick to day with this mountain fever.

Tues Sept 14 Traveled 10 miles. Found myself so I could ride to day. Lydia is quite sick yet. Found ourselves very tired come night. This morning we had to leave one of our big oxen and our big wagon. Campt to night on Burnt River. Found pretty good feed. Saw 12 dead cattle to day. Weather quite cool but pleasant and very windy. Saw 4 graves to day.

Wedns Sept 15 Traveled 14 miles, crossed the river about a dozen times. Found some pretty hard hills and rough road. Lydia and I found ourselves very tired come night and very weak. Saw 7 graves and 12 dead cattle. Campt near a small run. Found but little feed. The feed is mostly burnt off through here by some ill disposed persons. Weather cool and windy but pleasant.

Thurs Sept 16 Traveled about 14 miles. Found a rough uneven road. Crossed several streams. Saw 3 graves and 15 dead cattle. Campt on a small run. Found pretty good feed. Lydia and I found ourselves very tired and weak yet – Weather cool and very windy but pleasant.

Fri Sept 17 Traveled 20 miles. After traveling 5 miles we had to go 15 more before we came [to] water. Found a tremendous rough road. Lydia and I have nearly like to have died, it hurt us so to ride. Saw 20 dead cattle to day. It looks like misery along here. The cattle are a dying off and people are getting out of provision and a great many sick and some are dying. Weather cool and tremendous windy. Campt near a small run. Found but little water and poor feed.

Sat Sept 18 Lost our horses last night. Did not find them untill the middle of the afternoon. We then started on and went 5 miles to another creek. Saw 1 grave. Lydia and I found ourselves a little better to night. Found very good feed. Had a very cold night, froze water quite thick. It was quite cool through the day but pleasant.

Sun Sept 19 Traveled 18 miles to day – Found a pretty smooth road. Crossed Powder River 3 times, came to another small stream and campt. Found very good feed. Saw 5 graves and 13 dead cattle. Lydia and I found ourselves some better but very tired. Weather cool and windy

Mon Sept 20 Traveled about 14 miles. Found some tremendous hard stony Hills which come pretty hard on Lydia and I. Crossed 2 or 3 little runs. Came to what is called Grand Round. Found it to be nothing

but a level spot of ground 8 miles acrost and I don't
know how far the other way. We traveled 4 miles on
to it and campt. Saw 3 graves today and 13 dead cattle. Weather a little warmer to day but rather windy.

Tues   Sept 21   Traveled 20 miles. After traveling 4
miles we [unreadable] the other side of Grand Round.
We found a trading post each side where they [un-
readable] beef to sell and buy up [unreadable] lame
cattle. This is all there is here. Here we commence
climbing the Blue Mountains. After traveling ten
miles farther we came to Grand Round River. We
traveled 6 miles farther. Had to camp without water.
Found hard hills to day and very stony. Saw 5 graves
and 5 dead cattle. The weather cold and rainy.

Wedns   Sept 22   Traveled 12 miles. Started in the
morning without our breakfast, went about 3 miles to
water, stopt and got breakfast and then went on about
7 miles to a creek. Found no feed. Watered our teams
and took on some water to cook with and went on about
two miles to find feed. Found a rough hilly road again
to day. Saw 3 graves and 9 dead cattle. Weather cold
so that we suffer with the cold a riding. Lydia and I
have got pretty [unreadable] but not able to walk.

Thurs   Sept 23   Traveled 20 miles. After traveling
18 miles we left the mountains came into the valley.
The mountains are 40 miles and they are blue ones
indeed. They are covered with large pine timber, the
first timber we have seen since we left the Platte River
of any account. This valley we came into is on the
Umitilla River. Here is a large Indian town. We
counted 4 or 500 ponies. We traveled 6 miles down
the river and campt. Found poor feed. Saw 2 graves

and 6 dead cattle. Weather cold, froz[e] hard last
night and night before.

[*Here the diary comes to an end.*]

SECOND LETTER OF MARTHA S. READ to
Lorinda Sheldon, Norwich, Chenango County, New
York. Although there is no date on the letter, it was
evidently written just after they settled on their claim
south of Salem, Oregon. The date of settlement for
the claim was November 30, 1852. She says in the
letter, "We are a building a small frame house."

Dear brother and sister   I will attempt to write a few
lines in this far distant land to inform you of our health
and something respecting our long tedious journey
we are all well and eat every thing before us we have
such uncommon appetites. Clifton wrote you a few
lines when we left Missouri   I do not know whether
you received it or not   I cannot give you much of a
history of our journey on one sheet of paper   I have
a day book that I kept a journal of our travels – daily
– if I could send you that you could have a full detail
but I can tell you one thing we had a long tedious
journey   we were 6 months on the road   we were too
late   there was so much emigration before us that their
teams eat up the feed so that we found but little food
for our teams the latter part of our journey in particular so that we had to make short drives in order to
save our teams   there were a great many lost all their
teams: some by over-driving and not having foot
care and a great many died with the horn oil and some
by drinking alchalye. it wants a great deal of care and
attention to dumb beasts on this long journey. we count-

ed over 600 dead cattle and 50 horses, and there was
a great emigration behind us that would have a great
deal more. the feed would be so very poor we only left
one ox and picked up one horse that was left on the
road. our horses got tired out having such poor feed
we had to take them off from the wagon and have it.
we got through with one wagon and 7 oxen 2 cows and
horses and they all say they look the best of any teams
that have come through but they are very poor for all
that. you cant have no idea of the immense emigration
that has been through this year. we have seen a great
deal of sickness, sorrow, and death on the road. I
counted 750 graves on the road but I suppose that was
a small part, for there were so many campt of from
the road and buried their dead. It seemed to be a cholera that they died with on platte river although the
physicians did not call it a proper cholera. but they
were taken like the cholera and frequently died in a
few hours. they said there was 1000 grave on the south
side of the river. they said there had never been no sickness on the north side untill this year. we laid it to bad
water. we drank no water only what was made into
tea or coffee. we escaped sickness untill we got to the
mountains. Clifton was then taken with the mountain
fever. he was pretty sick for a week or so but we had
a man in our company that doctored him and we took
good care of him so that we soon raised him. after
that I was taken with diarrhea and fever together. I
was pretty sick for about two weeks. we laid by one
week. Lydia was taken soon after I was with the same
complaint. I had two or three attacks after that with
a diarrhea and Kitridge and Lucy had slight attacks
of it. that was pretty much all the sickness we had on

the road. you may depend it is a hard place to be sick on the road. and jolting along in a wagon through the day and a hard bed at night I will not undertake to tell you how often I wished myself back but I feel thankful that our lives were all spared. it was distressing to see how many widows and widowers and orphans were left on the road and a great many would suffered for want of provisions if the people from Oregon had not gone out with provisions to meet the emigrants. those that were not able to buy, they gave it to them. there were trading posts all along the road but provisions sold so high it took a great deal of money to buy a little we did not have to buy any untill we got to the cascade mountains there we found flour 50 cts a lb bacon 75 and coffee sugar and apple 75 cts a lb and tea 12 shilling this counts fast. we arrived this side of the Cascade mountains the 16 of Oct but we have had mountains to travel over or in sight all the way. I think it is curious plains for when we were on the platte river there was a ridge of bluffs on the opposite side of us all the way and most of the way we had to travel through deep sand sage brush a weed that resembles southern wood which grows thick and sometimes as high as my head. it was the hardest place on clothes and shoes that I ever saw. finally it was every thing but a delightful journey. after arriving this side of the Cascade mountains we came into what they call the Willamet Valley. we traveled about 50 miles up the valley most of the way it was very mountainous and thick heavy timber. the timber here consists principally of pine hemlock cedar and fir some oak and black maple. we stopt with a bachelor about a week 8 miles from Salem the seat of government. we found

we were too late to get through to the mines and rainy
season had commenced and we wanted to keep our
stock untill they were in condition to sell. so Clinton
thought he had a right to a home as well as the rest
of the folks so he looked around and made his claim
of 320 acres of land. it is prairie land with timber
enough on it for fire wood and a large tract of heavy
timbered land on the mountains about 3 miles from
us where he can get plenty of rail timber. we are about
3 miles from a saw mill and the best kind of timber
for building our folks say they can get hewing timber 100 feet long if they want we are 6 miles from
a grist mill where they make the best kind of flour.
they raise the best kind of wheat here to make flour
of we are 9 miles from Salem on the Willamett river
where steam boats run up. we are 40 miles from Oregon City. they have a meeting about 2 miles and some
schools all around us. we have none in our neighbour-
hood as yet but they will start one another summer.
we have three or four neighbours within half a mile.
we can see 8 or 9 houses in sight. it is rather hard times
for emigrants that have come in here with nothing.
provisions are so high there is such a call from the
mines that it has raised provisions to a high rate
flour is worth 12 dollars a hundred, wheat 3 dollars
per bushel beef 8 dollars pork 10 potatoes 12 shilling
per bushel onions 4 dollars and other vegitables accordingly. they raise the best kind of vegitables here
butter is worth 50 cts per lb cheese from 40 to 50
chickens $1 a piece   eggs 81 per dozen   groceries and
clothing are not much higher than they are there
wool is worth 50 cts per lb   socks at 1 to 8½ per pair
stoves from 40 to 100 dollars a piece. stock is high

horses from 3 to 500 hundred dollars a span oxen from
100 to 150 dollars a yoke cows from 60 to 125 dollars
a head   money is very plenty   most of the folks have
been to the mines and got money which makes them
negligent about farming they are most of them getting
up good buildings   Clifton thinks any one could soon
make a fortune a farming here and raising stock [un-
readable] grass just a springing up here   it looks here
now just about as it does in may with you. the grass
gets dry in the fall here and when the rainy season
sets in the grass springs up green and grows all winter
so that cattle get fat by spring. they have the fattest
cattle here I ever saw and no expense to raise them
no more than to call them up and salt them once in a
while. it is not so cold but what we live in our tent
very comfortable. they say we have seen as cold as we
shall see. we are building a small frame house   we
have got a good well of water   it is good soft water
here   Clifton thought he would get a farm a going
and let Kittridge farm it and he would go to the mines
and try his luck   we are only 150 miles from Rogue
river mines which is called as good as they is. they
have found gold in the Cascade mountains about 30
miles from here   they discovered it late this fall   they
concluded they would omit it untill spring   they are
then going into it   they think it will prove to be as
good diggings as any in California   Clifton thinks this
is the country to make money easy   I expect if the
country suits him as well as it does now he will spend
his days here but it seems to far off for me to think
of that and another thing I dont like the country very
well as yet. it is too uneven and mountainous and another thing I dont like the rainy seasons so far although

it does not rain half of the time and not much hard rain.
it is kind of a mist most of the time   I suppose I shall
not mind it so much when we get into a house. our
folks think it is fine they do not have to be out in the
cold a foddering. I forgot to tell you that Lucy was to
work out a getting her $2 per week   mens wages are
from 1½ to $2 per day on a farm these short days and
mechanics get from 5 to $10 per day   I want you to
make up your minds whether you will come to Oregon
or not   write immediately   direct your letters to Salem Marion Co   I must stop for want of room   I will
write the rest next time   Yours with respect

Twin Sisters on the Oregon Trail
⸶ Cecelia Adams & Parthenia Blank

INTRODUCTION

In 1904 there appeared in the *Transactions* of the Oregon Pioneer Association a diary entitled "Crossing the Plains in 1852." [1] The author's name was "Mrs. Cecelia Emily McMillen Adams."

Over the years since its publication this journal has been quoted in many standard works on the overland trails.

Originally it was our assumption that on the face of it this was a correct rendering of Cecelia Adams' diary, and that no major changes would be necessary in its publication in our series.

Never were we more wrong. Upon studying the original manuscript in the library of the Oregon Historical Society in Portland,[2] we found that there was a typewritten copy of it accompanying the handwritten original. It was transcribed by some unnamed volunteer who pointed out that there were two persons' handwriting alternating through the diary. Upon careful study of the manuscript we found this was true. As we studied it, it became clear that the diary was alternately kept by two women, but who was the other one? Then it became clear: There were twin sisters, Cecelia and Parthenia,[3] daughters of Joseph and Ruth McMillen. At the time of the overland journey the young

---

[1] Thirty-Second Annual Reunion, pp. 288-329.

[2] Ms. 1508.

[3] Occasionally there appear variations in the spelling of both names. Cecelia's name was often spelled "Cecilia"; Parthenia's name appears as "Perthenia." The name, Parthenia, derives from the same roots as the Parthenon. It means "maidenhood" or "maidenness."

women were 23 years old, having been born on February
16, 1829, at Lodi, New York.[4] Cecelia was married to a
medical doctor, William Adams,[5] in Elgin, Illinois, on June
30, 1849.[6] Parthenia was married to Stephen Blank, a
carpenter, in St. Charles, Illinois, on November 9, 1850.[7]

Many years after the 1852 overland journey William
Adams reminisced about the twins in a letter to George
Himes, Curator of the Oregon Historical Museum, Port-
land: [8]

> The twins were always together when circumstances would
> permit and if they ever disagreed or doubted each other I do not
> know it. In all the long journey thro the wilderness they, with
> their husbands, slept at night in the same wagon, Mr. Blank's,
> walking much of the day, and as the oxen began to weaken they
> *would* walk together *all* day, sometimes over 20 miles. They
> were rather short, and in short dresses, looked shorter, and when
> we took the short steamboat ride from the Cascades to Portland,
> a lady asked my brothers wife if those little girls mother was
> with them.

William Adams, in the same letter, said of his former
wife that Cecelia "was a born musician, Artist and teacher,
and worker too." Of Parthenia he wrote, "Her twin sister
was just like her but very different — taciturn, but never
gloomy, never sang nor played on instruments — had good
taste but no ambition in art — never taught nor wanted
to — steady, earnest, cheerful work."

---

4 *Transactions* of the Oregon Pioneer Association, *op. cit.*, p. 288.

5 Manuscript letter of William Adams to George Himes, Hillsboro, Oregon,
June 1, 1905 (Ms. 1508). Adams was a new graduate of Oberlin College,
Oberlin, Ohio.

6 *Genealogical Material in Oregon Donation Land Claims,* I, (Portland,
1957), Claim No. 1617.

7 This information is from Parthenia Blank's obituary, Forest Grove,
Oregon, *Washington County, News-Times,* Dec. 30, 1915. Stephen Blank is
usually designated either a "carpenter" or a "cabinet-maker." Beulah Hurst
and Beatrice M. Carstairs, *Early Oregon Cabinet Makers and Furniture
Manufacturers, 1826-1897* (N.p., 1935), mimeographed, p. 65.

8 This letter is in the same folder as the twins' journal in the Oregon
Historical Society collection. It has the same number also, ms. 1508.

Neither of the couples had any children; however, Parthenia and Stephen Blank adopted and raised ten orphans.[9]

Cecelia died on August 12, 1867,[10] at age 38, in her sister's home in Forest Grove. Parthenia lived on many years. Her death took place on December 25, 1915, at age 86.[11]

The Blanks lived out their lives in Forest Grove, and the Adamses resided in neighboring Hillsboro.

Another member of the 1852 party was Joseph McMillen, father of the twins. He had left his wife, Ruth, and three other younger children in Illinois. Joseph was a millwright. He would return from Oregon in 1856 by way of Panama. Once more he crossed over the Oregon Trail with the family. They settled and lived out their lives in Forest Grove. Joseph died at age 93 in 1890; Ruth also lived into her nineties.[12]

James H. McMillen, older brother of the twins, had emigrated to Oregon in 1845, was already well-known in the Oregon Country. He, too, was a millwright.[13] The overland party arrived just in time for the marriage of James to Tirzah Barton in the autumn of 1852.[14]

Also taking the overland trail with the 1852 party was Calvin H. Adams (brother of William) and his wife, Catherine. In writing his memorandum in 1905 William Adams told George Himes that he lived with his brother and "his invalid, aged wife" in Hillsboro. He added that Calvin, "now 85, often walks two miles to his work and back. . ."

It is with the permission of the Oregon Historical Society, Portland, that this record of two young women cross-

---

[9] William Adams, Letter, *op. cit.*

[10] Portland *Oregonian*, Aug. 19, 1867. See also William Adams, Letter, *op cit.*

[11] Forest Grove *Washington County News-Times*, Dec. 30. 1915.

[12] *Portrait and Biographical Record of the Willamette Valley, Oregon* (Chicago, 1903), pp. 107-08.

[13] Captain J. H. McMillen," in *History of the Pacific Northwest*, II (Portland, 1888), pp. 464-65.

[14] "Mrs. Tirzah Barton MacMillan," (*sic*), Joseph Gaston, *Portland, Oregon, Its History and Builders*, II (Chicago, 1911), p. 792.

ing the plains is printed. The society has also given permission to quote from the William Adams memo to George Himes.

The McMillens, Adams and Blank families were all active supporters of the Congregational educational institution in Forest Grove, now Pacific University. Then it was called "Pacific University and Tualatin Academy." Parthenia Blank took great delight in entertaining students in their home. William Adams even served as principal of the academy.[15]

KENNETH L. HOLMES

THE DIARY

[*Parthenia*] . . . behind us. Staid where we were for 3 hours. Started on. Had a hard rain & hail storm. made the roads bad and we soon camped. Made 14 miles

Wednesday 19th [May].   Found we were on the road to St. Joseph instead of the Mormon trace.[1] Passed through Gentryville about noon. Here we had a prairie to cross 15 miles without water, staid till sunset and went on about four miles and encamped on the Prairie carrying our wood with us   made 18 miles

Thursday 20th.   Traveled about six miles on the road to St. Jo. then took the Savannah state road and had rare fun in crossing some of the state mud holes for they beat anything we had before seen. Encamped on

---

[15] James R. Robertson, "Origin of Pacific University," *Oreg. Hist. Qtly.*, VI (June, 1905), pp. 109-46, especially p. 127.

[1] The Mormon trace or trail was from St. Joseph westward along the Santa Fe Trail in Kansas to 110-Mile Creek [now Dragon Creek], thence to Fort Riley, on to Fort Kearny, Nebraska, and finally to Salt Lake City. Louise Barry, *The Beginning of the West* (Topeka, Kansas, 1972), p. 1222.

the bank of the Platte [2] forded near Hunts mill. Made 20 m

Friday 21st [May]   Commenced raining soon after we started and continued to rain all day mostly. Went on to Ogle's mill on the river 102[?] which we forded and encamped. Bought 200 lbs. flour and 4 bushels meal. made 5 miles

Saturday 22d   started to day and it soon began to rain but did not continue more than 2 hours. After traveling about 7 miles we came upon the road leading from Savanna [Missouri] to the [Council] Bluffs. Passed through Newark and crossed the Nottaway [Nodaway] River by ferry. Made 12 miles. Could find no grass for our cattle and as it was near dark we tied them up and staid till morning

Sunday 23d   started for good feed and encamped about 3 miles from the river on a Prairie and had first rate grass. Here we staid all day. Made 3 miles

Monday 24.   Started early. Had rough roads bad dry and very Hilly. Found some gooseberries and had them at supper. Calvin discovered a litter of young skunks but afterwards found they were calves – Reached the Missouri bottom about noon and traveled under the bluff the rest of the day. Made 18 miles

Tuesday 25th   Crossed the Little Tarkio and then left the bottom and traveled over hills till we came to the Big Tarkio then took the mud for it. O dear! for about

[2] This was the "Little Platte River," so-called by Lewis and Clark. It flows in northwestern Missouri southward to join the Missouri River at Farley, some 15 miles northwest of Kansas City. The French call it *Petite Rivière Platte,* in contrast to the much larger Nebraska Platte River, which the overlanders would follow later. *Missouri, A Guide to the "Show Me State"* (New York, 1941), p. 388.

½ mile – Had some rain in the morning and roads not very good. Level ground is not known here. Made 20 miles

Wednesday 26th [May]   Had rain all last night and the roads bad in consequence. Traveled slowly till afternoon when we came to the town of Lynden. Here we found roads that had been traveled more and were very good and soon came again into the Missouri bottom and had good level roads for the rest of the day. Here we got our first sight of the Mo. river and encamped in sight of it on the banks of the Niskinabotany [Nishnabotna] which we crossed on a bridge. Made 17

Thursday 27th   Started early and traveled up the bottom for about 6 miles. Paid 25 cents for traveling the length of a ferry boat across a slough and then up the bluff again. Today we left the state if Missoury and entered Iowa. From this time we found but little bad roads. Mostly prairie and timber scarce. Passed near the town of Sidney. Made 18

Friday 28th   Roads still good – Traveled 17 miles.

Saturday 29th   Passed through Coonville and crossed Keg creek. To day we came upon the Mormon trace and traveled about three miles on it and encamped on Pony creek about 5 miles from Kanesville. made 20 miles

Sunday 30th [May]   In the morning found Esquire Hewitt from Dundee [Illinois] informed us that our company were encamped about a mile ahead of us. Hitched up our team and started about 11 o'clock but when we got where they had left, but we passed on and soon found them encamped again in a field on the Mis-

souri bottom about 2 miles from Kanesville. Of course
we camped too –

Wednesday   the same   Thursday [June 3d]   started
and went to the ferry – the old Traders Point – Council Bluffs P. O. 6 miles.

Friday 4th   This is a day long to be remembered for
hard work. Paid $1.00 per wagon and 25 cts. pr yoke
of oxen for the privalege of ferrying ourselves over the
Missouri in a flat boat which took us all day and till
after dark. Made one mile. Our company now consists
of six wagons, one of which is bound for California.
A great many Mormons are starting for the Salt Lake.
[*There follows a poem written in pencil signed by
Cecelia*:]
   Home
   what so sweet!
   So beautiful on Earth!   Oh!   so rare
   As kindred love and family repose!
            The busy world
   With all the tumult and the stir of life
   Pursues its wonted course; on pleasures some
   And some on commerce and ambition bent
   And all on happiness, while each one loves
   With natures holiest feelings. One sweet spot
   And calls it *Home*.   If sorrow is felt there
   It seems through many bosoms and a smile
   And if disease intrudes the sufferer finds
   Rest on the breast beloved

[*Parthenia*] Saturday 5th [June]   proceeded up a
pretty hilly road and but little of interest occurred.
Made 15 miles   [*Interlined by Cecelia*:] Just commenced keeping guard   Found some strawberries today.

[*Parthenia*] *Sunday* 6   proceeded on. At noon when we stopped for dinner the cattle took a stampede for about a mile, cause unknown. At night as we were about to encamp they took another with the wagons but did not do much damage and were soon stopped Made 18 miles   [*Added by Cecelia*:] Last night my clothes got out of the wagon & the oxen eat them up & I consider I have met with a great loss as it was my woolen dress

[*Parthenia*] *Monday* 7th   Nothing of much interest occurred to day except a cold night last night – Ferried across the Elkhorn and forded Rawhide and reached the bank of the Platt – Made 24 miles   [*Written in margin*] While we were crossing the Elkhorn it rained and hailed very hard   [*Cecelia*] To day we saw four Indian's graves   They were quite open I could see two buffalo robes within which had probably been wraped around the body   They were buried on the surface of the earth and mounds erected over them and an opening had been made in the side probably by the emigrants   As we were looking at them we saw four Indians comeing towards us on horseback which caused us to be leaveing   they had been stealing sheep from the Emigrants.

[*Parthenia*] *Tuesday* [*June*] *8th*   Proceeded on up the Platte   caught a few small fish. Roads fine and boundless level prairie   made 17 miles

[*Cecelia*] [*June*] 9th Wednesday. We are all very glad to get on our clocks [cloaks] and overcoats and mittens this morning   it is so very cold   North wind blows very hard – noon   here we find a new made grave   on the headboard is inscribed "D Hherer [*sic*]

died May 28th 1852   Aged 5 years" To day we met
Several teams on their way back   We made no enquires
as they had the small pox   We also saw some mormons
on their way back   they said the road was good and
no Indians on our way as far up as *Ft Larimie*   Made
19 miles

10 Thursday   hard South wind for several days followed up the Loup fork   This is a branch of the
Platte a very rapped stream filled with sand bars   Find
a few wild roses and yellow daisys   To night we encamped on a beautiful spot with plenty of wood and
grass   One of our oxen has become very lame   Timber is generaly very scarce. to day we saw two new
graves   On the head board was writen with a pencil
"Mary Morris aged 19 and M C Morris aged 9 yrs
we saw good clothing scatter around which caused us
to think they had died with some contagious disease
here we done some washing   made 18 miles

[June] 11th Friday   S. W.   Took an early start this
morning   P and myself walked on several miles   We
have very cold nights and not very warm days which
makes it fine for our cattle   12 o'clock stoped for dinner
this is all the time I get to write or read   The horse
flies are very bad today. I never saw such large ones
and so many of them before   The boys are all laying
under the wagons asleep   To day crossed looking glass
creek beaver creek plumb creek and Ash creek   We
find quite a number of dead oxen and horses   Encampd on the Loup fork bottom to night   we could
hear the Indians but did not see any   made 20 miles

12 *Sat*   W. W.   quite warm to day with a cool breeze
P and self walked on several miles   We came to an

old deserted Indian village We think by the looks
of the land that it has been cultivated in a few places
found some Cedar for the first time The soil is very
sandy Grass is very good here Cotton wood is the
principal timber on these rivers See no Buffalo yet.
this is a beautiful part of the country very level We
have some good neighbors in our company encamped
for the night on the Loup Fork had to go two miles
for wood made 19 miles

[June] 13 Sunday W. wind very hard This is a
lovely morning has the appearance of rain which
made us very anxious to ford the river so we started
on found it rather dangerous crossing on account of
quicksand Mr Millers waggon came very near going
down P. and self waded through took father for
our pilot we had a grand time as we had to follow
down the river half a mile so as to keep out of the
deepest water so that we traveled nearly a mile in the
water We feel all the better for our ducking It took
us nearly all day, but got across safe at last Seams
but little like the Sabbath find a few strange flowers
made 6½ miles Think of Anne [3] as it is her birth day

[June] 14 Mon very hard W wind took an early
start this morning calculating to stop and rest our teams
as soon as we come to good grass which our (*guide
book*) says will be two or three days travel. here we
we find toads with horns and long tails they are about
three inches long and very slender and tails as long
as the body they are spotted white yellow and brown
can run as fast as a man and very wild Musketoes

---

3 "Ann E. (age 12) is listed along with "Perthena" (age 21) in the 1850
census of Illinois as daughters of Joseph and Ruth "McMellen."

annoy us very much and sometimes the air seams to be filled with large bugs Dust is very troublesome roads good. water scarce. grass poor. no timber This afternoon we passed seven new made graves one had four bodys in it and to all appearances they were laid on the top of the ground and the dirt thrown over them. most of them were aged people it was writen on some of the head boards that they died with the cholera We find good bed clothes and clothing of all kinds but do not pretend to touch one of them Encamped for the night on the wide prairie creek find good grass & water but no wood but we brought wood with us as our (Guide) directed us to do Made 23 miles

15th *Tues* N. wind quite cool, rained very hard last night which was acceptable to us Did not take an early start this morn as we do not calculate to drive any great distance to day as our teams are getting very tired and our lame ox is no better I had the sick head ache last night and do not feel able to sit up much to day have a good bed in the waggon *Our folks had a new milk's cow to day*. Encamped on the *Platte* poor wood and grass. rained all day which makes it very disagreeable getting supper to night Made 11 ½ miles

[June] 16th *Wednes* Wind N. E Rainy this morning very disagreeable getting breakfast we concluded to go on slowly untill we find a better camping place A man died this morning with the Cholera in a company ahead of us find prickly pear. all the wood we find to day is quakeing Asp which is miserable for fuel Have no wild game yet altho our boys are on the chase most of the time Passed 11 new graves

Crossed weed creek encamped one mile from the
Platte poor wood and miserable water good grass
Made 13 miles Elected officers to night

17 Thursday very warm and sultry concluded to
stay and do our washing by takeing our clothes down
to the river we can wash very well Another man died
near us this morning The Doct gets some practice
Henry is quite unwell to day but as a general thing
we are blessed with excelent health and good spirets
3 O'clock concluded to pick up and go a little ways
as we shall have a long drive tomorrow Done a large
washing had the hardest water I ever saw Oxen
getting better Passed six new graves Encamped on
the prairie brought our wood and water with us
found water enough for our cattle Made 4 miles
Had a new milks cow to day

18 Friday Warm and sultry took an early start this
morning Our company at the present consists of eight
waggons 16 men and 10 ladies besides children A
large company passed us to day from Kane *Co* Ill
Elgin Dundee and St Charles all horse teams They
seemed like our own folks Another man died near
us to day and an old lady 56 *yrs* old The Doctors
think that they drank poison water out of a spring
near by
[*Parthenia*] here we find Lockspir and also a very
prety dark flower strangers to us they resemble the
moss rose, this afternoon we had a very heavy shower
accompanyed with hail and hard wind we have passed
21 new made graves to day it makes it seem very
gloomy to us to see so many of the emegrants burried
on the plains made 18 miles

[June] 19 Saturday   very warm   took an early start
crossed a very deep ravene with steep banks which was
entirely dry   Our boys have been hunting all the forenoon   just returned with a buffalo covered with feath-
ers about the size of a prairie hen   is all the game we
have yet. Passed thirteen graves today   We just met a
train from Ft Larime going to St Joseph with the mail
but would not wait for us to write any letters so mother
missed of one this time   encamped on Elm creek a
very beautiful spot   It seems too bad to see such pretty
places uninhabited   We see snipes turkey buzzards
and a few blackbirds   We seen no Indians yet   The
express men tell us we shall find none untill we get to
Frt L— made 16 miles   At noon father made us a
good cup of tea

[June] 20 Sunday   This is a beautiful morning   very
warm   did not expect to travel any to day   a few
sweet birds are singing and all nature seems to be prais-
ing their Maker   I cannot help thinking of our dear
home to day   I think I see them going to the house of
God to worship there   O! what a blessed privelege
Here I [am] on these wide prairie   we seldom here
the voice of prayer   But I trust a spirit of prayer and
praise is felt in all most every heart   We have great
reason to be   thankful for the many blessings and mer-
cies that daily attend us   Through dangers both seen
and unseen the hand of God has directed us and while
we see so many continualy falling around us   We
still live in the enjoyment of good health and spirits
"Bless the Lord oh my soul   let all that is within me
bless his holy name"   It seems best for us to travel
to day as we shall be obliged to stop again in a day or

two We have more time for reading and meditation when we are traveling than we do when we stop and spend a day we have so much to do when we stop it keeps us busy all day Passed 10 graves We lost our Guide Book on *Sat* which caused us to go much farther to day than we expected We find a great many sink holes they are round hollow places in the ground filled with Alkaly water if they dry up it leaves the earth covered with Saleratus We have to guard our cattle from them all the time We saw some buffalo to day for the first time Our hunting boys ran after them with their guns prepared but they ran towards them so fast it frightened them away They were most to anxious We encamped on the prairie carried our wood with us besides picking up buffalo chips for the fire Made 16 miles

[June] 21st *Mon* Wind N. E. very pleasant took an early start Mr Stoel [Stowell][4] came back to us last night has not been with us before for five weeks or more are glad to have our friend come back with us again very high wind this afternoon which makes it very bad traveling to day we can see teams on the other side of the Platte that is the road that James[5] traveled the bluffs are very high on that side to day five men direct from oregon they gave us the privelage of writing home last night we had music and dancing it makes it seem quite like home to hear the Accordian which Cecelia plays most every evening Not very good roads Made 20 miles

---

[4] This was John Stowell, a Tennessean, who, with his wife, Margaret, and their family, later settled near Eugene, Oregon. Addie Dyal, *1860 Federal Census of Lane County, Oregon* (Eugene, n.d.), p. 13.

[5] James H. McMillen, older brother of the twins, was already settled in Oregon, having traveled over the trail in 1845. *History of Pacific Northwest –Oregon and Washington* (Portland, 1889), II, pp. 464-65.

[*Cecelia*] Tuesday [June] 22   cool and pleasant   Stephen [Blank] is quite unwell to day   Some of our boys are hunting to day   some men from Oregon came along to day on their way back to the states   tell us we shall find plenty of grass ahead and no Indians We sent two letters home by them   One of them said he was acquainted with James [McMillen]   Passed 7 graves   if we should go by all the camping grounds we should see five times as many graves as we now do   At noon it rained very hard and continued so all after noon very hard wind   Had rather a disagreeable time getting supper   Our chips burn rather poor as they are so wet   It seems like a winter night it is so very cold   Made 14 miles

23 Wednesday   this is a gloomy morning, it rained so much last night. To day we come to some bluffs for the first time   sandy roads and hard drawing good grass   find some wood very poor   take some with us   poor water   crossed Skunk creek   encamped for the night with no wood or water excepting what we had with us   Passed 21 graves   Here we find a white poppy but they are so covered with thorns that we cannot pick them   Made 18 miles

June 24   Wind N. E.   very cold indeed this morning   took an early start   Found some good looking springs but dare not use any of the water, roads good very sandy   We can see teams on the other side of the Platte   the road that brother James traveled on But our road is much the best as there are so many bluffs on the other road   Passed 18 graves   We met another Oregon train to day on their way back to Iowa   It consisted of men women and children   they were packed on horses   had but one wagon   We inquired

if they were sick of Oregon   They said *no* expected
to go back next spring   They were in such a hurry
they would not stop to talk   To day we see the last
timber for 200 miles   *So our Guide* sayes   Made 18
miles

25 Friday   Wind E this morning   woke up and found
it raining very hard   We expected to do our washing
here to day but it rains so that we concluded to travel
The roads rather bad   use Platte water   it is a very
mudy stream   We can settle it with alum so that it is
very good. generally get a pint of mud out of every
pail of water   To day we passed a grave that had been
dug open by the wolves   all we could see of the remains were the clothes that it had been wraped up
in   We found the head board some distance from the
grave   on it was inscribed Henry Verdant Aged 52
from Edgar *Co* Ill   Crossed the North bluff fork
Passed 8 graves   traveled 4 miles on the bluffs   so
much sand that it is almost impossible to get over
them   Did not find a camping ground till very late
Muskuetoes very troublesom   Made 18 miles

[June] 26   Saturday   Wind E.   Did not Start very
early as we oversleept ourselves   Have a hard time
getting a fire to cook our breakfast as everything is so
wet   Some of our company had a regular fight to day
but all of our folks kept out of the muss   One or two
was knocked down but no injury done only they are
obliged to leave our company   Find prickly pairs in
great abundance   the flowers of one kind resemble the
pink China Aster   The pink ones are very beautiful
Passed through another dogtown to day   they resemble the fox Squarrel in shape and color   it is almost
impossible to kill one of them   they are so very shy

Passed some deep ravenes Passed 9 graves very sandy roads find some beautiful looking springs but dare not use the water Keep near the Platt good grass no wood Made 18 miles

27 Sunday This is a lovely mornig conclude to stay here to day and recruit our team they have stood the journey very well but want some rest But we find a great deal to do P done some washing and I baked bread and pumpkin and apple pies cooked beans and meat stewed apples and baked suckeyes in quantitys sufficient to last some time Besides making dutch cheese and took every thing out of the waggons to air A birth took place to day in one of the companies near us It threatened a hard storm this afternoon but only gave us a few drops and passed on Buffalo bones are scattered all over the plains We can see emigrants as far as the eye can reach I do not see any company that can get along better than we do We all take a great deal of comfort especially sister P and myself we have some jolly times if we are in the wilderness

[June] 28 Monday South W. cool and pleasant started early roads sandy crossed two small creeks Stoped for dinner opposit Cedar Bluffs on the other side of the Platte some of the boys are out on a hunting excursion Passed 11 graves Encamped for the night on the banks of the platte Some little sickness in some of the companys but we all enjoy good health which we consider a great blessing Made 19 miles

[June] 29 Tuesday Wind E last night about 12 o'clock the wind blew a perfect hurricane which made a scattering among the tents We slept in our waggon and it rocked like a cradle expected it to go over

every moment altho they were chained down   but it
is very calm this morning   After traveling some 4
miles of good road we came to some very high bluffs
the highest we have seen yet   P and myself forded a
little stream barefoot and walked over the bluffs which
are a mile in length   sand very deep   Passed 10 graves
Passed the lone tree the only stick of timber within
200 miles   this is about half way between   The tops
have all been cut off   it is cedar   We took a few splin-
ters in memory of it   Encamped on Cassel [Castle]
creek   Passed another dog town   Made 20 miles
Passed Ash Holler Station Where one man stays alone

30 Wed   W.N.   very pleasant   Last night had another hard wind and some little rain   The Bluffs look
very beautiful on the other side of the Platte but should
not like to travel over them   Good grass   Passed 10
graves   find considerable drift wood   Made 22 miles

July 1st *Thurs*   Wind S. E.   has the appearance of a
storm   We see Antilope very often but our hunters
have not caught any thing worth speaking of yet
have killed two or three yellow rattle snakes   Large
gray wolves are very plenty   they will kill buffalo and
the emigrants sometimes loose their cattle   Passed 8
graves   One of the men that left our *camp* is very
sick   one that had a quarrel with his son in law
Made 21 miles

2 Friday   Had a very hard wind last night   The sick
man is dead this morning   We stop to see him burried
They wraped him in bed clothes and layed him in the
ground without any coffin   We sung a hymn a had
prayer   O! it is so hard to leave friends in this wilderness   Some of the bluffs look like old castles. Are

in sight of chimney rock, can see it fifty miles off. Passed 8 graves. Follow on the Platte, very poor grass, quite warm, travel slowly. Made 16 miles.

3 Sat W.W very pleasant To day we come to the river opposite Chimney Rock which has been visible most of the way for the last 35 miles It is said to be 3 miles from the opposite side of the river but on these level prairies we cannot judge much of distances by the eye It does not appear more than half a mile It consists of a large square column of clay and sand mixed together with a base of conical form apperantly composed of sand, round base cone. and appears as if the column had been set up and the sand heaped around it to sustain it It is said to be 500 feet high but doubt it some Just back of it to the South is another structure of the same material which has the appearance of an Illinois Straw Stable [6] and a little to the west is a cluster which the imagination can easily make a barn and stacks and which bears this name We very much regret that we could not cross the river and get a closer view of it but we can see it very distinctly through our spyglass I love to look at it because I know that Brother James [McMillen] been on it We see a great many strange looking rock that look like old ruins but I could not discribe them accurately had I time *16*

[July] 4th *Sun* W.W. This is a delightful morning a few sweet birds are trying to sing their makers praise Our thoughts are continually turning homeward I suppose your all haveing a sabbath school celebration to day We would like to take a sly squint and see

---

[6] A "straw stable" or "straw shed" was a winter shelter for farm animals made of posts and covered with straw. Ramon F. Adams, *Western Words* (Norman, Oklahoma, 1968 rev.), p. 309.

what you are doing   This morning met a train from
Call [California] on their way to the States they tell
us we shall be rather late   but little trouble if any
with the Indians   Seemed much pleased with our new
stile of dress   To day Henry found an ox that had
been left because he was a little lame   they put some
shoes on him and think he will do us a great deal of
good   Passed 2 graves   Encamped on the Platte
Made 15 miles

5 Mon   W.W.   The wind blows hard every night
To day we see *Larime Peak*   It looks like a cloud   It
is over 100 miles from here   roads good   Passed 9
graves   Made 18 miles

6 Tues   W South   pleasant and cool   To day we
come to timber mostly cotten wood   a Mrs Wilson in
our company is quite sick so that we cannot go very fast
roads very good   Passed 6 graves   grass rather poor
Has the appearance of a hard storm   Made 9 miles

[July] 7   Wed   W.W. Last night we had a very
hard rain and O! how hard the wind blew   Our sick
woman much better   Started on and commenced raining but it soon passed off and has the appearance of
a pleasant day   Passed a tent where we found one
keeping a grocery store   Kept a little of every thing
but a person must want very bad before paying high
prices

[*Parthenia*] Roads good most of the day but towards
night sandy. camped 3 miles below Fort Larimie.
Plenty of wood a great luxury for it is the first time
we have had it for more than 200 miles

Thurs 8th   To day we do not travel for we want to
do some business at the fort and the women want to

wash   Idy [?] is quite sick to day but hope she will
be better soon

[*Cecelia*] [July] 9   Fri   W.W. Started on very
pleasant roads very sandy   Passed by the *Ft*   left 4
letters at the P.O   Saw some Indians   Find some
wild currents two kind black and yellow ones   Encamped on the bottom of the Platte   Made *14*

10 Sat   S.W.   very cold this morning   to day we
come into the Black hills   They seem to be solid rock
and very high and Steep covered with Pitch pine and
cedar   P and I climbed one of them and had as much
as we wanted to do to get down, it requires long toe
nails to go up and down them   Stoped for dinner but
could find nothing for our poor cattle neither grass
nor water   Passed 8 graves   Encamped on the Platte
poor grass   plenty of wood & water   made 14 miles

[July] 11   *Sun*   very cool north wind   Started very
late [h]our   go up hill and down again   Find some
beautiful yellow flowers that resemble the evening
beauties and some little blue bells and a white flower
resembling the lily and blue lark spur and the yellow Suflowers   Find wild sage for the first time   no
water   poor grass   Passed 15 graves   Encamped near
the Platte   made 13 miles

12 *Mon*   W.N   Cool and cloudy   Started early
find neither grass or water till 5 o'clock   To day we
left an ox   it was so lame but Henry's ox takes it
place   is cloudy every afternoon   Passed 5 graves
Poor grass   Made 15 miles

13 Tues   W S   very pleasant   Henry killed a mountain hen   it resembled a prairie hen but I think superior in flaver   is some larger   P. and I walked on

ahead of the rest of the *com*[pany] some distance
went down a steep hill   some Indians on horse back
came along   We were somewhat frightened we turned
back for our teams   found they were nearer than we
had expected and so we stood still and looked at them
They looked at us very smileing painted faces and long
hair hanging down on the back   We passed on and
left them Standing gazeing at us   Our boys are on a
buffalo hunt   hope they will get one   Well here they
come each one loaded with buffalo meat   have at last
had the chance of tasting the long wished for meat
We do not relish it as well as we had expected to, is
very much like beef, good roads   made 20 miles

[July] 14, 15 and 16   spent in resting our teams   by
swimming them across the Platte we found excellent
grass   Spent our time washing, repairing wagons and
makeing a new tent   Our boys killed an antilope which
we all relish very much   also caught some nice fish.
it is very warm –

17   Sat   W S   very pleasant this morning   did not
get started very early it took so long to get our cattle
over the river   find the roads very sandy and hilly   no
grass   Passed 3 graves   Encamped on the Platte
Made 14 miles

18   Sun   W W   very pleasant with a good breeze
Think of home a great deal to day   now and then see
a buffalo   no grass on this side of the river   we swim
our cattle over every night and back in the morning
4 graves   keep a constant guard by them   roads very
sandy   Encamped for the night on the Platte   Made
16 miles

19   Mon   W.W. cool and pleasant   roads very sandy

and dust very troublesome   We walked most of the day   Passed but 2 graves   The ground is covered with little purple, pink and white daisys   Misquetoes very annoying   Made 14 m

[July] 20 Tues   W E   cool breeze   To day met some men from *Call* [California] on the way back to the States   gave us much encouragement   We have nothing but sand to travel to day   We encamped to night on the Platte for the last time   see plenty of buffalo but can kill none of them   made 10 miles

July 21st   Wed   W.W.   concluded to spend the day here and repair their wagons and rest the teams   We do our washing   Find plenty of wild currents   they are very good but not equal to the tame   Find good grass and water

22 Thurs   W N   To day passed the ferry where James came over in our road   I have the sick head ache to day so that I am not able to sit up   met another train of Oregon men   would not stop to talk with us   The Indians are gathered around us to day they look very savage but we are well prepared for them   we go in large companies   very good roads To day we leave the Platte for good   Made 14 m

23 Fri   W.W.   This morning we started at three O'clock as we had 15 miles to go without water and wanted to travel in the cool of the day   did not stop to get any breakfast for our cattle or ourselves   Passed 7 graves   We encamped to night on willows spring find good grass by driving our cattle two miles off the road and keep a strict guard   Good water   all keep well   Made *15* miles

[July] 24   Sat   W.W.   very pleasant and warm

Did not start very early as we do not expect to go far
Stoped at noon on greece wood creek here we will
stay till morning Passed 3 graves Poor grass no
wood, good water Made 10 miles

25 Sun W.W. this morning we started at 3 o'clock
to feed and get breakfast Sand very deep and dust
very troublesome Stoped for dinner opposit Independance Rock It is a great curiosity but we were
all so tired that we could not go to the top of it It
is almost entirely covered with names of emigrants
Went on to the Devil's Gate and encamped this is
is a great curiosity but we have not time to visit it and
regret it very much Passed 3 graves Forded the
Sweet water. *M 16*

26 Mon W.W. cool mornings and evenings but warm
and sultry through the day Find a great many dead
cattle to day passed a Station here we traided off
a yoke of oxen for a yoke of cows our oxen were sore
footed Made 14 m

27 Tues W N very warm we can see nothing on
eather side but mountains roads very sandy and dust
troublesome keep on the sweet water River Find
goose berys they are very sour indeed Passed 3
graves Encamped on the river made 14 m

28 Wed W.W. warm and pleasant Perthenia and
I climbed a very steep rock some 4 or 5 hundred feet
high got very tired indeed, found a great many names
To day we can see the snow cap mountains for the first
time roads in some places very bad keep on the
sweet water Very poor grass Made 17

[July] 29 *Thur* This morning was obliged to start
at One o'clock and go 10 miles before we could find

any grass for our cattle   they had no supper last night
or water   We stoped at Sun rise and find every good
feed by driving our cattle 2 or 3 miles off   Mr Miller
is quite sick to day   fear he has the mountain fever
We shall stay here till noon   we do some washing
and bakeing   Started on at noon   went 6 miles   Encamped on the river near some willow springs, one
of Jame's camping grounds [interlined: "here the river
forks"] He is nine days in advance of us   very poor
grass   Passed 8 graves within two days   made *16*

30 Fri   W.N. Took an early start this morning. have
some very bad hills to climb to day   Passed some very
good springs and several Saluratus lakes   Last night
One of the Doct's cows died   To day I have kept an
account of the dead cattle we passed   the number to
day is 35   We passed a Station to day   here we saw
plenty of Indians   they seem very friendly they were
engaged in dressing some prairie dogs   They had several little Pappoos's   they look very cunning   Some
were makeing moccasins for sale they trim them very
nicely with beads   Went on a little farther and came
to another   here is a black smith shop   We saw one
white lady here   The men engaged in gambling and
playing cards   Passed five graves   Encamped on a
branch of the Sweet water   every afternoon it clouds
up and threatens a hard storm but generaly passes of
without raining but gave us a little last night   Mr
Miller is better   Poor grass to night   We use wild
sage for fuel   it grows very thrifty   I have seen some
8 ft high   it is very dry   Made *15*

[July] 31   Sat   W.W. cool and pleasant   Did not
Start very early as we do not expect to go far to day
roads very good   The snow cap mountains lie directly

north of us to day   here we find Strawberys and huck-
elberies   the latter not ripe yet   Encamped at noon
drive our cattle off three miles and get excellent feed
do some washing   clouds up and rains this after noon
made 12 miles

[*Parthenia*] August 1st Sunday   To day we left the
waters that flow into the Atlantic and proceed to those
of the Pacific   We let our cattle feed till about noon
and then started on, for the South pass 10 miles distant – It ill comports with the ideas we had formed
of a pass through the rocky Mountains, being merely
a vast level sandy plain sloping a little each way from
the summit and a few hills for we could not call them
mountains on each side. Some few snowy peaks in the
distance, and this is the South pass through the Rocky
mountains   From the summit we proceeded down a
gentle slope to the Pacific spring and creek 3 miles and
encamped for the night. Here we could find no grass
except on a deep slough formed by the springs covered
with turf and grass on which a man can stand and
shake the ground for several feet around him it is so
soft underneath. Upon this we put our cattle to feed
for it was the only chance and the sod was so tough
they did not break through a great deal   the Pacific
spring rises in the middle of this boiling up through
the sod as cold as ice itself – made 13 miles

2 Monday – To day left the spring for a long pull of
24 miles to little sandy creek. Crossed dry Sandy creek,
but it contained no good water and we made the
whole distance without any – soon after we started
we met a pack train from California on their way
home. Came about noon to the forks of the old Oregon

and Salt Lake road. Took the road to salt Lake with
the intention of going by Kinneys Cutoff [7] to avoid
the desert. Reached Little Sandy a little before sunset.
Found plenty of good water though somewhat muddy
like the Platte, but no grass for the cattle it having
been all eaten off. We let our cattle feed as well as
they could till dark and then tied them up to keep them
from wandering off for feed. Hardest time yet. the
road to day has been as level as you often find even in
Illinois slightly inclining to the south and west. You
hardly believe yourself among the mountains. Old
Cataraugus [Cattaraugus][8] beats it all hollow – 21 m.

[August] 3 Tuesday we started for the Big Sandy
in hopes of finding better grass, but did not find it
much better

[*Cecelia*] Stoped here at noon and concluded to stay
a day or more as Mr Miller is very sick   Find good
feed by going three miles off   We have very heavy
dews this side of the Pass   made 11

---

[7] "Kinney" Cutoff solved the problem of the desert crossing on Sublette's
Cutoff, which had been troublesome since 1844. To take the new cutoff one
followed the trail toward Fort Bridger down along the Big Sandy to within
a few miles of where that stream joined the Green. One then cut across the
angle between the two streams, a distance of about ten miles, and came to
the Green at a spot where a ferry was operated at times of high water. At
low water it could be forded. Then the traveler went on west along Slate
Creek until he rejoined the main cutoff. George R. Stewart, *The California
Trail* (New York, 1962), p. 304.

[8] The Cattaraugus hills are part of the Appalachian highland forty or
more miles directly south of Buffalo. They constitute a "relatively flat-topped
upland with deep intervening valleys." J. H. Thompson, Ed., *Geography of
New York State* (Syracuse, 1966), p. 33. The Federal Government's *Com-
prehensive Management and Use Plan* for selecting historic sites along the
Oregon Trail indicates that "South Pass is perhaps the most important landmark on the entire Oregon Trail," and then goes on to say, "As a physical
landmark, there is nothing dramatic about South Pass." *Oregon Trail: National Historic Trail,* Appendix III (Washington, D.C., Aug., 1981), p. 202.

4 Wed   Pleasant   we shall stay here to as Mr *M* is
not able to ride   it rains some to day   We meet a
great many mormons   Want us to go to Salt L

5 *Thurs*   Our sick man is better and we make a move
this morning in good spirits   roads rather sandy but
level   Encamp on big sandy   Made 17 mil

[August] 6   *Fri*   This morning we leave big sandy
for good   Have very sandy roads   met three men from
Oregon on their way to the states   We see no water
from morning till night   Encamped to night on the
long looked for Green river a very muddy Stream   the
water looks red. had a very heavy wind in the after
noon but very warm through the day   See no flowers
to day   Made *17*

7 Sat   very warm this morning   we ferry over green
river   have to pay three dollars per waggon. Here
is a station 3 or 4 white men and a few Indians
Passed but 8 graves within a week   traveled over
rough roads   Made 16 miles

8 *Sun*   very cold this morning   need over coats and
mittens   Father was very sick all night   is some better this *morn*   We take a late start on his account
This afternoon we climb some mountains worse than
any we have seen since we left the Black Hills
When we got to the top it rained and hailed very hard
and turned very cold sudenly   *Doct* and I were out
in most of the storm as we had staid so far from the
wagons   Encamp on a little stream   do not know the
name, see a few Indians of the Snake tribe. See few
strange flowers very pretty, very poor grass very cold
at night   Made 18 miles

9   Mon   freezing cold this morning but as soon as

the sun rises it is very warm   Father is much better
to day   Our road to day is very hilly and sandy but
the earth begins to look more furtile   Encamp to night
on Ham's Fork   here is an Indian village   it consists
of some 40 or 50 tents covered with buffalo skins   We
have plenty of visitors to night. They are very friendly
Passed 4 graves   Find good grass and a beautiful camp
ground   *16 m*

[August] 10 *Tues*   W S   Pleasant, conclud to stay
here till noon to rest our cattle   find plenty of goose-
burys   they   are   very   sour   and   smooth   We   do   a
little washing here   we caught some speckled trout.
had a very high mountain to climb   Encamped in a
beautiful grove of poplar   Good grass   Made 8 *mi*

11   *Wed*   W.W.   cool   and   pleasant   get   an   early
start this   morning   I   have   the   teeth   ache   to   day
roads very mountainous   Passed 10 graves in two days
Encamped on Bear river   Good grass   Willow for
fuel   made 18 mil   Passed through a beautiful grove
of Fir   find some pretty flowers

12   Thurs   traveled on till noon and then stoped to
repare our wagon   have some very hyh hills to climb,
good grass   Passed a station   Met some packers from
Oregon   find wild flax   red yellow and black currnts
Narrow dock and cranesbill and wild pie plant   made
8 *mil*

13   Friday   W.W. very sultry in the vallyes but cool
on the mountains   Come to another Station   here is
two bridges and by going over them we can take a
cut off Saving 7 miles of very bad mountains   have
to pay one dollar per wagon   see some Indians   Have
plenty of good water   some beautiful springs   Took

a new road leading on the banks of the river   it is two
miles farther but saves some very high mountains
Passed two graves   Encamped on the river   made *20m*

[August] 14 *Sat* very pleasant this morning   Find
a bury resembling the whortlebury rather larger. here
we met a man that had groceries and potatoes to sell
at 1½ *cts* per pound   Of course we bought some the
first we have seen since we left the states. The grasshoppers are so thick that they look like snow in the
air coming very fast   We can get a good pair of mock-
ersons for a dollar   Travel on the river bottom most
of the day   Made *16*

15 Sun   very pleasant   can see snow on the mountains Find good grass Passed 2 graves Encamp
to night at Soda springs
[*Parthenia*] These consist of springs of water of an
alkaline taste bubbling up through the rock and forming mounds of the mineral from 2 to 20 feet high and
with bases of proportional size and gas sufficient coming up to keep them constantly boiling like a pot and
the opening at the top resembles a large kettle   Some
are very cold and others less so. The water sweetend
and mixed with acid makes a beautiful efervesceing
draught. We saw some ten or 12 scattered over a surface of less than ½ mile square. in some places it boils
up in the bed of the river.   18

16   Monday. This morning passed one of these springs
about a mile from the camp which has received the
name of the Steam Boat spring. Here the gas rises
with such force as to throw the water some 18 inches
above the ground. Here we find a great many mounds
which have evidently been thrown up by the water but
have been cracked open and are now dry   We left the

track of the Californians to day for good about 6 miles
from the springs. Crossed a chasm in the rocky road
how long we could not tell and in places so deep we
could not see the bottom. Must have been caused by
an earthquake. About a mile from the road saw the
crater of an old volcano. Stopped at noon near another Soda Springs – Found a trading station at the
Steam Boat spring. Had a beautiful level road all day.
Crossed some beautiful mountain streams and fine
springs. Encamped for the night on a small stream 20

[August] 17 Tuesday. Found good level road for
about half the day. Crossed two small streams and
found trading stations at each. Then came to the dividing ridge between Snake and Bear rivers and had
some pretty hard hills to climb up and down. Upon
these hills we found a great many Sarvice berries very
good to eat. Found two of the finest springs we ever
saw. Encamped for the night in a valley among the
mountains upon a very rapid little stream. Grass good.
Made 21 m.

18 Wednesday started again down the mountains.
A good many steep pitches but on the whole road very
good. Followed down the stream on which we were
last night toward Snake River. Found some fine choke
cherries to day very large – Encamped at night on the
same stream Grass not very good. Here we fell in
with another company of 6 wagons mostly from Illinois with Mr. Hyland [9] of Plainfield for Captain and

---

9 Benjamin S. Hyland, b. 1804, emigrated to Oregon from Plainfield, Illinois, in 1852, with two sons, Amos D., b. 1837, and Burnham S., b. 1834.
He settled on a claim in Lane County, Oregon, on July 19, 1853. There is an
interesting note in the Oregon donation land records that reads, "1 Nov
1854, Salem, O. T., Hyland gave off that Abigail Hyland did not emigrate
to Oregon & they were legally divorced at Nov term U. S. Dist Court for

as we were now just on the borders of the Digger Indians Territory both companies thought best to increase our strength by combining our forces. We now have 14 wagons in company and 32 effective men and keep a guard of four men at night. We are now in the valley of the Snake River   Made 20.

[August] 19 Thursday   To day came to Fort Hall on snake River and passed it at one in the P.M. It is made of unburnt bricks and is little larger than a good sized barn. It is not now occupied by the soldiers but is used for a trading station. Some 50 or 100 wagons, markd U.S. in large letters stand there rotting. Encamped about 2 miles from the fort on Pannock creek and had very good feed – Made 14m

20 Friday – To day crossed the creek and came to the Port Neuf river two miles. This is a stream of considerable size and we had to raise our wag[on] boxes to cross it. All the streams we have seen since we crossed the Mo. River have been rapid and indeed all since we crossed the Mis but those on this side of the mountains are more so but the Snake River is the most rapid one I ever saw for so large a one. running over a rock bottom and every now and then taking an offset of some 3 to 10 feet in the course of a few rods. Traveled down the river all day and could see plenty of good feed nearly all the way but were afraid to put our cattle upon it for the alkali water in the bottom – 25 m   Did not camp till near sunset when we found a good spring and plenty of grass

2nd Judicial Dist of Ore. He further stated he had one minor heir in Ore." Genealogical Forum of Portland, Oregon, *Oregon Donation Land Claims,* IV (Portland, 1967), p. 90. See also A. G. Walling, *Illustrated History of Lane County, Oregon* (Portland, 1884), pp. 484, 490.

21st   Sat. Did not exactly like our camping place and concluded to go on a few miles and find a place better and stay over sunday – Passed to day the American Falls where the river falls about 50 feet in 15 rods it is about 20 rods across at this place. Capt Hyland went before to find grass and a good place for the Sunday camp – After traveling about 15 miles on the road without feed for our cattle we started out ourselves for grass and found very good about ½ mile from the road and stopped for the night while his company followed on about 5 miles and encamped without grass – In the morn

[August]   22   Sun   started on and traveled about 10 miles and found them encamped for Sunday on Fall River a very rapid little stream full of little falls of from 2 to 10 feet   Found good bunch grass on the hills. Here we staid the rest of the day. From the time we crossed the dividing ridge between Bear and Snake rivers the soil or surface has changed   Hitherto it has been composed mostly of coarse sand but now it has a mixture of clay with it and when tramped up by the numerous teams and wagons, makes the most beautiful cloud of dust you ever saw. Many times it is so thick you cannot see ten feet and you have to shut your eyes and go it blind – 12

23   Monday. To day got rather a late start and traveled over to Raft Creek a distance of 9 miles   found rather poor feed   9

24   Tuesday – Got a pretty early start as we had to travel 15 miles without water or grass. Had a very rough road over rocks varying from the size of a piece of chalk up to a fence block and so thick that they kept

the wagons constantly upon the jump   dust very troublesome. Killed a black tailed rabit. His ears and tail about six inches long – a terrible howling of wolves last night. Encamped on Bulroush creek a very swampy place. Grass all fed off except in the slough. Cattle did very well   15

[August] 25 Wednesday – Traveled on over a middling smooth road down the creek to Snake river and thence to Goose creek where we expect to find grass but were disappointed for it was all bare except sage brush, but we found a notice left there by some emigrant that about 3 miles ahead ½ mile from the road on the river there was plenty of grass. Proceeded there and found it so. Did not arrive till after sunset, put our cattle out to feed and let them feed till about 9 oclock then brought them into the Correll. 21 m

26 Thursday – found it so good feed that we concluded to remain the whole day and recruit our teams – doctored some for the hollow horn [10]

27 Friday – To day started again – Had a very dusty and rough road till noon reached the river again and gave our cattle water but found no grass. then on to Cut Rock creek. found it dry or nearly so. proceeded up it about 2 miles and found a hole where there was some water. Took some in our cans and proceeded up about a mile farther and found good grass, considering, and camped for the night. Did not put our cattle in correll but let them feed and guarded them outside as it was long after dark when we camped   25 m

28, Sat. Concluded to stay another day as we learn from our guide that we are to have very hard feed for

---

[10] See introduction to this volume for comments on cattle disease.

the next 70 miles. proceeded up the creek for about 3 miles for the sake of water. Here we found it coming out from between the mountains quite a stream but soon sinks away in the sand. Killed 2 black tailed rabbits. Country generally very sterile and sandy and a great many rocky hills. For the last week we have found a great many dead cattle – and the irons of a great many many wagons. the woodwork having been used for fuel. Timber is very scarce, very little except willow, wild sage constitutes much of our fuel. The river runs over a rocky bed and in most places has a high steep rocky bank – Our 3 miles to day dont count – Found a company here partly from Chicago who had lain here 3 days for the sake of finding 4 horses they had lost, probably taken by the indians. they did not guard them and they came up missing in the morning – To day one of them returned alone and taking this back track the men found tracks of indians who had followed him as far as they dared – Two of their men went forward to Rock Creek in search of the horses and were threatened with an attack by 7 indians who came out of the willows some of them armed with rifles and made an attempt to separate them but did not succeed and no shots were fired –

[August] 29th Sun. Remain to day also. Have a sermon from Capt. Hyland who is a methodist Preacher feed is not very good but fear we shall have worse before we have better. Had a good sing to day.

30, Mon. To day started for Rock Creek and had to retrace our three miles we traveled up stream and nine miles more. Last night we guarded our cattle out 3 miles from camp on account of feed – Had seven men out on guard with the cattle and two at camp. The

guard at camp shot an indian dog and heard and saw
other signs of indians – Supposed they came to steal
the captains horses but he was not there   9 m

[August]   31st   Tuesday – Traveled down Rock
Creek 12 miles – Found good feed and concluded to
stay till near night tomorrow and then start out on the
long pull of 35 miles at least without grass and 22
without water – which we intend to travel in part at
least in the night – Road very dusty and some rock –
mostly level for we follow the valley of the Snake – The
grass we found on Cut Rock was a kind of coarse grass
as high as your head nearly and has a head on like
blasted wheat. What we have found on this so far has
been bunch grass dried as thoroughly as any hay and
our cattle eat it with a good relish and it is hearty
food. For the last 3 days the weather has appeared
like the closing days of autumn in Illinois – Have had
very warm days generally and very cold nights. makes
it hard times for the guard at night. Rock Creek has
very high steep rocky banks and in the course of the
12 miles we have traveled we have found only two
places where a wagon could cross it   12 m

Sept 1st Wednesday – Our cattle are well filled
and in as good order as possible for the trip across the
desert. Crossed Rock creek about 4 O'clock and started
on our way. passed down the creek about 5 miles where
there was a poor chance to get water but we had supplied ourselves before leaving our camp – traveled on
till after dark and then halted till the moon rose about
9 o'clock and then started on again. Road in many
places very rough and rocky and all the way dusty but
the dust not near as bad as in the day time – weather
very cold so that a man could not keep warm in walking without an overcoat and my hands suffered with

cold – Came near the river once in the night but it was down a dreadful hill and we did not go to it. Just at sunrise we again came to the river down a very steep hill but here we found no grass and our cattle had kept so cool they were not very dry   Rested here about two hours and got our breakfast and started on in search of grass. Passed down the bottom with high rocky banks on each side nearly perpendicular – came to Salmon creek in about three miles but found no grass   Here is a fall in the river about equal to the American Falls – passed on ½ mile over bluff to the river again. Here we found a company with whom we were some acquanted who had been here 2 days and put their cattle over the river and found good grass and said they had been on before 7 miles to the commencement of the next desert of 33 miles and found no grass which would make us 40 miles more and that is too much for our cattle – It is dangerous crossing the river and they had drowned one horse and one ox in putting theirs over, but it was the only chance and so we put them over. and made a boat of one of the wagon boxes to ferry ourselves over all safe   Arrived here about noon and concluded to remain the rest of the day and to-morrow and recruit   find very good bunch grass and some bottom grass. Two large springs break out from the side of the mountain within 1 mile of each other at least 100 feet above the river and contain water enough to turn any mill in Kane Co [Illinois] – and dash down with great velocity to the river   32 m

Sept. 3rd Friday – To day staid at camp most of the day. tried fishing some but did not make out much, weather very warm. can see plenty of large salmon jumping out of the water but cant catch them

4   Sat. This morning brought our cattle over again
without any accident and prepared for the long pull –
in 3 miles passed some hot springs in river bank   came
to Bannoc creek but found no grass but found a notice
that five miles below was a ferry across the river and
plenty of grass on the other side. Went to it about 1
mile out of our way and the ferrymen recommended
the route as so much shorter and better supplied with
grass and water that we concluded to try it. The ferry
consists of 2 wagon boxes lashed together so as to make
a boat and a rope stretched across the river to pull it
across – and all they asked was three dollars a wagon
for ferrying. The day was so windy that we could not
cross so we had to stay on this side and swimm our
cattle across the river. found good grass about 1½
miles back. We have had some heavy sandy roads
today the first for some time   3 m   Here we find
some indians with some very nice salmon for sale and
we all got a good supply – they will trade them for
powder, lead & caps bread, beads, brass nails, old
shirts or almost anything you have and they seem to
have a great many. just below the ferry is another great
fall, Just above on the opposite bank very large springs
break out high up in the bank and fall into the river
with great noise a fine sight

[September]   5th Sunday   No wind this morning
and we ferried over in good season and proceeded on
our way – A few rods below the ferry is another salmon falls fall in the river of some 20 feet where the
indians catch their salmon in traps – found very rough
rocky road for the first mile then deep heavy sand for
five more when we came to a good sized creek in a
deep valley with plenty of grass and encamped. Here

are some 5 or six large springs breaking out high up in the rocky bank and running down part of the time above ground and part of the time below till they reach the creek which is very rapid. The water of these spring brooks has a greenish tint but otherwise is perfectly clear and the finest looking water I ever saw and good tasting but not very cold. The scenery for the last 3 days has been truly delightful and only wants a soil and what grows on a soil to make it one of the most beautiful spots on the earth– Within these three days mill seats enough for the whole state of Illinois and finer than I ever saw there. About a mile from us is the river and another great fall – The indians bring us salmon again but find dull sale for we are all supplied and the market is glutted   6 m

[September]   6 Monday – Had a steep rocky hill to climb this morning to start with then came to sand again which lasted 8 miles to another creek. very heavy road – Here the water fall down into a very narrow chasm some 40 feet and runs along it for half a mile or more dashing and foaming as it goes – a fine sight – Here we watered our cattle and proceeded on about a couple of miles where we found grass and stopped for dinner then proceeded on and did not find water till long after dark – when we came to a small creek. watered our cattle and put them into correl without any feed. Some indians camped on the same stream   24 m

7th   Tuesday. This morning found plenty of excellent bunch grass on the hills near camp and let our cattle feed then started and traveled down the stream about 7 miles and stopped for dinner – then passed over the hills about 10 miles without water when we came to the same creek again and encamped for the night. Have found plenty of bunch grass all the way to day – and sage of an enormous size and the general appearance of the country has been more like live then any we have seen for the last thousand miles – Have seen 14 graves in a week   17 m

[September] 8th Wed. Traveled over hills again about 8 miles to a dry creek but some little water standing in puddles. Here we stopped and took dinner. Plenty of dry bunch grass all the way. Afternoon started again and passed up a very rocky hill 3½ miles and in a most of the way steep. when we came upon a level table land and went about 3 miles more over a very rough rocky road when we came to another dry creek in a ravine with steep rocky banks – Here we encamped for the night   Find no good water and but little of it. Plenty of dry willows for the fuel   15 m

9 Thursday – Proceeded over a very rough road to another dry creek about 6 miles. Here we came upon the road leading from the ferry. 3 miles further on came to a fine stream and cold spring and several places some 10 feet across where water and mud boil up among the sand – Stopped here for dinner and had pretty good grass – Here we found ten graves all in a row – all had died from the 28th of July to the 4th of August. Disease unknown – About 7 miles farther on came to another stream from springs and stopped for the night. found plenty of grass about one mile below on the stream   16 m

10 Friday – Traveled about 8 miles to a stream of very black water and high colored – were afraid of it and did not let our cattle drink. About a mile further on came to a number of large boiling hot springs which

make a stream 2 ft wide and 3 or four inches deep –
Water very clear and not bad tasted – Here we stopped
and fed our cattle but did not let them drink – traveled
along the foot of mount about 5 miles to another creek
and stoped for the night – plenty of dry bunch grass –
no timber but willows and sage – Found 8 graves here
15 m

[September]   11th   Sat. came to another small creek
in about 2 miles   then found no more water for 8 miles
more. when we came to Charlotte creek down in valley
with steep rocky bank   The road for the last 3 days
has been mostly very rough and rockey but generally
level and the dust has been very troublesome. This dust
differs from sand in being mostly clay and is mixed
up by the teams to a depth of from 2 to 4 inches and
light as flour and under is a hard bottom so that a
wagon runs very well on it where there are no stone
in the way – but there is such a perfect cloud of dust
rising constantly that it almost suffocates our cattle and
is disagreeable to us. and we cannot keep anything clean
– We find plenty of dry bunch grass all the way but no
green feed have we had for some time. Our present
position must be high above the river for we have not
come down much since we climbed the long hill. All
the living creatures we see are a few ravens and black-
tailed rabbits and flies and white gnats and at night
hear some wolves. Here we found tolerably plenty of
dry grass from 1 to 2 miles back on the hills. Concluded to stay over sunday. plenty of willow for fuel
and some balm of Gilead.   10

13   Monday – Today started again. had rough. (rocky
and dusty) road along foot of Mount on right for about
5 miles then came to light sand and gravel and road

hard and smooth. About noon came to a deep broad
valley covered with dry grass as well as the hills. Begins
to look live but our cattle are beginning to be tired of
dry grass – Here we found a dry creek, some poor
water. Traveled on till we came to a small spring. Had
very scanty supply of water and it soon got rily. Hard
case – Land covered with dry grass. Looks like a large
wheat field   14

September   14 Tues – Traveled over hilly road of
sand and gravel – In about 2 miles came to a small
stream in deep ravine   Water sinks away in the sand
in a few rods – then in about 5 miles more came to
White Horse creek. Here we watered our cattle and
drove on about 2 miles and fed. Then traveled on about
10 miles to another small spring a rather worse case
then the other and stopped for the night   We have
no trouble for grass – such as it is. Roads smooth but
hilly   16

15 – Wed. To day traveled up a long hill some 4 miles
road good – ascent very gradual   when we arived at
the top a grand view of the Boise River valley. It is all
filled or covered with dry grass and a few trees immediately along the bank the first we have seen for
more than a month. We traveled for some 4 miles on
a high level plain then came down a steep hill about
200 feet to another equally level on which we traveled
about 3 miles then took another offset of about 100
feet and in about a mile and a half came to another
offset about the same. and we were nearly on a level
with the river. This is a fine clear stream and there are
plenty of indians scattered along its banks. They bring
us a great many salmon trout but no salmon – We have

seen no fish since day after we left the ferry till now and we are getting hungry for some – These indians have a great many fine ponies and most of them have guns and ammunition and many of them have almost a complete suit of clothes which they have got of the emigrants. They will trade a very good pony for a good rifle or a coat. Our company traded 2 guns for 2 ponies – Last night we had a very heavy wind all night and it sprinkled slightly for about ½ minute the first rain we had since time immemorial. On the other side of the river are lofty rolling mountains – 14 m

[September]   16   Thursday – Traveled down the river. in about 3 miles ascended to platform No. 2 and traveled on it, level road, nearly all day then came down to the river. These offsets are about as steep as sand and gravel can be laid without mortar – pretty dusty most of the day – Saw the most rabbits to day 5 [miles] that I ever saw in the same length of time. Frank shot 18 in about an hour   To night have pretty good green grass for our cattle. Indians bring fish and rabbits   15

17   Friday. Some traders who are camped about 2 miles above came down and bought some of our lame and worn out cattle. Traveled down the bottom, Road sandy in many places and begin to find some sage again – Camped on river   13

18. Sat. Proceeded down the river – Road sandy and very dusty in places. A great deal of Grease-wood and some sage. Country looks about as desolate as ever – About 4, 1, clock crossed Boise river – Very good ford – This river is skirted with timber all the way consisting of Cotton wood, Willow and Balm of Gilead.

Large quantities of balm might be procured here. Camped on the river. Had good feed and fuel 15

[September] 19 Sunday – Thought we would just drive down to the fort as we thought it could not be more than 5 miles. Drove all day but did not see it Camped about sunset on river – Saw the most fish to day in the river that I ever saw 16

20 Monday – To day drove down to the fort about 4 miles. Crosed the ferry, It is built of unburnt brick a large yard inclosed by a wall some 12 feet high and 2 buildings of the same about 14 feet square and one story high   It is tenanted by a rough looking Scotchman [11] and a few indians and squaws – It is a station of the Hudson's Bay Co – A great many had depended on getting provisions here but failed entirely of getting anything except fish – There is a little sugar for sale here at ,75, cents pr pound – Prospects seem to darken around us a good deal for some families are already entirely out of bread and many more will be in the course of one or two weeks – We have enough to last us through but we shall have to divide if necessary

21st   Tuesday – To day Mr. McMillen,[12] Mr. Stowell and Mr Raymond left us to pack their way through to the Dalls in company with eleven others from our company – They have 3 ponies among them which

---

[11] This has been thought to have been James Craigie, longtime Hudson's Bay Company employee, who was stationed at Fort Boise for many years. The "Scotchman," however, was Archibald McIntyre, who had taken over from Craigie. They both had Indian wives. Annie L. Bird, *Boise, the Peace Valley* (Caldwell, Id., 1934), p. 74. The government donation land records indicate that Craigie filed an intention to become an American citizen on August 13, 1852, in Clackamas County, Oregon, and he settled on his claim (#3268) in western Oregon on Nov. 2, 1852. *Oregon Donation Land Claims, op. cit.*, II, p. 40.

[12] This was Joseph McMillen, the twins' father.

carry the most of their provisions. They expect to make the trip (300 miles) in ten days while it will probably take our teams in their present condition at least 20 days and perhaps more. Had some difficulty in finding our cattle this morning as we do not keep guard over them now for we are not much afraid of the indians stealing them. Found them about noon and started them on the way. Had first rate green feed for them last night Proceeded about five miles against an increasing west wind over a very dusty road till it became so bad that we could not see our teams or hardly breathe and were obliged to heave to for a season. After a while the wind shifted more into the north and blew the dust across the road and then we proceeded on – followed up a deep ravine about three miles more and encamped for the night with out water or grass. plenty of sage. Cold   8

[September]   22   Wed. Started early. Followed up same ravine to summit. then followed another down to Malkeurs [Malheur] River. the most sluggish stream I have seen for some time   Here we found but poor feed but thought best to stay the rest of the day as the next stopping place was too distant to reach to day Find plenty of willow – water not very good   7 m

23   Thurs. To day traveled over a smooth level road for about 15 miles when we came to a sulphur spring. Here we watered our cattle but did not find much grass. Country very poor – Nothing but sage and grease wood – From the spring we began to ascend hills and the country began to improve. Hills mostly covered with dry grass. Traveled till after dark without finding water. Camped in valley among hills. Plenty of thrifty sage. Plenty dry grass. Tied our cattle to sage

brush Mr. Miller thought he saw a bear in the night. The last three nights have been very cold froze some 22

24 Friday – After giving our cattle time to feed we started. In about a mile came to Birch Creek. Water not very good. does not run more than half the way above the surface. Stands in pools. Tastes of sulphur – In about 4 miles more over hills came to Snake River for the last time. Here it runs between lofty and inaccessible mountains. so farewell Snake – Traveled over high mount to Burnt River 4 miles. Here we stopped and fed our cattle on dry grass – They are getting tired of it for it is too dry. This river is fine clear water about 20 feet wide on an average and flows between very lofty mounts with just room to pass – Traveled up its banks about 4 miles and encamped. Plenty dry grass   13

[September]   25 Sat. To day crossed the river three times in going 5 miles, and climbed over high bluffs the most of the rest of the way. Soon left the river banks and traveled over bluffs very hilly for about 6 miles to a small creek and stopt for the night. Find very little sage or grease wood. Dry grass   12

26 Sun – Traveled down the creek to the river 2 miles. Here the mountains are so high and so close that they leave no room for bluffs and when they close down upon us on one side of the river our only alternative is to flee to the other. Crossed the river 5 times in about 6 miles. These mounts are as near as I can judge about 1200 feet high on an average and as steep as they know how to be Mostly covered with dry grass, except where it is burnt off – See a good many fine

fish but cant catch them – To day found a place where there were a good many green rushes and a good many Birch trees. Here we stopped for the rest of the day 8   River bottom at this place some 6 rods wide   covered with timber as is the bottom most of the way – Birch, Cotton Wood and Willow and some Balm of Gilead [13] a few scattering pines and cedars on the mount high above us. Scenery fine.

[September]   27   Mon. To day crossed the river for the last time 9 times in all about ½ mile from camp and started up a small creek. very rapid. got up hill pretty fast by following it – crossed it 9 times in going 4 miles – then turned from it up steep long hill in ravine and descending came to another small stream and spring. Here watered our cattle and drove up another steep hill and stopt to feed on some bunch grass – The grass along here has been mostly burnt off and we have to get it where we can catch it – Drove down the hill, found a spring brook which we followed down for some 2 miles then crossed over ridge to another creek and soon came again near Burnt river and camped on it – Grass good – Some packers overtook us from behind hurrying on to procure provisions. They give a sad account of the destitution of those who are behind. Say there are but few who have more than 5 days provisions   14

28th   Tuesday   This morning met some traders from

---

[13] The "Balm of Gilead" she writes of was the black cottonwood, a poplar. Charles R. Ross in his *Trees to Know in Oregon* (Corvallis, 1967), p. 61, describes it as a "friend of the pioneers." He adds, "To pioneers on the Old Oregon Trail the cottonwood was the most important tree. For nearly 1000 miles of their journey it was the only shade tree to be found." It was called Balm of Gilead because when the spring buds burst it emits a refreshing balmy odor. See also diary entries for October 10 and 24.

Oregon buying lame cattle   River forks some little
distance above camp and we take the right hand fork.
Follow up it all day among hills and camp on it at
night   10

29 Wed. Cross the stream twice then leave it and
follow up small creek to a spring and water our cattle
as we are to have 18 miles without water   Traveled
over hills till afternoon then came to a pretty level
piece of land covered with sage on which we traveled
till nearly night and then descended to another beautiful smooth plain several miles in extent bounded by
grass covered hills except on the west which is bounded
by the Blue Mountains beautiful in the distance covered with Pine   looks as if we were coming some-
where – Camped among the sage without water   Plenty of grass for our cattle on hill near by   18 m

[September] 30 Thurs. After going about 4 miles
found a kind of dry creek where was plenty of water
standing in pools but poor stuff – Here we watered
our cattle – Drove on about five miles and got badly
fooled by the willows growing very abundantly about
2 miles to the left as we supposed it was Powder
River – Stopped on some good feed for our cattle and
[page torn] there for water to get our dinner but found
none but dirty pools – The soil on this plain is much
better than we have seen before – Grass in many places
fresh and abundant. In about a mile's travel came to
a small stream a branch of Powder river. very sluggish, water poor, bad ford – and in about 6 miles more
came to one of the main branches of Powder River and
stopped for the night. found good grass – and fine
water   Found some more Oregon traders here – They
say we must hurry if we get over the Blue Mountains –

Rains some in the valley and snows on the mountains – very cold all day   15 m

Oct. 1. Friday. Let our cattle feed till after noon. One of the packers we had seen before came back – Had been to the Grand Ronde and bought 50 pounds of flour for $30.00 and was hurrying back to the relief of his friends. Traveled about 2 miles down the stream then crossed it and in about 5 miles crossed another branch of Powder River. fine stream, then crossed several small streams and ascended to a high table land and went about 6 miles upon it before finding water. Nearly dark when we camped on a small stream – Water not very good – Grass tolerable – No wood but green – willows. very cold. Rained some in fore part of the day – Plenty of snow to be seen on mountains. Roads good, no dust – the first time we have been free from it for a long time. Have seen 35 graves since leaving Ft. Boise   12 m

[October]   2d   Sat. Could not raise fire enough to cook breakfast. Powerful cold – Started early and in about 3 miles came to foot of mount – Climbed the mount. Ascent very gradual – about 3 miles – when we came to a fine little valley with some springs in it. and plenty of grass. followed up it about a mile then up mount 2 miles when we came in sight of the Grand Ronde a beautiful level valley nearly round   I should think some 15 miles in diameter – but O the getting down to it over a long steep and stony hill is equal to any getting down stairs I ever saw, and I have seen some on this road – Arrived at the bottom   found feed had been mostly burnt off but found enough for our cattle. Here we found another trading station from Oregon – They sell flour for 60 cts. pr lb. Salt at 50

cts. and first rate fat beef which they brought with
them or drove at 20 to 25. Stopped and fed and then
traveled on about 5 miles to a spring and camped
Good water and grass. but no wood except a kind of
green stuff that *wont burn no how*. Still cold and freezes
considerably – Did not get very near any snow nor to
timber – The traders say they drove their beef cattle
from the Dalles in 8 days – The soil of this valley
is fine   16 m

3d   Sunday. Have not seen any of the clover spoken
of by others but have found plenty of red top grass.
both here and on Powder River and it grows very
thrifty. The indians have all left for their winter quarters. Traders say they were very thick here about 2
weeks ago – are said to be very rich in ponies and
trade a good many for cows. considerably civilized.
Raise some cattle and some vegetables for sale – but
they did not leave much marks of civilization on the
road or near it to be seen. Traveled along the west
side of the valley at foot of mount about 3 miles when
we came to a small stream and then commenced ascending the mountain, very steep in many places and
continues to ascend for about 6 miles. very hard drive
but at the top found the grass burnt off and there was
no water, so had to go on till we came to Grand
Ronde, ten miles, worst hill to go down that we have
found yet. long, steep and rocky. Our road to day has
been mostly through lofty pines as fine as I ever saw
and to night we have plenty of dry pine for fires. The
feed here has been very thoroughly fed off but we found
plenty on the mountain side among the pines. This
river runs through the middle of the Grand Ronde,
a fine little stream, rapid and shallow – 15 m

[October]   4th   Mon. This morning got a late start and commenced climbing again – very steep hill to start with about a mile long. then had hills to ascend and descend all day, many of them steep. About night found a place where we could find some standing water about ½ mile from the road, down a very steep hill all the way – poor stuff but it was the best we could do. Camped and turned our cattle out to grass but did not drive them down to water as it was almost dark. Plenty of pine   Today saw two very small black squirrels   15 m

5th   Tues   Staid till near noon and let our cattle feed   The grass is very good and quite fresh in many places among the pines. We find Pine, Spruce, Tamarack and Fir here – Mr Millers co. from Iowa are here entirely out of flour. Have some loose cattle which they kill now and then for food. Traded them some flour for beef, sold them some and lent them some to be repaid at the Dalles. Hard times. many cattle are failing and all are very poor and a good many get lost among the thick timber. A good many wagons are left, some broken and some good and sound because the cattle are not able to take them along. So much good pine here they do not burn them. The general appearance of the country is altogether changed. The soil even on the mountains is quite good and in the valleys it is excellent. In many places the road has to twist round a good deal among the trees. Traveled on about 7 miles on a mountain ridge sometimes on one side sometimes on the other. pretty sideling in places – Do not have to rise and fall as many notes as common to day   begin to hope we are getting out of the mounts. Camped on mount. A good spring about ¼ mile off down at the foot of mount. Timber very thick to day. Good grass – 7 m

[October] 6th Wed. Concluded to rest to day and recruit our cattle as we have good feed and they have had a hard pull of it for the last 4 days – Spent the day in cooking and hunting for cattle lost in the brush as a great many have been lost here.

7th Thurs. To day staid till about noon and then started on about 6 miles to another spring still in the thick timber very thick. Find plenty of good grass all the way 6

[October] 8th Friday – Started for the Umatilla river. Road slightly descending nearly all the way and in some places steep. At last came in sight of the valley covered entirely with dry grass except a small skirt of timber along the river – and literally dotted with indian ponies – and cattle. Commenced the descent into the valley very gradual. said to be five miles down hill. Dont think is was much overrated. The grass here is very poor having been fed off by the ponies and cattle. Soil excellent. This valley is the head quarters of the Cayuse Indians. They are more civilized than any we have seen before Bought a few potatoes of them. They are killing some very fat cattle and sell the beef at 15 to 20 cts. pr lb. No other provisions can be had here and that is a death blow to the hopes of many hungry people. Found a man here who had left our company some time ago and been on to the Dalles and returned with a pony load of provisions. Gives a very discouraging account of the prospect before us. Grass is very poor all the way. No provisions for sale between here and the Dalls. 15 m

9th Sat. Our friend from the Dalls advises us to stay

and recruit our cattle as we shall have no more as good grass as we have here. but the prospect here is nothing but starvation for ourselves and teams. Started off after noon and went down the river 6 miles. put our cattle over bluffs but found poor feed. Find some prairie chickens   6

10th   Sunday – Traveled down river, passed over bluffs, some sand, crossed river passed down some 3 miles and camped – Find a great many mice living in holes in the ground – Timber mostly Balm of Gilead – some willow. 9 m

[October]   11   Mon. Climbed the bluff, ascent very gradual but some 3 miles long. after passing some 7 miles found good feed, dry grass and stopped for noon. then passed on some 7 miles more and stopped for the night. No water. Road good, plenty dry grass. mice very plenty   14

12th   Tues. put our cattle down to the river about 2 miles for drink and got one of them stuck in the mud. Spent the forenoon in trying to get him out, but failing we killed him – Started on and came to the river in about 3 miles and traveled down it about 3 miles and camped on it. poor feed – 6 m

13   Wednesday, Traveled down 3 miles to the Indian Agency, the first framed house we have seen since we left the Mo. River – and they have actually got a stoned up well. The agent was gone to the Dalles. but we left 2 of our wagons there and sold 3 cattle to some traders and put all the teams to Stephens wagon and proceeded. Our loads are light but our cattle are getting powerful weak and we think best to favor them as much as possible. An indian here has some flour for sale at

50. cts. pr. lb   A white man has some corn brought
from Ft. Wallawalla which he sells at the rate of six
pint cupfuls for a dollar and it sells fast. Traveled on
about 5 miles after crossing the river and leaving it
Road very sandy the heaviest I ever saw for so long
a distance. Camped on the open prairie   no water.
Burn grease wood of which we have seen a good deal
to day – Looks familiar but old fashioned. We find it
to our advantage to camp between the watering places
on account of grass – 70 graves since leaving Ft
Boise   8

14th   Thursday – Started on again and traveled over
the same heavy sand about 5 miles more to Alder creek.
A sluggish dirty stream. some willow on banks
[*Cecelia*] Here we saw Mr. Torance[14] the Indian
agent on his way back to the Station from Milwaukie [Oregon] loaded with provisions   Seemed much
pleased to see us told us a great deal about James as
he is well acquainted with him   After dinner started
on   carried water with us   very warm and sunny
encamped on the prairie   no wood or water for our
cattle   Warm nights   11 m

[October]   15   Friday   looks very much like rain,
cool   Frank and Doct have concluded to start on a
head as Stephen bought an Indian pony & they will
take it & go to the dalls and there meet us   Encamped
at a spring of miserable water   Here we met Lot

---

14 William S. Torrance had settled a claim in the Milwaukie, Oregon,
area in 1849, *Oregon Donation Land Claims, op. cit.*, I, p. 30, claim #725.
The pioneer Oregon City newspaper, the *Oregon Spectator*, contains many
reports of his traveling to The Dalles and even to Salt Lake City on mail
contracts. He seemed to have a passion for giving aid to the overlanders
approaching the Columbia River. (Oct. 28, 1847; July 13, 1848; May 22,
1851; Aug. 19, 1853.)

Whitcomb [15] direct from Oregon   told us a great deal
about Oregon   was well acquainted with James and
spoke very highly of him   He had provisions but not
to sell but gives to all he finds in want and are not able
to buy. Took supper and breakfast with us   Traveled
all day   Made 15 miles over deep 16 sand and dust
had no water till night   Encamped on Willow creek
the water stands in holes but found three good springs.
Made 18 miles.

17   Sunday   warm and pleasant   Stay here to day to
rest our teams   some cedar and willow   see no Indians   drive our cattle over the bluffs some three miles
[*Parthenia*] find very poor feed all along here – Here
are 12 graves all together. We hope this is the last
sabbath we shall spend on the road

[October]   18   Monday   Very cloudy. Started on
and it soon began to rain. As we left the creek we had
a very long steep hill to climb. The train we started
with are all behind and we travel alone. At noon it
rained very hard and we all got wet which was very
reviving   Pleasant in the afternoon. Road very hilly
all day and dusty. Camped without wood or water and
with little grass. 13

19   Tuesday   Cool and pleasant. High W. wind.
Road lay through a deep narrow valley, but very barren. At noon camped by a small spring coming out of
a hill. No grass here. From here pass over high bluffs
and descend a very steep hill to John Day's River a
very rapid stream. No wood here except a few very

15 Lot Whitcomb was a well-known old time riverman on the Columbia, everybody's favorite. He is reputed to have named the Oregon town of Milwaukie. His river boat was named the *Lot Whitcomb*. Howard M. Corning, *Dictionary of Oregon History* (Portland, 1956), p. 263.

small willows. All the country from the indian agency
to this place is about as barren and desolate as any
we have passed over and we have seen nothing that
could be fairly called wood since we left the Umatilla 13

20 Wednesday Very pleasant this morning. Our
first act was to pass up a very long rocky and sandy
hill as bad as any we have had all things considered
and when arrived at the top stopped for dinner. Here
we have good grass. the first since we left Umatilla.
Here the Doct. met us on his way back from the Dalls.
Franklin had gone down by the boat. He brought some
flour, pork, Salt, and saleratus. Prices are coming down
at the dalls. flour can be had at 15 cts. Pork at 37½,
Salt at 25, Saleratus 25, Sugar 25 to 30 Afternoon
traveled on about 6 miles and encamped on the prairie
Plenty of dry grass. but no wood or water. country
quite changed land all covered with a fine growth of
dry grass. Pretty hilly. Soil good 9 m

[October] 21st Thurs. Travel on. Road good but
rather hilly. Plenty of grass all the way. Came to a
spring of poor water in about 9 miles, stopped and
watered our cattle but did not feed. passed on about
3 miles more 12 and camped for the night. grass excellent for dry – but no water

22nd. Friday. Rose early and drove down to the great
Columbia River for wood and water for breakfast.
Had a very long but not very steep hill to descend. At
the foot found a trading station. Sell flour, pork, Sugar
and tobacco at 40 cts. pr. lb. Stopped and got our
breakfast – no wood but very poor willows and some
grease wood. Drove on to DeChutes River 3 miles.

No grass in the bottom, all eaten off. The Columbia here is a very rapid and shallow stream apparently about the size of Rock River Ills. flowing over a rocky bottom with frequent falls and not navigable for sap troughs [16] or canoes. Banks very high steep and rocky and bottom very narrow and in some places sandy. DeChutes river is to appearances nearly as large as the Columbia though it must be much smaller and comes dashing down over the rocks – as rapid as water can come on a plane inclined one foot in 20. Here is a ferry at $2.00 for those who have money and a ford for those who have not. The latter is the most numerous class – After crossing this river we climbed a very steep and long hill but good road and passed on about a mile on the level and camped for the night. Here is a good spring on the hill. Found rather poor grass but thought best to stop for fear we could not climb the other hill   7 m

[October]   23   Sat   Traveled on about 2 miles and came to another hill as bad as the last. Hard pull our cattle are so much weakened, but it is the last we shall have. Then down steep hill to Olney's creek. Here is a house and a white man Mr Olney [17] living with a squaw. There are also 2 houses at DeChute river. and some tents belonging to the Walla Walla indians who do some ferrying and act as guides to those who ford. Pretty shrewd fellows for money – but very civil

---

[16] Sap troughs were hollowed out logs made to collect maple syrup. In an emergency they could be used as dug-out boats.

[17] Nathan Olney was a friend of northwest Indians. His wife, Annette Hallicula, was a Wasco Indian. He traded all around the Deschutes-The Dalles area. Roscoe Sheller's book, *The Name was Olney,* is a somewhat romanticized story of the life of Nathan and his Indian "princess" wife and other Olneys. (Yakima, Wa., 1965), pp. 55-66.

From thence we went over bluffs ascent and descent very gradual to a creek 5 miles from the Dalles called 5 miles creek and encamped for the night. Stephen had gone before to the Dalls and returned bringing the intelligence that Mr. [Joseph] McMillen had returned there with some provisions for us from the valley. Staid all night and did some cooking for the journey down by the water. Have long been convinced that we are too late to cross the Cascade Mountains with safety so we concluded to leave our cattle and wagon at the Dalls and proceed down by water. Hire a man to take care of the cattle at $6.00 pr head and deliver them in the vally in the spring as soon as it is safe to travel over the mountains   9 m

24   Sun. Traveled to the Dalls, 5 miles, and found a boat ready for sail   Put our loading on board and got on ourselves and were ready to be off   Stephen staied to take care of the cattle and some other business and the rest of us went on – It was an open kiel boat rowed by three men and we went on at a pretty good rate. The appearance of the river here changes from being a rapid, shallow, and narrow stream   it becomes a wide deep and still on in places more than a mile wide and too deep to be sounded – The water is clear and fine and the banks are precipitous and rocky and several hundred feet high in most places. We had a very favorable run for the weather was calm. This is said to be a very windy stream and the channel being so deep it follows it up and often prevents boats from running for 3 or 4 days. During the night it rained a good deal and we got pretty thoroughly wet. About 2 oclock hove to, to wait for daylight. Went on shore and got breakfast. Rained hard nearly all the time.

Here is a narrow bottom and some balm of Gilead growing, some of the trees more than 4 feet in diameter. We are now only 6 miles from the Cascades. The mounts, are covered with a thick growth of lofty pines and fir and the pack trail which passes along here seems almost impassable the mounts are so very steep – Passed down to the cascades which consists of an emmense pile of loose rocks across the stream over which the water runs with great rapidity for 6 miles. The indians have a tradition that many years ago the Columbia ran above here the same as above the Dalls but the mountains got into a fight and threw large rocks at each other which falling into the river dammed it up and indeed the river appears like a vast millpond. The distance from the Dalls to the cascades is 45 miles. Here is a large warehouse and from it proceeds a rail road 3 miles long made of scantling and plank without iron. On this runs a small car propelled by a mule attached to by a long rope for an engine and a pair of thills[18] between which the engineer stations himself and walks and guides the car. on this the charge is 75 cts. per cwt. but takes no passengers. At the end of the railroad the goods have to be let down perpendicularly some 150 feet to the river from whence they are taken on a boat to the steam boat landing about 3 miles more. Charge 75 cts. in all. Rained hard most of the day. Women walked down on land and expected their goods that night but could not get them down. Had no tent, no beds, and no feed except what they bought. Mr. Miller staid with the goods and the rest of us went the tavern to stay. The steamer Multnomah

---

18 Thills were wagon or buggy shafts used one on each side of a single animal.

came up about dark and staid till morning. Here we came across Mr. Stowell who had been detained by sickness. Early in the morning Mr Miller came down with the goods and we all got on board the steamer. Charge 6 pr. passenger. distance to Portland 65 miles – The appearance of the river below the Cascades is about the same as above. Rises and falls with the tide in the Pacific. Had a very pleasant ride. Much better than an ox team where you have to work your passage by running on foot. The banks soon began to grow less steep and high and soon we were in the valley but could see nothing except timber on shore. but that was fine. Passed some timber farms and good dwellings and one saw mill belonging to the Hudsons Bay Co Passed Ft. Vancouver pleasantly situated on the N.W. side of the river. About 2 O'clock came into the Willamette (pro. Will am' et) River. Much like the Columbia wide, deep and slow. and soon were at Portland the largest town now in the Territory and a fine town it is and would compare favorably with many eastern cities. At the head of ship navigation it is bound to be the great commercial emporium of the North west. Here we remained 3 days nearly – when brother James came for us with his team and we started for his farm 10 miles distant

Index

Adams, Calvin H. and Catherine: 255, 257

Adams, Cecelia (Emily?): 253-54; death, 255; diary of, 256-312; ill, 281; married, 254; musician, 266; traits, 254

Adams, William: 254-56

Agriculture and crops: *see also* livestock, wheat

Ague: 41

Alcoholism: 33; *see also* liquor

Alder Creek (OR): 125, 306

Alfred Univ. (NY): 174-75, 201

Alkali: 62, 77, 223, 225, 266

American Falls (of Snake R.): 96, 197, 285

Anderson, Stinson and Naomi: 34

Antelope: 56, 270, 274

Anthrax (Murrain, hollow horn): cattle disease, 15-16, 197, 233, 246, 286

Arapaho Indians: 14

Ash Creek (NE): 261

Ash Hollow (NE): 63, 190, 270

Aumsville (OR): 208

Baker, Edwin Dickenson: 24

Balm of Gilead trees: 87, 293, 295, 298, 311; *see also* cottonwood

Barlow's Gate (OR): 131

Barrell, Lydia: 35

Barton, Tirzah: 255

Battle, Mr.: 215-16

Bear River (UT/ID): 86-92, 195-96, 234-35, 281-83

Beaver Creek (KS/NE): 261

Bedding and blankets: 28-29

Beef: 303-04

Bentley, William P.: 203

Berries and nuts: 196, 236-37, 278; *see also* chokecherries, currants, salal, strawberries

Birch Creek (OR): 115, 298

Birds: 265, 271

Black Hills (WY): 67, 191, 273

Blacksmithing: 277

Blank, Parthenia: 253-54; adopts orphans, 255; death, 255; diary of, 256-312;

married, 254; sister Ann E., 262; traits, 254

Bloomer costume: described, 180

Blue Mts. (OR): 122, 245, 300-301

Blue River (KS/NE): 52, 55-56

Bluff Creek (NE): 224

Boiling springs: *see* hot springs

Boise River (ID): 241-42, 294-96

Botsford, Charles: 79

Brimhall, Noah: 235

Brown, James: 203-04

Browne, R. Edwin: 26, 139-40

Buffalo (Bison): 60-62, 221, 223; hunting of, 265-66, 274; meat of, 60, 229, 274; robes, 55

Buffalo chips: 57, 67, 80, 191, 224, 230, 266

Buffalo Creek (NE): 223

Bullrush Creek (ID): 286

Buoy, John: 37-38

Burnt River (OR): 115-18, 243, 298-99

Butler (driver): 38

Cactus: 263, 268

Caffee, Charles Clifford: 34

Caffee, Edward Taylor: 34

Caffee, Levi: 30, 96n, 98n, 101n, 112n, 119n, 134n, 163, 166; alcoholic, 33, 128n; wife, 34; ill, 44-45, 141, 143, 146

Caffee, Martha Roelofson, "Mattie": 34, 98n, 111n, 133n, 153; ill, 55-56

Caldwell: mountaineer, 93

Cañon Creek (ID): 201

Carleton College (MN): 26

Cascade Mts. (OR/WA): 131

Cascades: of Columbia R., 311

Cascades Massacre: 248

Castle River (NE): 63, 270

Catherine Creek (ID): 107

Cattle: 62, 181, 310; die, 14-15, 103, 108, 207, 216, 287, 305; milk cows, 30; stampede, 82, 229, 260

Cayuse Indians: 304

Cedar Bluffs (NE): 224, 269
Cedar Creek (NE): 221
Cedar Rapids (IA): 181
Cedar trees and wood: 64, 66, 69, 191, 262
Chamberlain, J.B.: 35-36, 48, 148, 150; death, 49n
Champoeg (OR): 32-33, 163, 166
Chariton River (IA/MO): 30, 45
Charlottes Creek (ID): 201, 293
Cheyenne Indians: 14
Chickens: 42; see also sagehens
Childbirth: 269
Chimney Rock (NE): 65, 190, 225, 271
Chokecherries: 124, 283
Cholera: 62n, 115, 156n, 189, 220-23, 247, 263
Christian church: 208
Clackamas County (OR): 32
Clason, John H.: 35, 136; death, 119, 166
Clothing: for overland trip, 27; see also bloomer
Coats, John: 200n
Coats, Thomas J. and Carolyn: 200n
Coburn, Catherine Scott: 21, 27
Coburn, John R.: 33
Coffee: 134n
Columbia River: 128, 308-12
Congregational Church: 256
Cook, Amos: portrait, 11; career, 32; 162n, 170
Cooking: on trail, 269; see also stoves
Coon, Cornelia Evelyn: 175, 205
Coon, Delia M.: 174n, 201
Coon, Polly L. (Crandall): portrait, 11; death, 176; 202; diary illus., 12; 13; 174-77; family, children, 175; journal, 177-201; marries Stephen Price, 176, 205-06
Coon, Samuel L.: 184, 186, 198
Coon, Thomas Lewis: 175-76, 203, 205; death, 176
Corn: for feed, 44-45, 214, 216, 306
Cornell, William: 15
Cottonwood trees: 55, 74-75, 191, 261, 270, 295, 298; see also Balm of Gilead
Council Bluffs (IA): 259
Court House Rock (NE): 64, 190, 225

Coyotes: see wolves
Crandall, Amanda: 177, 204
Crandall, Clark P.: 177, 203-05
Crandall, Cornelia: 204
Crandall, Emily Jane B.: 177, 205; illness, death, 198-200
Crandall, John: 174n
Crandall, Luke S.: 177, 206
Crandall, Paul and Sally (Stillman): 174-76, 192, 202; children, 202-03; Paul's parents, 201
Crandall, Phoebe G.: 177, 204
Crandall, Ray: 205
Crandall, Webster: 203-04, 206
Crow Indians: 14, 194
Currants: 90, 229, 235, 273, 275, 281
Cut Rock Creek (ID): 286, 288

Dalles: see The Dalles
Darby, W.H.: 209
Davenport, Dr. Benjamin: 205
Dead Ox Flat (ID): 16
Deady, Judge M.P.: 162n
Deaths on trails: 59, 61, 67, 71, 96, 117, 119, 187-89, 192, 198, 200, 222-23, 263-64, 270; in OR, 29
Deer Creek (WY): 75
Des Moines River: 184, 215
Deschutes River (OR): 129, 132, 308-09
Devil's Back Bone: 85
Devil's Gate (WY): 78, 193, 230, 275
Diaries and journals: sources of, 21, 171, 209, 253
Diarrhea: 52-53, 62, 71
Digger Indians: 284
Diseases: of cattle, 14-15; see also ague, cholera, illnesses, pleurisy, pneumonia, smallpox, typhus
Dixon, John: 35, 101n, 109n, 136, 166
Dixon, Robert: 35, 101n, 136, 166; wife, 35
Doctors: 45, 48; see also medicine
Dogs: 30
Dolley, Horace: 79
Donation claims of land: 34, 37-38, 175, 200n, 208-09, 246, 249, 283n
Drownings: 100, 182, 192, 214

Dubuque (IA): 180

Dunbar, Rice: 205; daughter Eliza, 205

Duniway, Abigail Scott: portrait, 10; *see also* Scott, Abigail

Duniway, Benjamin Charles: 21, 27, 170

Duniway, Clyde A.: 5, 26, 29

Duniway, David C.: 13, 26-27, 140

Duniway, Robert E.: 27

Duniway, Willis S., II: 27

Dunmore, Sherman: murdered, 87-88

Eagle Ferry (WI): 180

"Elephant, seeing the": 120, 167, 188

Elk Creek (NE): 223

Elkhorn River (NE): 186, 219, 260

Elm Creek (NE): 265

Emigrants: number of, 50; returning parties, 190

Estes, Charles: 37

Fairview (IL): 40

Fall River (ID): 285

Farnham, Thomas J.: 24

Feed for livestock: *see* grass

Fernside, George: 25

Ferries: 45, 213, 215, 257; accident, 182; on Bear R., 281; on Columbia R., 129; fees, 77, 113, 129, 187, 233, 242, 286, 309; on Green R., 84, 233, 280; on Mississippi R., 43, 213; on Missouri R., 186, 259; on Platte R., 77; on Snake R., 113, 290

Fights: among emigrants, 268, 270

Fillmore, Pres. Millard: 14

Firearms: *see* guns

Fish: bought of Indians, 234, 295; in trail streams, 99, 235, 260, 274, 281, 296; *see also* salmon

Fisk, Mountain (driver): 30, 37

Fitzpatrick, Thomas: 14

Five-mile Creek (OR): 129

Flag Creek (ID): 238

Flax: 281

Flemming, Henry: 196

Flour: 79, 94, 121, 126, 249; price of, 237, 301, 306; *see also* mills (grist)

Flowers: 47, 51, 60, 69, 71, 74, 85, 193, 225-26, 261, 264, 267-68, 273-74, 281

Food: *see* beef, potatoes, provisions

Forest Grove (OR): 255

Fort Boise (ID): 32, 112, 296

Fort Hall (ID): 94, 197, 237, 284

Fort Kearny (new, NE, on Platte R.): 57

Fort Laramie (WY): 68, 191, 272-73; treaty council, 14

Fort Vancouver (WA): 312

Foss, Gladys: 173-74n

Free Emigrant Road Co.: 36

Fuel for fires: *see* buffalo chips, sagebrush, wood

Game, wild: *see* buffalo, grouse, pheasant, prairie chicken, sagehens

Garden of the World (OR): 128

Gay, Franklin B.: 30, 36, 75n, 109n, 166, 172

Geer, Isaac: 177

Gold: 75, 77; mines, in OR, 250; mines inflate provision prices, 249

Goodrich, Anson: 178, 181, 188, 193, 202, 204

Goose Creek (ID/UT): 99, 286

Gooseberries: 194-95, 257, 276, 281

Goudy, Malinda Jane Brown: 34, 130n, 141, 143

Goudy, Mary: 34

Goudy, William H. "Bill": 30, 34, 36, 130n, 166; wives, 34

Gowdy, Cyrus F. and Tabitha R.: 34

Gowdy, John Tucker "Teet": 30, 34, 38, 136, 170; wife, 34

Gowdy, Stinson: 34

Gowdy, W.H.: 136

Grand Island (NE): 57

Grande Ronde River and Valley (OR): 120-21, 244-45, 301-02

Grass: *passim*; bunch grass, 104, 292, 299; in plenty, 47, 76, 89-90, 123, 220, 297-98; scarcity on trails, 108, 246; wait for growth, 250

Grasshoppers: 282

Graves: on trails, 50, 52-53, 56, 59, 61-66, 68-69, 74, 76-77, 79-83, 86, 90, 105, 112, 157, 185-86, 189, 191, 194, 207, 219-32, 247, 259-61, 263-81, 301

Greasewood: 75, 108, 295
Greasewood Creek (WY): 276, 306
Green (French mountaineer): 89
Green Creek (WY): 77
Green River (WY): 83-87, 195, 233-34, 280
Grouse: 124
Guidebooks: 52
Guns: 28, 93, 218, 295

Hail storms: 77, 86, 102, 190, 256
Hares: 56; see also rabbits
Harpers Creek (WY): 77
Hay: 41, 44, 144, 180
Haywood, Ben: 181-82
Hewitt, Esquire: 258
Hillsboro (OR): 255
Himes, George: 254-55
Hollow horn: cattle disease, see anthrax
Hood River (OR): 176
Horned toads: 262
Horseflies: 261
Horses: passim; die, 216, 221; drowned,
    101; emigrant use, 30, 130; of Indians,
    104, 121, 295
Hot springs: 197, 200, 292
Hudson's Bay Co.: 112, 312
Hutton, John: 177
Hyland, Benjamin S.: 283, 285, 287; sons
    Amos D. and Burnham S., 283n

Ice Springs (WY): 194
Idaho: 14
Illinois: 22, 24, 27, 39-43, 207, 212-13,
    254, 264
Illnesses: 41, 62, 67, 108, 111-12; colds,
    178, 182; see also ague, cholera,
    diarrhea, diseases, lung fever, medicine,
    mountain fever, pleurisy, smallpox,
    typhus
Independence Rock (WY): 78, 193, 230,
    276
Indians: 14, 55, 181, 217-18, 227, 302;
    fear of, 88; friendly, 124, 129, 187, 195,
    274; graves, 260; horses of, see horses;
    steal guns, clothes, 295; steal livestock,
    218, 228, 260, 277, 287; treaty council,
    14; see also tribal names; squaw wives

Injuries: Indian death, 89; by wagons, 184,
    193; see also deaths
Iowa: 179-85, 213-17, 257-58
Iowa City (IA): 213
Iowa River: 182
Iron ore: 55

Jackrabbits: see rabbits
John Day River (OR): 30, 127, 307
Johnson, Alexander: 99
Johnson, Foster: 128, 131, 158, 166, 170
Johnson, John: 128n, 170
Johnson, John Lawrence: 127, 128, 131,
    158, 166
Johnson, Rev. Neill: 24, 30, 99, 127n, 156,
    166, 170
Jordan, John: 37, 102, 104n
July Fourth: recognized, 81, 229

Kanesville (IA): 186, 217, 258
Kelty, James Munroe: 33
Kemp, Ann Eliza: 34
Kentucky: 22
King, Robert H. "Bob": 30, 35, 75n, 109n,
    119n, 136, 145, 166, 172
Kinney, Giles: 182
Kinney Cutoff (WY): 279
Kirksville (MO): 45
Knight, Isaac: 21-22

La Grange (MO): 31, 43n
Lafayette (OR): 32-33, 35, 157-69
Land claims: see Donation Claims
Lane County (OR): 38, 283n
Laramie Peak (WY): 66-67, 70, 272
Latter-Day Saints: see Mormons
Laundering: 264, passim
Laurel Hill (OR): 133, 204
Lee, Jason: 23-24
Lee's Encampment (OR): 122-23
Lewis River (ID): see Snake R.
Liquor and temperance: 79, 128n
Livestock: dead, 185, 216-17, 261; prices
    of, 249-50; see also cattle, oxen, sheep
Lockley, Fred: 30
Logan, David: 162n
Lone Cedar Tree (NE): 190, 270

Looking Glass River (NE): 220, 261
Loup Fork River (NE): 187, 220-21, 261-62
Lung fever: 41
Lyford, Mr.: 31, 37, 149

McCord, William R.: 33
McCornack, Helen: 38
McDonald, John: 37; drowned, 100-101n, 103, 166
McIntyre, Archibald: 296n
McKesson, John: 140
McMillen, James H.: '45 southsider, 266-67, 271; marries, 255; in OR, 255, 306-07, 312
McMillen, Joseph and Ruth: 253; to OR, 255, 296, 310; twin daughters Cecelia and Parthenia, 253
Madison Creek (MO): 46
Mail: carriers, 68, 189, 265
Malheur River (OR): 113-14, 297
Mansfield, Mr.: 222
Marion County (OR): 34, 175, 203, 209
Marshy Creek (ID): 97
Maxon, Dr. G.: 199n
Measles: 50, 53, 206
Medicine and doctoring: 189; cures for livestock, 92
Methodists: 165
Mice: 305
Mills: grist, 249
Milwaukie (OR): 35
Mining: see gold
Mississippi River: 43
Missouri: 43-48, 256-57
Missouri Bottom (MO): 257-58
Missouri River: 219; crossing of, 49, 258-59
Mitchell (driver): 30, 36, 95-96, 166
Mormon Trail or Trace: 256
Mormons: as diarists, 261; emigrant numbers, 189, 259; friendly to emigrants, 280; at Kanesville, 217
Morrison, Crawford: 37, 110n, 167
Morrison, Dorothy N.: 21
Mosquitoes: 76, 90, 220-21, 262, 275
Mount Hood (OR): 124-25, 129, 132

Mount Jefferson (OR): 129
Mount St. Helens (OR): 125, 129
Mountain fever: 96, 195, 208, 233, 247, 277
Mountain sheep: 80
Moynihan, Ruth Barnes: 21
Multnomah: steamboat, 311
Murders: 56, 79, 87-88, 192, 194
Murrain: see anthrax
Murray, Katherine Duniway: 27
Music: 266; see also recreation

Nebraska: 51-66
Nemaha River (NE/KS): 51
Nishnabotna River (IA): 185, 217, 258
Nodaway River (IA): 185, 257
Norton, Thomas H. and Emeline: 200

Oats: wild, 83
Oberlin College (OH): 254n
Olmstead, Daniel: 86-87
Olney, Nathan: 309
Omaha Indians: 218
Oregon: emigrants to, 175-76; overland parties to, 21, 173, 207, 253; see also Donation claims
Oregon City (OR): 35, 135
Oregon Historical Museum: 254
Oregon Historical Society: 253, 254n, 255
Oregon Provisional Emigration Soc.: 24
Oregonian: magazine, 24
Organization of emigrant parties: elect officers, 264
Outfit for journeys: 27-29, 210
Owyhee River (OR): 112
Oxen: death of, 81, 116, 122, 124, 185, 196-98, 219-21, 276-77; as draft animals, 27, 30; price of, 136; lame, 241, 243, 261, 276; strayed, 192

Pacific Creek (WY): 82, 195
Pacific Spring (WY): 82, 195, 232, 278
Pacific University (OR): 33, 140, 256
Palmer, Isaac A.: 33
Palmiter, Henry: 178n, 196, 204
Palmiter, Jonathan: 178n, 183, 204
Pannock Creek (ID): 284
Panthers: 214

Pawnee Indians: 14, 53, 220
Pekin (IL): 27, 139
Peoria (IL): 39
Peoria party (1839): 23, 32
Pheasants: 44, 124-25
Photographer: 35
Platt, Philip L.: guidebook, 52-53
Platte River (IA/MO): 257
Platte River (NE/WY): 57-63, 186-93, 219-29, 260-75; North, 63-78, 191
Pleurisy: 44
Plum Creek (NE): 261
Pneumonia: 48; *see also* lung fever
Portland (OR): 33-34, 312
Portneuf River (ID): 95, 197, 237, 284
Potatoes: 131, 304
Powder River (OR): 119, 244, 300-301
Poyer, John: 214
Prairie chickens: 305
Prairie dogs: 60, 268, 270, 277
Prairie schooners: *see* wagons
Presbyterian Church: 23
Price, Eugene Crandall: 176
Price, Phillip S.: 173-74n
Price, Stephen: 176
Prices: of provisions, 84, 121, 126, 131, 134, 137, 237, 248; in OR, 249
Prichard, William D.: 15
Provisions for the trail: relief parties, 248; *see also* beef, flour, potatoes, prices
Purvine, Rosaline (Goudy): 34

Quincy (IL): 43

Rabbits and jackrabbits: 286-87, 293, 295; *see also* hares
Raccoon River (IA): 184, 215
Raft River (ID): 97, 285
Railroads: along Columbia R., 311
Rain: *passim*; 48, 55
Rattlesnakes: 185, 270
Raw Hide Creek (WY): 260
Read, Clifton Kittridge: 207, 246, 250; death, 209; ill, 233, 247; land claim, 208
Read, Clifton "Kittridge," Jr.: 207, 250; ill, 247

Read, Lucy M.: 208, 211; ill, 247; works, 251
Read, Lydia Mariah: 207; ill, 243-44, 247
Read, Martha Stone: 13-14; portrait, 11; children, 207; death, 209; diary, letters, 207-51; family, 210-11; ill, 243-44, 247; marries C.K. Read, 207
Recreation: 84, 178, 266
Red Buttes (WY): 76
Reed, William: 37
Reeves, Margaret: 173-74n, 177
Richards brothers: 37
Rivers and creeks: crossing of, 47, 92, 289; *see also* ferries, river names
Roads: dusty, 108, 198-99, 242, 274-76, 291-93; muddy, 41-42, 45, 180-81; rocky, 70, 95, 105, 285, 293; rough, 239; sandy, 61, 94, 202, 224-25, 238-39, 267
Rock Creek (ID): 104, 239, 287-88
Roelofson, Lawrence and Mary: 156; letters to, 141, 161
Roelofson family: 21-22, 24, 140
Rogue River (OR): mines, 250
Ross, Rev. Floyd A.: 134
Rover, John: 215
Ryan, Dorothy Duniway: 27

Sage Creek (WY): 77
Sagebrush: 73, 75, 80, 82, 229, 235, 237, 240, 292-93
Sagehens: 273
St. Joseph (MO): 31, 48
Salal berries: 133-34n
Salem (OR): 33, 248
Saleratus: 77, 230, 266, 277, 238
Salmon: 105, 240, 289-91
Salmon Fall Creek (ID): 105, 239, 289
Salmon Falls (ID): 199
Sandy River: Big, 55, 83-84, 195; Dry, 82; Little, 53-54, 83, 195; in WY, 232, 278-80
Savannah (MO): 256
Schools: in OR, 249
Scott, Abigail Jane "Jenny" (Duniway): 32; portrait, 10; has cholera, 66; journal of, 21-135; letters of, 143, 148, 150-51;

marries, 159; novels by, 26; poem of, 154-56; suffrage movement, 21

Scott, Ann (Roelofson): 22, 31, 34; ill, 42, 143, 146; death and burial, 32, 71-72, 111n, 151, 156-57

Scott, Anna: 25

Scott, Catherine Amanda, "Kit": 33; letter of, 157; married John Coburn, 33; narrative of, 138

Scott, Chloe Riggs: 24

Scott, Frances: portrait, 11

Scott, Harriet Louise "Duck" or"Etty": 26, 30-31, 58n, 114n, 122n; portrait, 10; letters of, 159-60; marriages, 33; memoirs of, 138

Scott, Harvey Whitefield: 21, 26, 30, 32-33, 111n, 138

Scott, James: 22, 24, 26, 33, 127n; letters to, 143-69

Scott, James and Keziah Terry: 22, 172

Scott, John Henry "Jerry" or "Sonny": 30, 33, 145, 168

Scott, John Tucker: 22-26, 30-33, 52n, 101n; accounts of, 136-38; career, 32; children, 24; diarist, 66, 68, 97, 107, 115, 128; ill, 108, 111, 115-16, 134n, 170-71; poem by, 72-73; widowed, re-married, 32, 38, 263

Scott, Lawson: 127-28n, 158, 166, 169, 172

Scott, Leslie M.: 26-27, 29, 38, 52n, 98n, 138

Scott, Louise J.: 35

Scott, Margaret Ann "Mag": 110n, 111n, 133n; portrait, 10; death, 25, 32; diarist, 66, 68, 131; letters of, 141, 145, 161, 165, 169; marries George Fernside, 25

Scott, Maria "Chat": 33, 145, 168, 172

Scott, Mary Francis "Fanny": 26, 29, 32, 49n, 94n, 96n, 111n, 130n, 133n; portrait, 11; interview of, 138; letter of, 168; marries Amos Cook, 32, 169

Scott, Peter: 24, 35, 127n, 172

Scott, William Neill "Willie": 33, 169-70; ill, 111, 113n, 115-16; death, 117, 156n, 158

Scotts Bluff (NE): 66

Service berries: 283

Sheep: 194, 260

Sheldon, Lorinda: 209, 246

Shell Creek (NE): 187

Sherwood, D.: 203

Shoshone Indians: 14, 83

Silver Creek (OR): 203, 205

Silverton County (OR): 175-76, 205

Sioux Indians: 14, 68

Skunk Creek (NE): 60-61, 267

Skunk River (IA): 184, 215

Slavery (MO): 33, 43-44

Smallpox: 261

Smith, Helen Krebs: 21

Smith, Peter: 37

Smith's Fork (WY): 86, 196

Snake Indians: 83, 194, 233-34, 280

Snake (or Lewis) River (ID/OR): 15, 32, 36-37, 94-95, 97, 99-112, 197-201, 237-43, 283-90, 298

Snakes: 185, 214; see also rattlesnakes

Snow: 39-41, 179

Soda Springs (ID): 91, 196, 236, 282

Sommers: emigrant, 35, 136

South Pass (WY): 82, 195, 278

Spring Creek (NE): 66

Springfield (IL): 59

Springs: salt, 69-10; see also hot springs

Squaw wives: 81

Squirrels: 44, 303

Steamboat Springs (ID): 91, 282

Steamboats: 311-12; fares on, 218

Steeves, Sarah Hunt: 174n, 201

Stevenson, George: 38, 55, 121n, 130n; ill, 130

Stevenson, Jacob George: 38

Stevenson, Ruth Eckler: 32, 38, 130n, 163n

Stillman, Charlotte P.: 178n, 194, 198, 204

Stillman, Dr. Clarke: 178, 181, 188-89, 193

Stillman, Henry: 204

Stillman, Sally: 174, 202; parents, 202; marries Crandall, 202

Stoves: 210

Stowell, John: 266, 296, 312

Strawberries: 232, 259, 278

Sulphur Springs: in ID, 242; in OR, 114-15
Sunbonnets: 27
Sunday observance: 40, 46, 144, 165, 265
Surveying: 36
Swearingen, Evaline Buoy: 38
Swearingen, Isaac Stull: 38, 45n, 101n,
    104, 110n, 121, 136, 145, 166
Swearingen, Lydia J.: 38
Sweetwater River (WY): 78-82, 193-94,
    230-32, 276-78

Tarkio River (MO/IA): 257
Tazewell County (IL): 22-24
Tents: 61, 65, 210, 250
Terry, Benjamin: 22
Teton Mountains: 94
The Dalles (OR): 29, 310-11
Thomas Fork (Bear R.): 89, 196
Thompson, Martha Stone: 207; see also
    Martha Read
Thunder, lightning: 60, 183, 213-14, 222
Tillamook Bay (OR): 25
Timber: in OR, 119, 121-22, 302-03; on
    plains, 60, 132, 245, 248; in UT, 86
Torrance, William S.: Indian agent, 306
Trading posts: 68, 79, 81, 91, 230, 236,
    245, 248, 283, 301
Tualatin Academy (OR): 25, 256
Turkey: 46, 145
Typhus fever: 186

Umatilla River (OR): 124-25, 245, 304

Vanderwort, Jefferson: 37, 166
Verdant, Henry: grave, 268
Village Creek (OR): 130-31
Virginia: 22

Wade, Daraleen: 207, 209
Wafer, J.L.: 31, 35, 136, 149
Wagons: abandoned, 109, 303; beds as

boats, 106-09; numbers of, 30, 178;
    upset, 68, 95
Walla Walla Indians: 309
Water: passim; purchased, 27; scarcity on
    trails, 59, 188, 198, 227
Weather: cold, 80, 178, 244, 260, 267,
    280, 289; heat, 59, 63; see also hail,
    rain, snow, thunder, winds
Weber, Dr.: dies, 198
Well Springs (OR): 126
Wells, William: 190
Wheat: 249
Whitcomb, Lot: 307
White, Charles: 203
White Horse Creek (ID): 294
Whortleberries: 196n, 282
Wickes, Mr.: 215-16
Willamette River (OR): 312; transport on,
    249
Willamette Valley (OR): 204, 208, 248
Willow Creek: in NE, 222; in OR, 126,
    307; in WY, 229;
Willow Spring (WY): 76-77
Winbourne, John N.: 14
Wind River Mts. (WY): 80
Winds: 44, 64, 188, 261-62, 269; see also
    weather
Winterset (IA): 216
Wisconsin: 174, 202
Wolf Springs (NE): 62
Wolves and coyotes: 223, 226, 270, 286
Wood: on islands, 60-61; lack of, 188,
    191, 222, 263-64, 308; willow, 241,
    292-93; see also greasewood, sagebrush
Wood River (NE): 189, 222

Yakima Indian War: 32-33
Yamhill County (OR): 32-34, 157-69
Yamhill River (OR): 170

Zigzag Creek (OR): 133-34